Python for Asset Management

The asset management industry is undergoing a paradigm shift toward automation, transparency, and data-driven decision-making. Traditional tools (Excel, Bloomberg) are being replaced by programmable, scalable solutions. Yet most finance professionals lack accessible, practical training in applying Python to real portfolio problems.

Python for Asset Management fills that gap. The book empowers non-programmers – portfolio managers, risk analysts, and students – to implement advanced models themselves. It responds to the growing demand for quantitative literacy in finance, especially in sustainable investing and smart beta strategies, areas of active research for both of the authors.

Features

- 31 hands-on Python exercises with real data and executable code.
- Complete GitHub repository (MIT License) with all scripts, data pipelines, and results.
- Step-by-step implementation of VaR (historical, parametric, Monte Carlo), bond immunization, and factor models.
- Real-world decision tools – e.g., build a bullet/barbell/ladder bond portfolio, run Brinson–Fachler attribution, or backtest smart beta vs. index.
- Immediate applicability – every exercise produces a deliverable (e.g., optimal weights, risk report, attribution table) ready for client meetings.
- Focus on practical asset management workflows, not just theory.

Ignacio Cervera holds a PhD in business administration from Universidad Pontificia Comillas (Madrid) and an MBA from Instituto de Empresa (IE-Madrid) and is Professor of Corporate Finance and Portfolio Management & Investments. Since 2015, he has been an advisor on financial matters for the Pontificia Comillas University. He is currently co-director of the Asset Management Chair of this university. Lines of research are sustainability, investment funds, financial analysts, and financial and energy markets. He worked as Director of the Administrative and Financial Department at Tecnológica SA, Central de Aprovisionamiento y Diseño para Tecnología Espacial (Supply and Design Center for Space Technology) (1987–1990).

Natalia Cassinello holds a PhD in business administration and an executive master's in behavioral economics from LSE and is Professor in Finance and ESG and Co-Director of the Asset Management Chair at Universidad Pontificia Comillas at Madrid Campus. She is the Deputy Chief Financial Officer at the university. Lines of research are sustainability, investment funds, and health economics. Her teaching has been combined with professional activity in the private sector, having worked from 1990 to 2006 first as a strategic consultant at the consulting firm McKinsey & Co (1990–1994), then as a financial and tax advisor at the law firms Consultores&Asociados and Ramón y Cajal Abogados (1995–2003), and finally as Director of the Recruitment Department at the consulting firm Boston Consulting Group (2003–2006).

Chapman & Hall/CRC Financial Mathematics Series

Rama Cont, Mathematical Institute, University of Oxford, UK

Robert A. Jarrow, Ronald P. & Susan E. Lynch Professor of Investment Management at Samuel Curtis Johnson Graduate School of Management, Cornell University, USA

Peter Tankov, ENSAE, Institute Polytechnique de Paris, France

Recently Published Titles

Quantitative Finance with Case Studies in Python
A Practical Guide to Investment Management, Trading and Financial Engineering
Chris Kelliher

XVA Analysis
Probabilistic, Risk Measure, and Machine Learning Issues
Stéphane Crépey

Risk Analysis in Finance and Insurance
Alexander Melnikov

Handbook of Sustainable Mathematical Finance
Peter Tankov and Ruixun Zhang

Foundations of Quantitative Finance
Book VII: Brownian Motion and Other Stochastic Processes
Robert R. Reitano

An Introduction to Generalized Poisson Processes with Applications
Enzo Orsingher, Riccardo Cesari, and Vieri Mosco

Python for Asset Management
Ignacio Cervera and Natalia Cassinello

For more information about this series please visit: https://www.routledge.com/Chapman-and-HallCRC-Financial-Mathematics-Series/book-series/CHFINANCMTH

Python for Asset Management

Ignacio Cervera and Natalia Cassinello

CRC Press
Taylor & Francis Group
Boca Raton London New York

CRC Press is an imprint of the
Taylor & Francis Group, an **informa** business
A CHAPMAN & HALL BOOK

Designed cover image: Shutterstock

First edition published 2027
by CRC Press
2385 NW Executive Center Drive, Suite 320, Boca Raton FL 33431

and by CRC Press
4 Park Square, Milton Park, Abingdon, Oxon, OX14 4RN

CRC Press is an imprint of Taylor & Francis Group, LLC

ISBN: 978-1-041-30832-4 (hbk)
ISBN: 978-1-041-31936-8 (pbk)
ISBN: 978-1-003-78139-4 (ebk)

DOI: 10.1201/9781003781394

Typeset in Minion
by Apex CoVantage, LLC

Contents

Practical Exercises

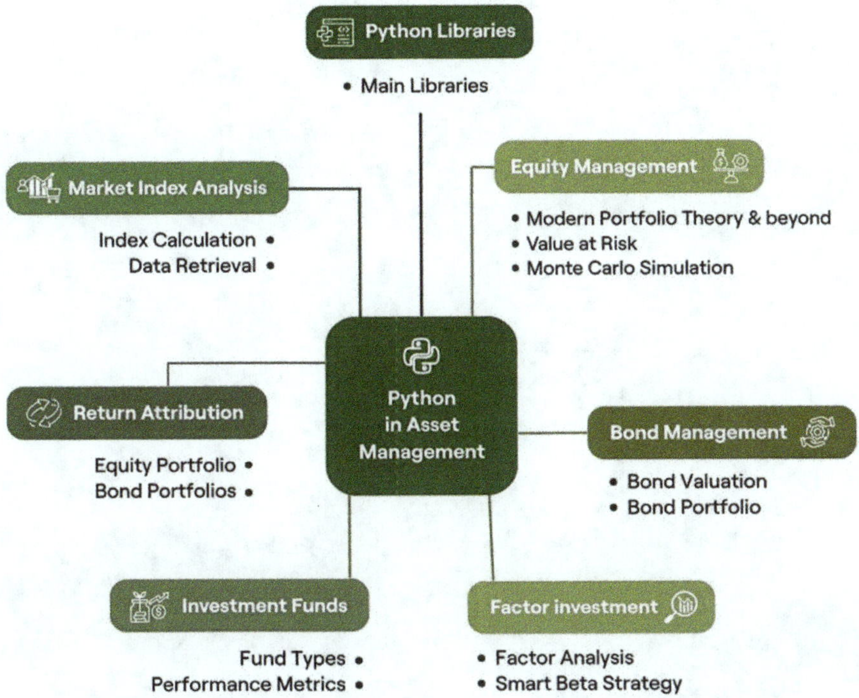

FIGURE 0.1 Python in Asset Management: Comprehensive Integration

Prologue

ASSET MANAGEMENT IS, at its heart, a discipline of decisions – decisions based on data, analysis, and, increasingly, automation and speed. For decades, these decisions were powered by spreadsheets, instinct, and experience. But the landscape has changed. The quantity of data, the complexity of financial products, and the demand for transparency and efficiency have transformed the skill set required of today's asset management professionals.

This book is not just about Python. It is about a shift in mindset. It is about equipping portfolio managers, analysts, risk professionals, and even students of finance with the ability to bridge the gap between financial reasoning and technological execution.

The financial industry has learned – sometimes reluctantly – that knowing how to analyze a portfolio is no longer enough. Understanding how to translate that analysis into automated workflows, scalable models, and data-driven insights is becoming an essential skill. Python is not the only tool, but it is the tool that has democratized access to this new way of working. It is flexible, open, and powerful enough to allow finance professionals, even those without formal programming training, to build their own solutions.

This book was written with that spirit in mind: not to turn asset managers into software engineers but to empower them to take control of their data, test ideas faster, reduce operational risk, and speak the language of modern finance.

You do not need to be a coder to use this book. You need curiosity, a willingness to learn, and the ambition to make better, more informed decisions. The pages that follow are an invitation to that journey.

Along the way, we have been fortunate to receive generous feedback and support from colleagues and institutions. We are grateful to Enrique Marazuela, CFA; Professor Teresa Corzo Santamaría; and Professor

Eduardo César Garrido Merchán for their invaluable suggestions. We also thank the sponsors of the Asset Management Chair at ICADE (Universidad Pontificia Comillas) – J.P. Morgan AM, M&G Investments, Schroders, BBVA AM, Santander AM, AQR, and DWS – for their support of this book.

Introduction

Asset Management in the Era of Analytics

IN THE EVOLVING LANDSCAPE OF FINANCE, the integration of technology and data analytics has revolutionized traditional practices, bringing about a new era of efficiency, accuracy, and innovation. One of the most significant developments in this regard is the adoption of Python as a powerful tool in the domain of asset management. Python, a high-level programming language, has gained widespread popularity across various industries due to its simplicity, versatility, and robust ecosystem of libraries and frameworks. In asset management, Python has emerged as an indispensable tool, enabling professionals to analyze financial data, develop models, and implement complex strategies with unprecedented ease and efficiency.

Asset management, which involves the systematic process of developing, operating, maintaining, and selling assets in a cost-effective manner, is inherently data driven. The ability to analyze large datasets, extract meaningful insights, and automate decision-making processes is crucial for success in this field. Traditional tools, such as Excel and proprietary software, often fall short when it comes to handling the vast volumes of data and the complex analyses required in modern asset management. Python, with its extensive libraries for data manipulation, statistical analysis, and machine learning, offers a compelling alternative that addresses these challenges.

The rise of Python in asset management can be attributed to several key factors. First, Python's readability and simplicity make it accessible to a wide range of users, from novice programmers to seasoned developers. This accessibility has facilitated its adoption across the finance industry, enabling professionals who may not have a formal background in programming to leverage its capabilities. Second, Python's open-source nature and active community support ensure that it is constantly evolving, with new libraries and tools being developed to meet the changing needs of the industry. This dynamic ecosystem allows asset managers to stay at the forefront of technological advancements and incorporate the latest techniques into their workflows.

Moreover, Python's ability to integrate seamlessly with other technologies and platforms enhances its utility in asset management. For instance, Python can be easily combined with databases, web applications, and cloud services, providing a comprehensive solution for managing the end-to-end asset lifecycle. This integration capability is particularly important in the current era of big data, where asset managers must deal with diverse data sources and formats. Python's flexibility allows for the development of customized solutions that can accommodate specific organizational requirements and objectives.

In this book, we will explore the application of Python in various aspects of asset management. We will begin with an overview of the fundamental Python libraries that are commonly used in this field, such as *Pandas, NumPy, Matplotlib, and Scikit-learn.* These libraries provide essential building blocks for data manipulation, statistical analysis, and visualization. We will then delve into specific use of Python in the management of different asset classes, illustrating with practical exercises how Python can be employed to develop models and strategies.

As we navigate through the technical details, it is important to recognize the broader implications of Python's adoption in asset management. The shift towards Python represents not just a change in tools but a fundamental transformation in the way asset managers approach their work. By embracing Python, asset managers can unlock new levels of efficiency, creativity, and insight, ultimately driving better outcomes for their clients and stakeholders.

In conclusion, Python is more than just a programming language; it is a catalyst for innovation in asset management. As industry continues to evolve, those who harness the power of Python will be well positioned to thrive in a data-driven world. This book aims to provide a comprehensive introduction to Python applied to asset management, equipping readers with the knowledge and skills to leverage this versatile tool in their own professional practice.

The structure of this book is as follows:

1 Brief introduction to the main libraries used in this book. This section will provide an overview of the Python libraries such as Pandas, NumPy, Matplotlib, and SciPy, which are instrumental in performing financial analysis and modeling.

2 Python applied to market index analysis. Focuses on using Python to analyze stock market indexes, including techniques for trend analysis, volatility measurement, and comparative index performance.

3 Python applied to equity management through modern portfolio theory. Although we will explore models that outperform the CAPM model, these models will be examined in more detail in the fourth section. This part will discuss the application of Python in optimizing equity portfolios using variance minimization and expected return maximization under the framework of modern portfolio theory (MPT).

4 Python applied to bond management, forming portfolios with a duration objective, an immunization objective, or to meet the cash flows of a liability. This segment will cover strategies for managing bond investments to achieve specified financial goals using Python, focusing on duration matching and immunization techniques.

5 Python applied to return attribution explores how to decompose the performance of a portfolio into the contributions of allocation decisions and selection decisions, providing clarity on investment strategies' effectiveness.

6 Python applied to investment funds discusses the use of Python in managing investment funds, focusing on performance evaluation.

7 Python applied to factor investing, where certain factors will serve as a reference for portfolio analysis. This part delves into the identification and utilization of risk factors like size, value, and momentum to enhance portfolio returns and manage risk more effectively.

8 Python applied to ESG investment. This final chapter presents the evolution and relevance of ESG investing, explaining why it matters for finance and asset management. It reviews the main ESG data providers and shows how to access and transform ESG metrics into usable indicators with Python. Finally, it introduces practical ESG integration approaches – such as screening, ESG tilts, and portfolio

constraints – illustrating how ESG criteria can be incorporated into portfolio construction and evaluation.

In each section We will explain the main concepts involved in each part, providing practical exercises solved with Python codes, for better understanding. These codes are hosted in a GitHub repository, which can be accessed via the following link: https://github.com/icervecon/PythonAssetMagement.

CHAPTER 1

Python Libraries

1.1 CHAPTER OVERVIEW

This chapter provides a comprehensive introduction to key Python libraries, emphasizing their importance in simplifying programming tasks by offering pre-written code for various functionalities. It categorizes libraries based on their applications, such as data manipulation (*Pandas*, *NumPy*), scientific computing (*Statsmodels*, *SciPy*), optimization (*PuLP*), financial analysis (*Yfinance*, *Empyrical*), web interaction (*Requests*, *OS*), data visualization (*Matplotlib*, *Seaborn*), and input/output operations (*Zipfile*). Each library is briefly described, highlighting its primary functions and common use cases.

1.2 BRIEF INTRODUCTION TO THE MAIN PYTHON LIBRARIES

Libraries in Python play a critical role in simplifying and accelerating programming tasks by providing pre-written code for a wide range of functionalities. Python libraries are collections of pre-written code that provide specific functionality, allowing developers to avoid writing code from scratch for common tasks.

Python libraries span a wide spectrum in terms of functionality and use cases, from general-purpose utilities to highly specialized tools tailored for specific domains (e.g., data analysis, machine learning). General-purpose libraries are often foundational and are combined with specialized libraries to build robust solutions.

Libraries allow you to focus on solving the problem at hand rather than implementing low-level details. Libraries provide pre-written code for common functionalities, eliminating the need to reinvent the wheel.

DOI: 10.1201/9781003781394-1

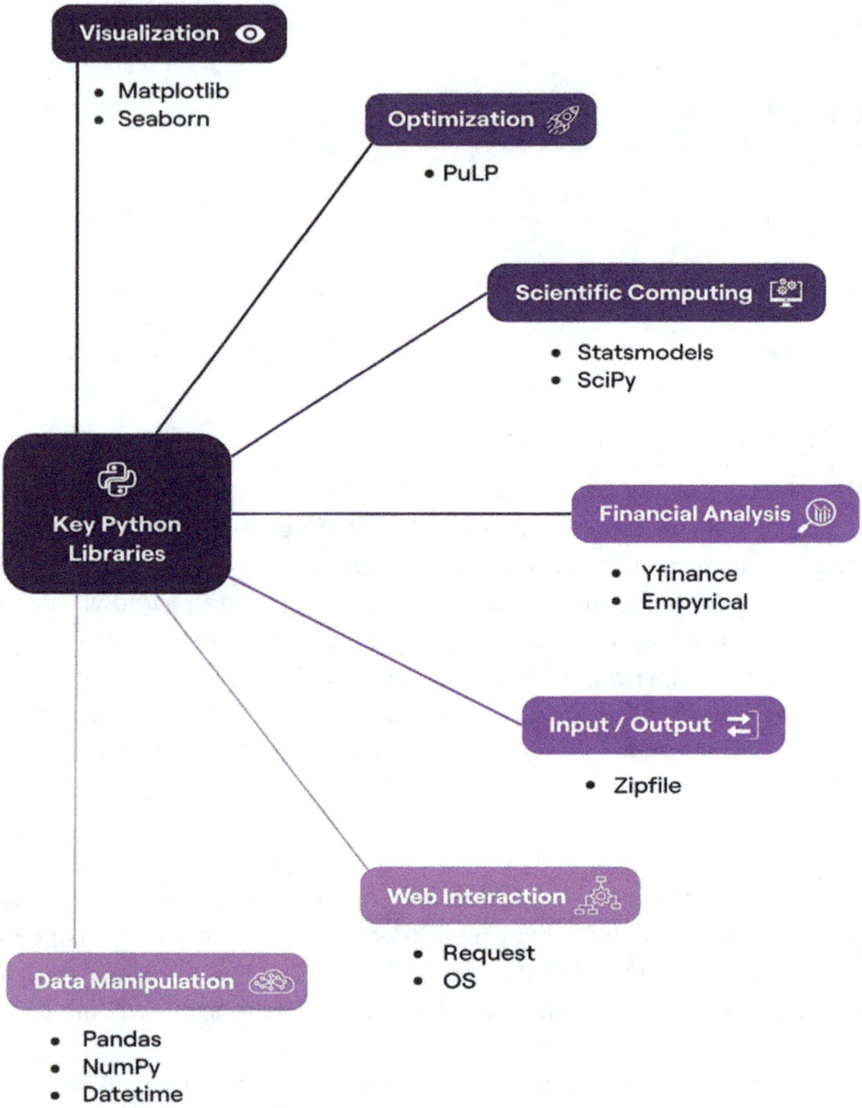

FIGURE 1.1 Key Python Libraries and Their Applications

Developers can use these tools without worrying about the internal implementation details.

The following Python libraries have been used in this book. Following is a brief description of each of them.

1.2.1 *Pandas*

Pandas is a powerful and flexible data manipulation and analysis library for Python. It provides data structures like series and dataframes, which are essential for handling and analyzing structured data, such as tables with rows and columns. *Pandas* is widely used for data cleaning, preparation, and analysis tasks, making it a staple in data science and financial analysis.

1.2.2 *NumPy*

NumPy (Numerical Python) is a fundamental package for scientific computing in Python. It provides support for large, multi-dimensional arrays and matrices, along with a vast library of mathematical functions to operate on these arrays. *NumPy* is essential for numerical computations and forms the foundation for many other scientific libraries in Python.

1.2.3 *Statsmodels*

Statsmodels is a Python library that provides classes and functions for the estimation of many different statistical models, as well as for conducting statistical tests and data exploration. It is particularly useful for performing regression analysis and time series forecasting, making it a valuable tool in econometrics and financial modeling.

1.2.4 *SciPy*

SciPy is an open-source Python library used for scientific and technical computing. It builds on *NumPy* and provides additional functionality, including modules for optimization, integration, interpolation, eigenvalue problems, and signal processing. *SciPy* is a key tool for performing complex mathematical and scientific computations. *SciPy* is better suited for nonlinear, unconstrained, or gradient-based optimization problems, as well as for solving equations numerically as part of broader scientific computations.

1.2.5 *PuLP*

PuLP is a Python library for linear programming and mixed-integer linear programming. It allows users to describe optimization problems mathematically and solve them using various solvers. *PuLP* is used in operations research and optimization tasks, such as resource allocation, production planning, and portfolio optimization. *PuLP* is ideal for linear and mixed-integer linear programming, especially when you need precise control over the formulation and constraints.

1.2.6 *Yfinance*

Yfinance is a Python library that allows easy access to financial data from Yahoo Finance. It can be used to download historical market data, retrieve current stock prices, and analyze financial data. *Yfinance* is especially useful for financial analysts and traders who need to pull real-time or historical market data into their Python scripts.

1.2.7 *empyrical*

The *empyrical* library is a Python package designed specifically for financial analysis, especially performance and risk assessment of investment portfolios. It's commonly used by financial analysts and portfolio managers to calculate various important metrics: Sharpe ratio, Sortino ratio, annual returns, cumulative returns, alpha, beta, information ratio, volatility, maximum drawdown, downside risk, and tail risk metrics. The functions are straightforward and take simple inputs like return series, making it accessible even to beginners.

1.2.8 *Requests*

Requests is a simple yet powerful Python library for making HTTP requests. It abstracts the complexities of making requests behind a straightforward API, allowing users to send HTTP requests and interact with web services easily. *Requests* is commonly used for web scraping, API interactions, and downloading files from the internet.

1.2.9 *OS*

The *OS* module in Python provides a way of using operating system-dependent functionality like reading or writing to the file system, handling directories, and managing environment variables. It is essential for tasks that involve file management, executing system commands, or interacting with the underlying operating system.

1.2.10 *Matplotlib*

Matplotlib is a popular plotting library in Python used for creating static, interactive, and animated visualizations. It provides a variety of plots, including line graphs, bar charts, histograms, and scatter plots. *Matplotlib* is highly customizable, allowing users to create complex figures with fine control over every aspect of the plot.

1.2.11 *Seaborn*

Seaborn is a Python data visualization library based on Matplotlib that provides a high-level interface for drawing attractive and informative statistical graphics. It is particularly useful for visualizing complex datasets, making it easier to explore data through heatmaps, violin plots, and pair plots.

1.2.12 *datetime*

The *datetime* module in Python supplies classes for manipulating dates and times. It allows users to perform arithmetic on dates and times, such as calculating differences between dates, parsing date strings, and formatting dates. *datetime* is crucial for any application involving time-based data, such as time series analysis or timestamp management.

1.2.13 *Zipfile*

Zipfile is a built-in Python module that provides tools for creating, reading, writing, and extracting ZIP files. It is useful for compressing and decompressing files, making it easier to handle large datasets or share files more efficiently.

In Python, the choice of library largely depends on the specific operations or tasks one intends to perform. The following is an overview of various common operations, and the libraries typically used for each.:

- Data Manipulation and Analysis: *Pandas* and *Numpy*
- Data Visualization: *Matplotlib* and *Seaborn*
- Web Interaction: *Requests* and *OS*
- Scientific Computing: *Statsmodels* and *SciPy*
- Financial Analysis: *empyrical* and *Yfinance*
- Optimization: *PuLP*
- Input/Output: *Zipfile*

In every practical exercise we provide a code that starts indicating the libraries to import.

To learn more about using Python, we recommend checking out the work of Heydt (2015), Hilpish (2019), Ramalho (2015), Weiming (2015), Yang (2014), and Brooks (2019).

CHAPTER 2

Python Applied to Market Index Analysis

2.1 CHAPTER OVERVIEW

This section introduces the fundamentals of market indexes and their significance in financial markets. It explains how indexes, such as the S&P 500, Dow Jones Industrial Average, and Euro Stoxx 50, serve as key benchmarks for investors, offering insights into market trends and economic performance. This section lays the foundation for applying Python to financial market analysis, helping investors use data-driven approaches for portfolio management.

2.2 INTRODUCTION TO MARKET INDEXES

There is probably a common question that every investor, broker, or trader asks daily: *What is the market doing today?* Or over the past month? Or this year? The most common answer to this question typically refers to an index like the S&P 500, indicating whether it has gone up or down and highlighting which sectors and stocks have performed best and worst. Most people rely on indexes as their primary reference.

An index, such as a stock exchange index, provides a quick and straightforward way to gauge market performance over a given period using a representative sample of assets. Therefore, indexes serve not only as statistical measures but also as key market indicators that investors must understand and incorporate into their decision-making processes.

DOI: 10.1201/9781003781394-2

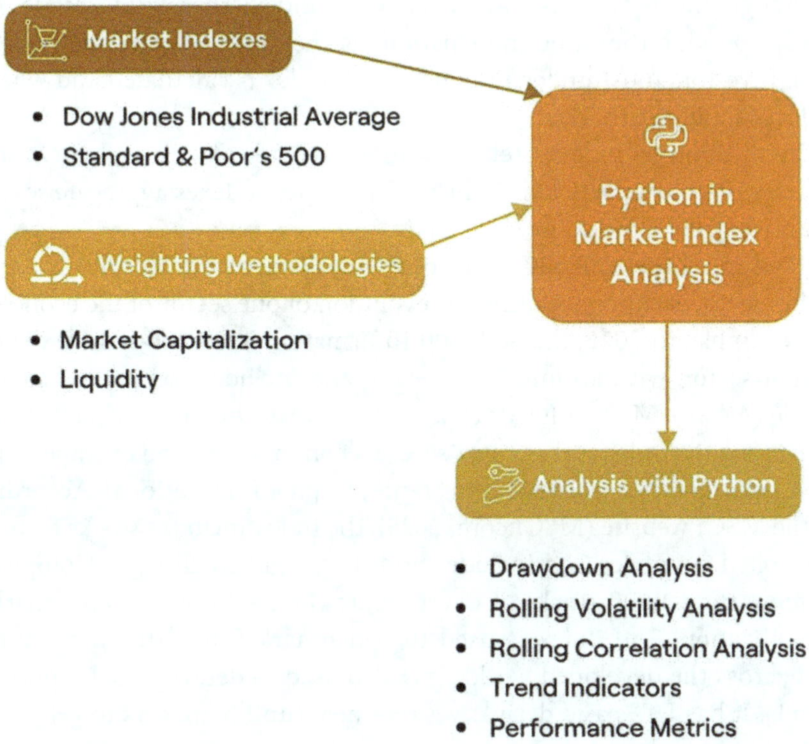

FIGURE 2.1 Python in Market Index Analysis

The main stock market indexes include:

- United States: Dow Jones Industrial Average, Standard & Poor's 500 (S&P 500), New York Stock Exchange Index, and Nasdaq.
- Europe: Euro Stoxx 50, Ibex-35 (Spain), CAC 40 (France), DAX 40 (Germany).
- United Kingdom: FTSE 100.
- Japan: Nikkei 225.
- China: Shanghai Composite Index (SSE Composite), Shenzhen Composite Index, and Hang Seng Index (HSI).

Although most markets have a primary index, these indexes do not always provide the same information, as they use different methodologies. Investors must understand how each index is calculated and what it reflects about the market.

In addition to indexes referring to a particular stock exchange, sub-indexes refer to a particular industry, and super-indexes aggregate several countries in one index.

Looking at the S&P 500, this global index is decomposed into 11 sectorial indexes, each representing the evolution of one sector of the economy. For example, in 2025, the S&P 500 Information Technology Index is the largest sector, with around 28% weight, and includes companies such as Apple (AAPL), Microsoft (MSFT), NVIDIA (NVDA), and Intel (INTC).

Among the indexes that cover several economies, a good example is the MSCI World Index from Morgan Stanley Capital International. According to the MSCI website (MSCI.com, 2025), the index includes stocks from 23 developed countries and includes both large and small caps. Composed of more than 1,500 stocks, it covers more than 85% of free float market capitalization. The index is used to benchmark funds that are diversified across the developed world. It is also used to detect global economic trends. It has ETFs and derivatives that help fund managers to get global exposure or hedge easily.

In addition, MSCI also publishes other global indexes, such as the MSCI Emerging Markets Index (including emerging markets like China or Brazil) and MSCI ACWI, which includes both developed and emerging markets. A different category is the ESG-related indexes. Amongst these are the MSCI World ESG Leaders Index, which is mostly weighted by companies highly ESG rated, or the MSCI ACWI ESG Screened Index, which excludes controversial industries such as tobacco or fossil fuels.

The index industry is not exclusive to the equity world. There are also indexes for bond markets, although they are less popular for retail investors. One of the oldest bond indexes is the Dow Jones Bond Average, which was created at the beginning of the 20th century. Nowadays, among others, a good example is Moody's Bond Yields, which refers to the average yields on corporate bonds categorized by their credit ratings (eg, Moody's Aaa Corporate Bond Yield). They are very much followed to assess the pricing of the credit rating in the bond market. The iTraxx is a family of credit default swap indexes measuring the credit risk of corporate bonds in different regions. It is also a good benchmark to hedge or speculate on the fixed-rate market.

2.2.1 Calculation of Indexes

Understanding how indexes are calculated is crucial for their proper use in portfolio construction and benchmarking. Two key aspects in analyzing indexes are:

a) The type of return they measure.

b) The weighting methodology used in their calculation.

2.2.1.1 Difference between Price Return, Total Return, and Net Return Indexes

There are three main types of index return calculations: Price Return, Total Return, and Net Return indexes.

a) Price Return Indexes: These indexes reflect only the price changes of their components, excluding any additional benefits such as dividends, taxes, or other corporate actions. They strictly track price appreciation and do not account for income distributions.

b) Total Return Indexes: These indexes include both price changes and any monetary distributions, such as dividends paid to shareholders. An example of this is the S&P 500 Total Return Index, which reinvests dividends to provide a more comprehensive measure of investment performance.

c) Net Return Indexes: Unlike total return indexes, net return indexes account for the impact of applicable taxes on monetary distributions. While price return indexes provide the most basic measure, net return indexes offer a more complete view. However, they are highly dependent on investor-specific tax situations, making them difficult to calculate accurately. As a result, total return indexes have become the most widely used benchmarks.

2.2.1.2 Differences in Weighting

Stock market indexes are primarily calculated by weighting the prices of their constituent securities. The two main weighting factors are:

- Market Capitalization: Companies are weighted based on their total market value (stock price × number of outstanding shares).
- Liquidity: Companies are weighted based on the dollar volume of shares traded.

Different indexes use different weighting methodologies, which can significantly impact performance comparisons. Some indexes, such as the S&P 500, are fully weighted by market capitalization, while others, like the Dow Jones Industrial Average (DJIA), are price-weighted, meaning they give more influence to higher-priced stocks regardless of the company's overall market value. The MSCI World Index is weighted with the free float market cap of each stock.

The impact of these methodologies can be seen in performance differences. For example, as of January 19, 2025, the DJIA posted a 12-month return of 16.06%, whereas the S&P 500 returned 25.43%. While differences in index composition contribute to this variation, a significant portion of the gap is due to the calculation methodology.

Understanding how each index is constructed highlights the importance of selecting an appropriate benchmark for investment analysis. We will see this with American market indexes.

2.2.1.2.1 Dow Jones Industrial Average

The Dow Jones Industrial Average (DJIA) is calculated using a price-weighted average methodology. This means that each stock's influence on the index is determined by its price rather than its market capitalization. Unlike market-cap-weighted indexes, where larger companies have more impact, in the DJIA, a stock with a higher price has a greater effect on the index value, regardless of the company's total market value.

Here's how the DJIA is calculated:

a) Sum of Component Stock Prices – The current prices of all 30 stocks in the index are added together.

b) Use of the Dow Divisor – The sum is then divided by the Dow Divisor, a specific adjustment factor that accounts for stock splits, dividends, and other corporate actions to maintain index continuity.

$$\text{DJIA} = \frac{\sum \text{Stock Prices}}{\text{Dow Divisor}}.$$

Initially, the Dow Divisor was simply the number of stocks in the index (30). However, due to various market events, it has since evolved into a much different value. The actual divisor is published by S&P Dow Jones Indexes and is updated in real-time to ensure the index remains consistent despite structural changes.

Several events can affect the divisor, including:

- Stock Splits: When a stock splits, the total value of the company remains unchanged, but the number of shares increases, reducing the price per share. Since the DJIA is price-weighted, this would artificially lower the index value. To prevent this, the divisor is adjusted accordingly so that stock splits do not impact the index.
- Special Dividend Payments: In cases where a company issues an unusually large or one-time dividend, the stock price may drop significantly after the dividend payout. To prevent this from distorting the index value, the divisor is modified to compensate for the price adjustment.
- Changes in Index Composition: When a company is removed from the index and replaced with another, the incoming stock often has a different price. For example, if a stock priced at $20 replaces one priced at $100, the index would drop purely due to the price difference. To avoid this artificial distortion, the divisor is adjusted to maintain the continuity of the DJIA.

Because of its price-weighted methodology, stocks with higher prices have a greater influence on the Dow Jones Industrial Average (DJIA), regardless of the company's overall market size. For example, a stock priced at $300 will have ten times the impact on the index as a stock priced at $30, even if the lower-priced stock belongs to a much larger company.

To better understand how the DJIA is constructed, consider a simplified example where the index consists of three stocks:

TABLE 2.1 Simplified DJIA Index

Company	Stock Price	Shares Outstanding	Market Capitalization
A	$50	1,000,000	$50,000,000
B	$100	500,000	$50,000,000
C	$150	100,000	$15,000,000

and the divisor is 0.5:

$$\text{DJIA} = 50 + 100 + 150/0.5 = 600$$

As can be easily understood, the stock priced at $150 is the one that impacts the most in the index, regardless of its market cap. If it goes up to 300 (+100%), the index would move to 900. In other words, the index would go up 50%, regardless of the fact that the only company with a change in price only represents 13% of total market cap (15 million over 115 million).

2.2.1.2.2 Standard & Poor's 500 The calculation of the S&P 500 is more complex than that of the DJIA because it uses a market capitalization-weighted methodology. This means that each company's influence on the index is proportional to its total market value, rather than its stock price alone. Here's how it is calculated:

$$S\&P500 = \frac{\sum(\text{Stock Prices}_i \times \text{Shares Oustanding}_i)}{\text{Divisor}}$$

- The numerator represents the total market capitalization calculated as Stock Price × Shares Outstanding.
- The weight of each company determines how much a change in a company's stock price will impact the value of the index. It is calculated as:

$$Weight = \frac{Company's\ Market\ Capitalization}{Total\ Market\ Capitalization\ of\ the\ Index}$$

- Index Divisor: Similar to the Dow Jones, the S&P 500 has an adjusted divisor to maintain the index's continuity in response to events such as:
    - Issuance of new shares.
    - Stock buybacks.
    - Mergers and acquisitions.
    - Changes in the index's composition.

  The divisor is not published, and it is calculated by S&P Dow Jones Indexes to make sure the continuity and consistency of the index.

A simplified example of how the index is built is the following: Suppose the S&P 500 only includes three companies:

TABLE 2.2 Simplified S&P500 Index

Company	Stock Price	Shares Outstanding	Market Capitalization
A	$20	1,000,000	$20,000,000
B	$30	500,000	$15,000.000
C	$40	100,000	$4,000,000

Total Market Capitalization = 20,000,000 + 15,000,000 + 4,000,000 = 39,000,000

If the divisor is, for example, 1000, the index value would be:

$$\text{Index} = 39{,}000{,}000/1{,}000 = 39{,}000$$

As can be seen, the company that impacts the index the most is the one with the highest market cap, in this case company A. This happens regardless of the fact that the price of one share is the lowest. In the case of the DJIA, as explained, it would have been company C.

The S&P 500 is considered a more representative measure of the U.S. stock market than the DJIA because it includes 500 companies and accounts for market capitalization.

Apple and Microsoft are present in both the S&P 500 and DJIA. Market cap changes in both companies have a very different effect on the change of each index. How would a 10% increase in the stock price of both companies impact each index? Additionally, how would this effect have differed over the past 20 years? The expected difference in the answer is an important element when using indexes as part of portfolio management. For this exercise, it should be assumed that the price change is not due to any effect that could affect the divisor.

2.2.2 Optimal Replication of Indexes

Index tracker funds are quite popular passive funds that aim to replicate an index as accurately as possible. Investing in a complete index involves buying all the stocks in proportion to their weight. At the extreme, there are indexes that are themselves composed of other indexes, providing a more global view of market evolution.

As an alternative, index replica could be executed with futures, but these are influenced by interest rates and do not necessarily move in exact correlation with the index.

Replication of indexes present the following issues:

- Transaction costs affect profitability. For instance, indexes such as S&P 500 require a large number of transactions to replicate.
- Need for continuous adjustments due to corporate events that affect the number of shares per company.
- High administrative costs due to the variety of stocks.

2.3 RETRIEVING MARKET INDEX DATA

Market indexes serve as key indicators of financial market performance, helping investors analyze trends, benchmark portfolios, and make informed investment decisions. To effectively work with indexes, it is essential to retrieve accurate and timely market data from reliable sources. This section explores various data providers and methods for accessing index data using Python.

2.3.1 Data Sources for Index Analysis

Market index data can be obtained from a variety of sources, ranging from free public databases to premium institutional platforms. The choice of a data source depends on the depth of information required, data frequency, and budget constraints.

Free Sources:

These platforms offer access to historical and real-time market data, often with some limitations:

- Yahoo Finance (yfinance library) – Provides historical daily prices, adjusted close values, and trading volume.
- Alpha Vantage – Alpha Vantage does not provide direct access to certain market indexes, such as the S&P 500 or the Dow Jones Industrial Average, through its API. Instead, users can obtain data for Exchange-Traded Funds (ETFs) that track these indexes. For example, the SPDR S&P 500 ETF Trust (SPY) tracks the S&P 500 Index, and the SPDR Dow Jones Industrial Average ETF Trust (DIA) tracks the Dow Jones Industrial Average.
- Quandl (now Nasdaq Data Link) – Features a mix of free and premium financial datasets, including market indexes.
- St. Louis Federal Reserve (FRED) – Provides macroeconomic and financial index data, useful for economic analysis.

Paid Sources:

- Bloomberg Terminal – Extensive financial data and analytics.
- Refinitiv (formerly Thomson Reuters) – Real-time and historical market data.
- FactSet – Institutional-grade financial data.
- S&P Capital IQ – Equity and index data for asset managers.

PRACTICAL EXERCISE #2.01 RETRIEVING MARKET INDEXES DATA

Request: Download data about the following indexes: S&P 500, Nasdaq, Dow Jones Industrial, and Russell 2000.

Summary of the script. –

The following Python script downloads and processes historical market index data from Yahoo Finance using the *yfinance* library. It retrieves data for the S&P 500, NASDAQ 100, Dow Jones Industrial Average, and Russell 2000 from 2010 to 2025. The script:

- Fetches data for each index, selecting the adjusted close price when available.
- Handles missing data, ensuring no empty datasets are processed.
- Stores the data in a dictionary and converts it into a pandas DataFrame.
- Cleans the data, removing missing values.
- Plots the historical prices of all indexes for visualization.
- If no valid data is found, it raises an error.

This script efficiently retrieves and visualizes financial index data while ensuring error handling, data integrity, and clear visualization.

TABLE 2.3 Summary of Key Functions and Their Purposes

Function/Method	Purpose
yfinance.download(symbol, start, end)	Fetches historical stock/index data from Yahoo Finance.
if not index_data:	Ensures at least one valid index was retrieved before proceeding.
pd.DataFrame(index_data)	Converts the dictionary of time series data into a DataFrame.
df.dropna(inplace=True)	Removes missing values to maintain data integrity.
plt.legend( )	Adds a legend to distinguish the different indexes in the plot.

Script execution and outputs. –

```
import yfinance as yf
import pandas as pd
import matplotlib.pyplot as plt

# Define market index symbols
indexes = {
    "S&P 500": "^GSPC",
    "NASDAQ 100": "^NDX",
    "Dow Jones Industrial": "^DJI",
    "Russell 2000": "^RUT"
}

# Download historical data
start_date = "2010-01-01"
end_date = "2025-01-01"
index_data = {}

for name, symbol in indexes.items():
    print(f" Downloading data for {name} ({symbol})...")
    data = yf.download(symbol, start=start_date,
end=end_date,auto_adjust=False, actions=False)['Adj Close']
    index_data[name] = data.squeeze()
    print(f" Data stored for {name}, first few rows:")
    print(index_data[name].head())

if not index_data:
    raise ValueError("No valid data found for any indexes.")

df = pd.DataFrame(index_data)
df.dropna(inplace=True)



# Plotting
fig, ax1 = plt.subplots(figsize=(14, 7))

# Left Y-axis: S&P 500 and Russell 2000
color1 = 'tab:blue'
color2 = 'tab:green'
ax1.set_xlabel('Date')
ax1.set_ylabel('S&P 500 / Russell 2000', color=color1)
ax1.plot(df.index, df['S&P 500'], label='S&P 500', color=color1)
ax1.plot(df.index, df['Russell 2000'], label='Russell 2000',
color=color2)
ax1.tick_params(axis='y', labelcolor=color1)

# Right Y-axis: NASDAQ 100 and Dow Jones
ax2 = ax1.twinx()
color3 = 'tab:orange'
```

```
color4 = 'tab:red'
ax2.set_ylabel('NASDAQ 100 / Dow Jones', color=color3)
ax2.plot(df.index, df['NASDAQ 100'], label='NASDAQ 100',
color=color3)
ax2.plot(df.index, df['Dow Jones Industrial'], label='Dow
Jones Industrial', color=color4)
ax2.tick_params(axis='y', labelcolor=color3)

# Combine legends from both axes
lines1, labels1 = ax1.get_legend_handles_labels()
lines2, labels2 = ax2.get_legend_handles_labels()
ax1.legend(lines1 + lines2, labels1 + labels2, loc='upper left')

plt.title("Market Indexes with Dual Y-Axis (2010-2025)")
plt.grid()
plt.tight_layout()
plt.show()
```

Output:

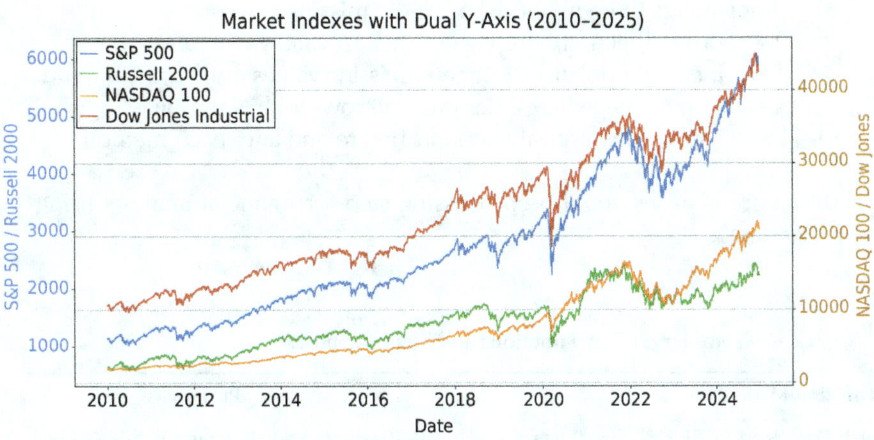

2.3.2 Preprocessing Index Data

Preprocessing index data is essential to ensure accurate and comparable financial analysis. This involves three key steps:

- Handling missing values
- Adjusting for splits and dividends
- Rebasing the index

Financial data can have missing values due to market holidays, connectivity issues, or incomplete datasets. To handle missing values, we can proceed as follows:

- Interpolation: Estimate missing values based on adjacent data points.
- Forward-fill: Use the last available value before the missing one.
- Dropping missing values: Suitable when missing data is minimal.

PRACTICAL EXERCISE #2.02 HANDLING MISSING VALUES

Request: Download data about the following indexes: S&P 500, Nasdaq, and Dow Jones Industrial and handle the missing values.

Summary of the script. –

This script retrieves historical S&P 500 data from FRED (Federal Reserve Economic Data) and handles missing values to ensure data integrity. Steps performed in the script:

- Fetches S&P 500 data from FRED using pandas datareader.
- Checks for missing values in the dataset.
- Implements three methods to handle missing values:
    - Forward-fill (ffill): Propagates the last valid value forward.
    - Linear interpolation: Estimates missing values using a linear trend.
    - Drop missing values: Removes all rows with NaN values.
    - Displays missing value counts before and after each method.

This script is an essential preprocessing step for financial analysis using FRED data.

TABLE 2.4 Summary of Key Functions and Their Purposes

Function/Method	Purpose
web.DataReader("SP500", "fred", start, end)	Retrieves S&P 500 data from FRED.
sp500.isnull( ).sum( )	Counts missing values in the dataset.
sp500.ffill( )	Forward-fills missing values with the last available data point.
sp500.interpolate(method='linear')	Interpolates missing values linearly.
sp500.dropna( )	Removes rows containing missing values.
sp500.isnull( ).sum( ).sum( )	Counts total missing values after each treatment.

Script execution and outputs. –

```
import pandas as pd
import numpy as np
import pandas_datareader.data as web
import datetime

# Define date range
start_date = datetime.datetime(2010, 1, 1)
end_date = datetime.datetime.today()

# Attempt to get S&P 500 from FRED
try:
    sp500 = web.DataReader("SP500", "fred", start_date, end_date)
    print("S&P 500 data retrieved from FRED")
except Exception as e:
    print(f"Error retrieving S&P 500 from FRED: {e}")

# Check for missing values
print("Missing values before treatment:\n", sp500.isnull().
sum())

# Option 1: Forward-fill (repeat last valid value)
sp500_ffill = sp500.ffill()

# Option 2: Linear interpolation
sp500_interp = sp500.interpolate(method='linear')

# Option 3: Drop missing values
sp500_dropna = sp500.dropna()

# Show results
print("Missing values after forward-fill:",
sp500_ffill.isnull().sum().sum())
print("Missing values after interpolation:",
sp500_interp.isnull().sum().sum())
print("Missing values after dropping rows:",
sp500_dropna.isnull().sum().sum())
```

Output:

```
S&P 500 data retrieved from FRED
Missing values before treatment:
 SP500    95
dtype: int64
Missing values after forward-fill: 0
Missing values after interpolation: 0
Missing values after dropping rows: 0
```

2.4 DESCRIPTIVE ANALYSIS OF MARKET INDEXES

This section performs descriptive statistical analysis on major market indexes, focusing on returns, risk, and drawdowns. The goal is to evaluate the performance and volatility of these indexes over time.

2.4.1 Summary Statistics and Performance Metrics

We compute key financial metrics:

- Annualized Return: Measures the average yearly return, assuming 252 trading days per year.
- Annualized Standard Deviation (Volatility): Measures the risk associated with returns (how much they fluctuate).
- Sharpe Ratio: Evaluates risk-adjusted performance:

$$Sharpe\,ratio = \frac{Annualized\,Return - Risk\_Free\,Rate}{Annualized\,Standard\,Deviation}$$

We assume a risk-free rate of 0% for simplicity.

2.4.2 Rolling Statistics for Market Trends

In financial markets, traders and analysts rely on moving averages to confirm trends and identify buy/sell signals. By smoothing out price fluctuations, moving averages make it easier to detect momentum shifts, reversals, and long-term trends. One of the most widely followed signals occurs when the 50-day simple moving average (SMA) crosses the 200-day SMA, known as the golden cross (bullish) or death cross (bearish). Unlike SMA, the exponential moving average (EMA) assigns more weight to recent prices, making it more responsive to price changes.

Moving averages serve as dynamic indicators, helping investors navigate market volatility with greater clarity. Instead of reacting to daily price swings, moving averages offer a broader perspective, making them essential tools for both short-term traders and long-term investors.

2.4.3 Correlation and Intermarket Analysis

Financial markets are interconnected and understanding how different indexes move together is crucial for investors and portfolio managers. This analysis explores the relationship between major stock indexes, focusing on correlation analysis and market regime detection through rolling correlations.

While long-term correlation values provide useful insights, market relationships are not static, they evolve over time due to macroeconomic events, interest rate changes, and investor sentiment. This is where rolling correlation analysis becomes valuable.

By calculating 50-day rolling correlations, we can observe how the relationship between indexes shifts over different market conditions. A high correlation environment often signals a risk-on market, where investors are confident, and equities move together. In contrast, a low or negative correlation environment may indicate a risk-off period, where capital shifts from stocks to bonds, gold, or other defensive assets.

PRACTICAL EXERCISE #2.03 DESCRIPTIVE ANALYSIS OF MARKET INDEXES

Request: Perform descriptive analysis of the following: S&P 500, and US Aggregate Bond ETF.

Summary of the script. –

This script retrieves, analyzes, and visualizes market data for S&P 500 and US Aggregate Bond ETF (AGG) as a proxy of US Bond Index from Yahoo Finance. It explores the relationship between stocks and bonds, capturing risk metrics, drawdowns, trends, and correlations.

The script performs financial analysis and market trend detection using:

a) Data retrieval and processing: Fetches data from Yahoo Finance.
b) Risk and performance metrics: Computes annualized return, volatility, and Sharpe ratio.
c) Drawdown analysis: Identifies max drawdowns and recovery periods.
d) Trend detection: Uses moving averages (SMA and EMA) and rolling volatility.
e) Correlation analysis: Examines the rolling correlation between S&P 500 and Bonds, highlighting shifts in market sentiment.

The primary goal is to evaluate stock-bond relationships, helping investors understand portfolio diversification and risk management.

TABLE 2.5 Summary of Key Functions and Their Purpose

Function Name	Purpose
annualized_metrics(returns)	Computes annualized return, volatility, and Sharpe ratio to assess risk and reward.
drawdown_analysis(series)	Calculates max drawdowns and recovery periods, helping detect market crashes.
rolling(50).mean( )	Computes 50-day SMA and 200-day SMA to track long-term trends.
returns.rolling(50).corr( )	Computes rolling correlation between S&P 500 and AGG to analyze market sentiment shifts.

Script execution and outputs. –

```
import pandas as pd
import numpy as np
import yfinance as yf
import matplotlib.pyplot as plt

# Define symbols
symbols = ["^GSPC", "AGG"]  # S&P 500 and US Aggregate Bond ETF

# Define date range
start_date = "2010-01-01"
end_date = None  # Gets the most recent data available

# Fetch data from Yahoo Finance

data = yf.download(symbols, start=start_date, end=end_date,
auto_adjust=False, actions=False)['Adj Close']


# Rename columns for clarity
data.columns = ["US Aggregate Bond ETF", "S&P 500"]


# Compute moving averages
data["SMA_50"] = data["S&P 500"].rolling(50).mean()
data["SMA_200"] = data["S&P 500"].rolling(200).mean()
data["EMA_50"]=data["S&P500"].ewm(span=50,adjust=False).mean()

# Compute daily returns
returns = data.pct_change().dropna()

# Compute risk and performance metrics
def annualized_metrics(returns):
    annualized_return = returns.mean() * 252
    annualized_volatility = returns.std() * np.sqrt(252)
    sharpe_ratio = annualized_return / annualized_volatility
    return annualized_return, annualized_volatility, sharpe_
    ratio

sp500_metrics = annualized_metrics(returns["S&P 500"])
bond_metrics  =  annualized_metrics(returns["US  Aggregate
Bond ETF"])

print("\n Performance Metrics:")
print(f"S&P 500 - Annualized Return: {sp500_metrics[0]:.2%},
Volatility: {sp500_metrics[1]:.2%}, Sharpe Ratio: {sp500_me
trics[2]:.2f}")
print(f"US Aggregate Bond ETF - Annualized Return: {bond_
metrics[0]:.2%}, Volatility: {bond_metrics[1]:.2%}, Sharpe
Ratio: {bond_metrics[2]:.2f}")
```

```
# Compute drawdown analysis
def drawdown_analysis(series):
    cumulative = (1 + series).cumprod()
    peak = cumulative.cummax()
    drawdown = (cumulative - peak) / peak
    return drawdown

data["Drawdown S&P 500"] = drawdown_analysis(returns["S&P 500"])
data["Drawdown Bonds"] = drawdown_analysis(returns["US Aggregate Bond ETF"])

# Compute rolling volatility
data["Rolling Volatility"] = returns["S&P 500"].rolling(50).std() * np.sqrt(252)

# Plot S&P 500 with moving averages
fig, ax1 = plt.subplots(figsize=(12, 6))

ax1.set_xlabel("Date")
ax1.set_ylabel("S&P 500 Price", color="grey")
ax1.plot(data.index, data["S&P 500"], label="S&P 500", color="black")
ax1.plot(data.index, data["SMA_50"], label="50-Day SMA", linestyle="--", color="blue")
ax1.plot(data.index, data["SMA_200"], label="200-Day SMA", linestyle="--", color="red")
ax1.plot(data.index, data["EMA_50"], label="50-Day EMA", linestyle="--", color="green")
ax1.tick_params(axis="y", labelcolor="black")

# Create secondary y-axis for Bonds
ax2 = ax1.twinx()
ax2.set_ylabel("US Aggregate Bond ETF Price", color="blue")
ax2.plot(data.index, data["US Aggregate Bond ETF"], label="US Aggregate Bond ETF", color="blue")
ax2.tick_params(axis="y", labelcolor="blue")

# Title, legend, and grid
plt.title("S&P 500 vs US Aggregate Bond ETF - Adj Closing Prices & Trend Indicators")
fig.tight_layout()
ax1.legend(loc="upper left")
ax2.legend(loc="upper right")
plt.grid()
plt.show()

# Plot rolling volatility
plt.figure(figsize=(12, 6))
plt.plot(data.index, data["Rolling Volatility"],
```

```
label="50-Day Rolling Volatility", color="purple")
plt.title("S&P 500 Rolling Volatility (50-Day Window)")
plt.legend()
plt.grid(True)
plt.show()

# Plot drawdowns
fig, ax = plt.subplots(figsize=(12, 6))
ax.plot(data.index, data["Drawdown S&P 500"], label="S&P
500 Drawdown", color="black")
ax.plot(data.index, data["Drawdown Bonds"], label="US
Aggregate Bond ETF Drawdown", color="blue")
ax.set_ylabel("Drawdown (%)")
ax.set_xlabel("Date")
ax.set_title("Drawdown Analysis: S&P 500 vs US Aggregate
Bond ETF")
ax.axhline(0, color="red", linestyle="--", linewidth=1)
ax.legend()
plt.grid(True)
plt.show()

# Compute rolling correlation
data["Rolling Correlation"] = returns["S&P 500"].rolling(5
0).corr(returns["US Aggregate Bond ETF"])

# Plot rolling correlation
plt.figure(figsize=(12, 6))
plt.plot(data.index, data["Rolling Correlation"],
label="Rolling Correlation (S&P 500 vs. Bonds)",
color="orange")
plt.axhline(0, color="black", linestyle="--", linewidth=1)
plt.title("Rolling Correlation between S&P 500 and US
Aggregate Bond ETF Returns (50-Day Window)")
plt.legend()
plt.grid(True)
plt.show()
```

Output:

```
Performance Metrics:
S&P 500 - Annualized Return: 13.15%, Volatility: 17.28%, Sharpe
Ratio: 0.76
US Aggregate Bond ETF - Annualized Return: 2.37%, Volatility:
4.81%, Sharpe Ratio: 0.49
```

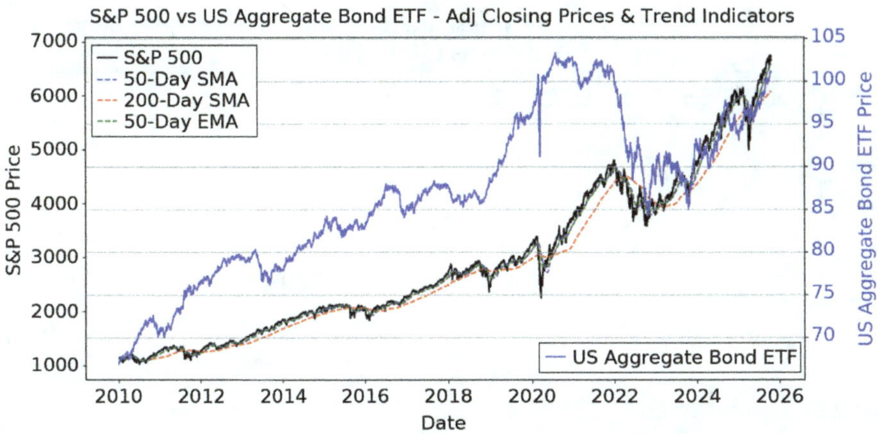
S&P 500 vs US Aggregate Bond ETF - Adj Closing Prices & Trend Indicators
S&P 500
50-Day SMA
200-Day SMA
50-Day EMA
US Aggregate Bond ETF
S&P 500 Price
US Aggregate Bond ETF Price
Date
1000
2000
3000
4000
5000
6000
7000
70
75
80
85
90
95
100
105
2010
2012
2014
2016
2018
2020
2022
2024
2026

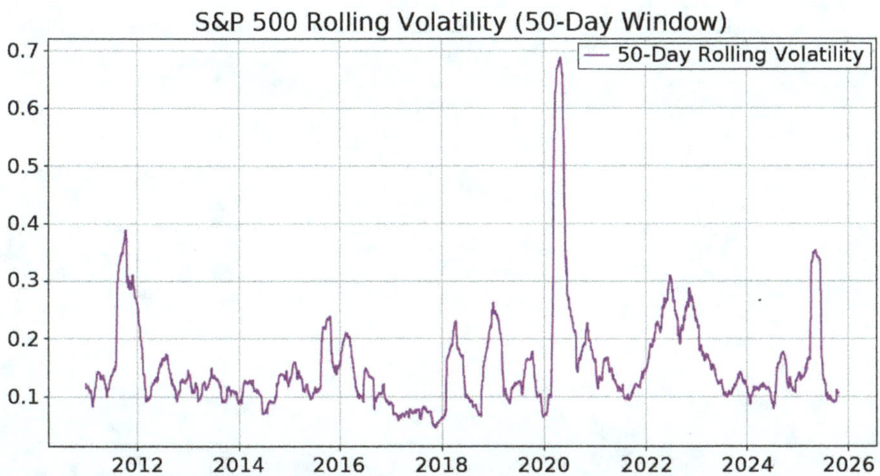
S&P 500 Rolling Volatility (50-Day Window)
50-Day Rolling Volatility
0.1
0.2
0.3
0.4
0.5
0.6
0.7
2012
2014
2016
2018
2020
2022
2024
2026

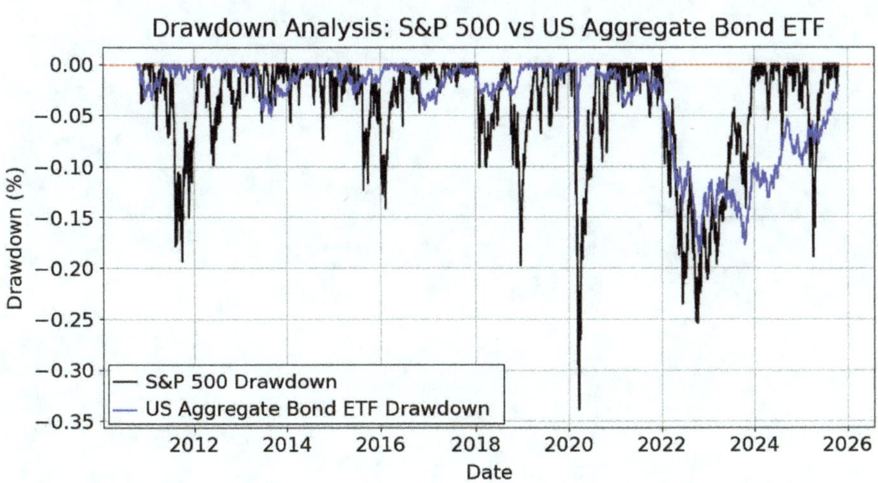
Drawdown Analysis: S&P 500 vs US Aggregate Bond ETF
S&P 500 Drawdown
US Aggregate Bond ETF Drawdown
Drawdown (%)
Date
0.00
−0.05
−0.10
−0.15
−0.20
−0.25
−0.30
−0.35
2012
2014
2016
2018
2020
2022
2024
2026

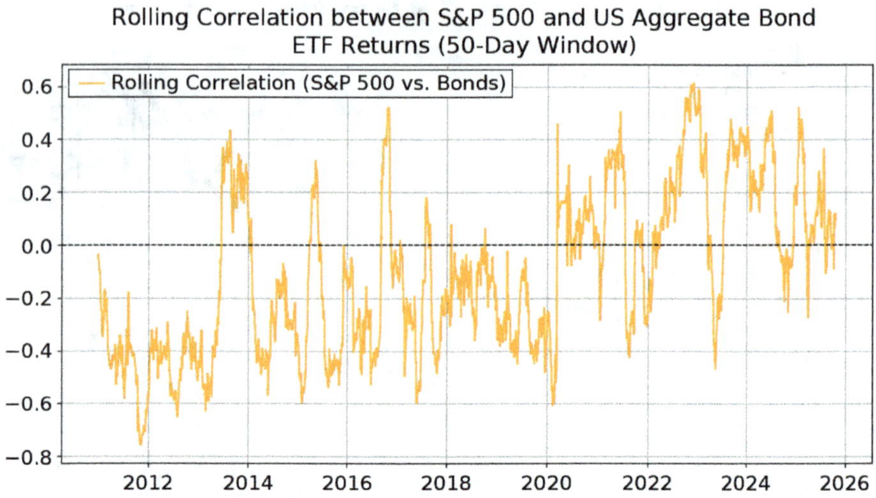
Rolling Correlation between S&P 500 and US Aggregate Bond ETF Returns (50-Day Window)
Rolling Correlation (S&P 500 vs. Bonds)
0.6
0.4
0.2
0.0
−0.2
−0.4
−0.6
−0.8
2012
2014
2016
2018
2020
2022
2024
2026

CHAPTER 3

Python Applied to Equity Management

3.1 CHAPTER OVERVIEW

This chapter explores the application of Python in equity management, focusing on portfolio construction, risk assessment, and performance evaluation. It introduces key financial concepts such as modern portfolio theory (MPT), the capital asset pricing model (CAPM), and the efficient frontier, demonstrating how Python can be used to optimize portfolios and analyze market data. Through practical exercises, it covers data retrieval using *yfinance*, statistical analysis with *pandas* and *numpy*, and portfolio optimization with *scipy*. Additionally, it discusses alternative asset pricing models beyond CAPM, performance evaluation metrics like the Sharpe and Treynor ratios, and the efficient market hypothesis (EMH). By integrating Python into equity management, the chapter provides a hands-on approach to making data-driven investment decisions.

3.2 PYTHON APPLIED TO EQUITY MANAGEMENT

In the complex world of finance, equity management plays a crucial role in achieving investment goals, balancing risk, and optimizing returns. As investors navigate fluctuating markets, the principles and practices of equity management provide a structured approach to constructing and maintaining portfolios that align with their financial objectives.

At its core, equity management involves the selection, monitoring, and adjustment of a portfolio of stocks with the goal of maximizing returns

DOI: 10.1201/9781003781394-3

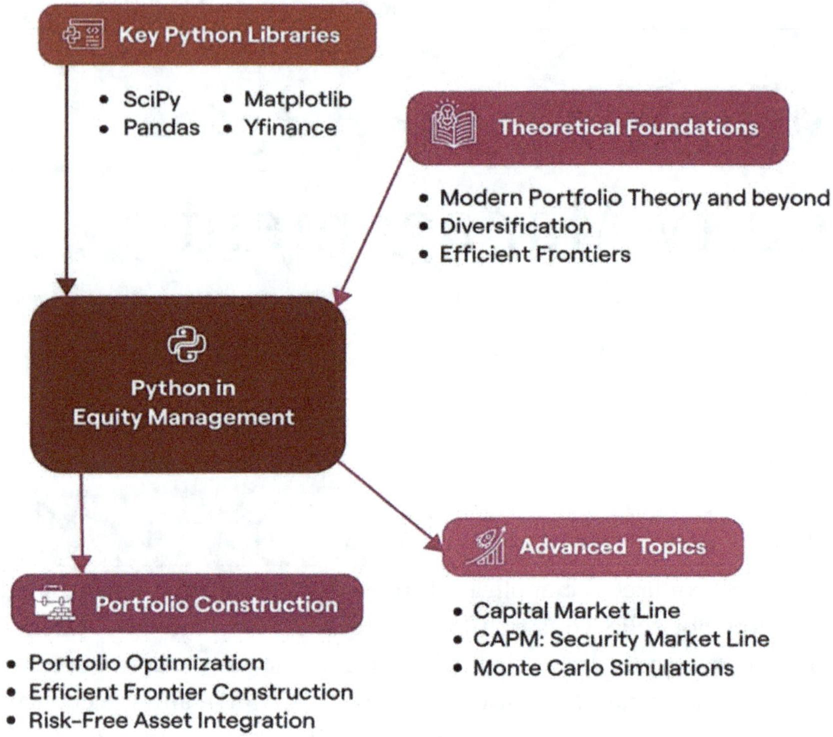

FIGURE 3.1 Python in Equity Management: Models and Applications

while managing risk. This process requires a deep understanding of financial markets, company fundamentals, and economic indicators. Successful equity management hinges on the ability to analyze vast amounts of data, identify opportunities, and make informed decisions that contribute to the long-term growth of the portfolio.

One of the most influential frameworks in equity management is modern portfolio theory (MPT), developed by Harry Markowitz in the 1950s (Markowitz, 1952, 1959). MPT revolutionized the way investors think about portfolio construction by introducing the concept of diversification as a means to optimize the risk-return trade-off.

According to MPT, it is not enough to evaluate investments in isolation. Instead, investors should consider how each asset contributes to the overall portfolio's risk and return. By combining assets with varying levels of correlation, investors can create a portfolio that minimizes risk for a given level of expected return, or conversely, maximizes return for a given level of risk. This optimal combination of assets lies on the so-called "efficient frontier," representing the best possible portfolios that offer the highest return for the least amount of risk.

Diversification, a key tenet of MPT, is achieved by investing in a variety of assets that respond differently to market conditions. By spreading investments across different sectors, industries, and geographical regions, the impact of a poor-performing asset can be mitigated, reducing the overall risk of the portfolio.

Python allows equity managers to implement MPT and beyond. For instance, portfolio managers can develop and backtest strategies that outperform the capital asset pricing model (CAPM), a single-factor model derived from MPT. Python's flexibility also extends to more advanced models like the Fama–French three-factor model, which can be implemented to better capture market anomalies.

Python's powerful optimization libraries, such as *SciPy* and *PuLP*, allow for the precise calculation of optimal asset weights that achieve the desired balance of risk and return.

In the following we will focus on the construction of equity portfolios following different models, calculating the Value at Risk (VaR) as an intuitive risk measure and the projection of the value of a portfolio following the Monte Carlo simulation.

3.3 MODERN PORTFOLIO THEORY (MPT) AND BEYOND

3.3.1 Introduction: Modern Portfolio Theory (MPT)

Modern portfolio theory has been the fundamental basis of portfolio management for over 50 years. MPT is due to Harry Markowitz, a prestigious economist of the Chicago school, who, in March 1952, published an article, "Portfolio Selection," where he established the basic principles of security selection for the formation of securities portfolios.

To be able to integrate a balanced investment portfolio, the most important thing is diversification, which is why diversification is the central concept in MPT, i.e. the fact that with a well-chosen combination of assets a higher return can be achieved with a lower risk than in any of the individually chosen assets.

Markowitz's theory and model were taken up by William Sharpe and Merton Miller, who carried out innovative work that strengthened the field of financial economics and corporate finance, thanks to their great contributions in the analysis of markets and risk distinction. Sharpe widely disseminated his models for analyzing investor portfolios and founded the Sharpe–Russell Research Institute for Finance.

Markowitz is credited with the development of the mean-variance model, which is a pioneering attempt to approach the demand for risky assets. To Sharpe and Miller we owe their contributions to the understanding of the equilibrium of capital markets.

William Sharpe, Harry Markowitz, and Merton Miller received the Nobel Prize in Economics in 1990 for proposing diversification models.

The exemplification of the models has been carried out with the Python program using Collab Google as its interpreter.

3.3.2 The Markowitz Model

Markowitz warned that the problem with investment selection is that it was always done in a context of uncertainty that carries risk, which meant recognizing that any financial investment has more than one possible outcome in terms of return and that, at best, it is only possible to know or infer a probability distribution for the outcome of the investment. If there were no uncertainty all investors would invest in the asset offering the highest rate of return, which is equivalent to saying that there could be only one investment asset. On the other hand, if only the expected value of returns is considered, the investment chosen would be the asset with the highest expected value. In both cases, the problem of asset diversification would not arise. On the other hand, the context of uncertainty in which the investment process necessarily takes place requires the incorporation of some hypothesis of the investor's behavior when faced with investment options, not knowing with certainty the future outcome of the same. These hypotheses are the following:

a) Investors are risk averse and want, for each level of expected return, the lowest possible risk.

b) The expected return of all assets is known, as well as their risk (variances and covariances). This is sufficient to determine the optimal portfolios.

c) There are no transaction costs or taxes.

d) Investors maximize expected utility each period, and utility curves show decreasing marginal utility.

e) Portfolios include all of an investor's assets and liabilities.

Under these assumptions, a portfolio is efficient if no other asset or set of assets offers a higher return for the same (or lower) risk; or lower risk for the same (or higher) return.

Harry Markowitz developed a measure for the return and risk of a portfolio. To do this, he first determined the expected return ($E(R_i)$) and risk (σ_i) of a financial asset with the statistical measures of the mean and variance (although the standard deviation is more commonly used) of a distribution of returns. If the observed returns are equiprobable (for example, when working with historical price series), the expected return is:

$$E(R_i) = \bar{R} = \sum_{i=1}^{k} \frac{R_i}{k}$$

where R_i at time t is

$$R_i = \frac{P_t - P_{t-1} + Div}{P_{t-1}}$$

If the observed returns are not equiprobable, then the expected return is:

$$E(R_i) = \sum_{i=1}^{k} R_i * p_i$$

where p_i is the probability that the return of asset i is R_i, for all i = {1 . . . k}. We measure the risk of the security or asset as the standard deviation of its returns:

$$\sigma_i = \sqrt{\sigma_i^2}$$

where

$$\sigma_i^2 = \sum_{i=1}^{k} \frac{\left(R_i - E(R_i)\right)^2}{k}$$

From here, the expected return of a portfolio (E(Rp)) is established as the weighted average of the expected returns of the assets in the portfolio:

$$E(R_p) = \sum_{i=1}^{N} E(R_i) w_i$$

However, when calculating the risk of the portfolio, one cannot lose sight of the fact that the variability of each of its financial assets is not independent of the variability of the rest, i.e. the variation in the profitability of one asset influences the variation of another asset. Therefore, the risk of a portfolio is expressed as follows:

$$\sigma_p = \sqrt{\sum_{i=1}^{N} w_i^2 \sigma_i^2 + \sum_{i=1}^{N}\sum_{j=1}^{N} w_i w_j \text{cov}_{ij}}$$

where

$$w_i, w_j \geq 0$$

$$\text{cov}_{ij} = \frac{1}{N}\sum_{i,j=1}^{N}\left[\left(R_i - E\left(R_i\right)\right)\left(R_j - E\left(R_j\right)\right)\right]$$

The expression of the risk of a portfolio in its matrix notation is as follows:

$$\sigma_P^2 = W \times S \times W' = \begin{pmatrix} w_1 & \cdots & w_N \end{pmatrix} \times \begin{bmatrix} \sigma_1^2 & \cdots & \sigma_{1N} \\ \vdots & \ddots & \vdots \\ \sigma_{N1} & \cdots & \sigma_N^2 \end{bmatrix} \times \begin{pmatrix} w_1 \\ \vdots \\ w_N \end{pmatrix}$$

where:

- W: 1xN vector of security weights
- S: NxN matrix of covariances between securities
- W': Nx1 vector transposed from vector W

By combining assets that do not perfectly correlate with each other, the overall risk of the portfolio can be reduced, as the negative performance of some assets can be offset by the positive performance of others. Stocks with low correlations to one another contribute significantly to reducing portfolio risk.

Investors aim to maximize returns for the amount of risk they are willing to take or minimize risk for a given level of expected returns. The Markowitz model quantifies this trade-off and helps investors make informed decisions.

In the Markowitz model, the trade-off can be formulated as an optimization problem:

- Maximize expected return for a given risk: *max E(Rp) subject to σp ≤ target risk level*

- Minimize risk for a given expected return: *min σp subject to E(Rp) ≥ target return level*

The following sections provide the code for the practical exercises along with the corresponding results (outputs).

PRACTICAL EXERCISE #3.01 EQUITY OPTIMAL PORTFOLIOS

Request: The Markowitz model helps optimize equity portfolios by balancing risk and return. It is based on the idea that investors seek to maximize their returns for a given level of risk or minimize risk for a desired level of return. Let's construct a portfolio with several US stocks ("The Magnificent Seven") for a given target risk.

Summary of the script. –

The script analyzes and optimizes a portfolio of selected technology stocks using historical data from Yahoo Finance. It:

a) Collects Data: Downloads adjusted closing prices for stocks (AAPL, AMZN, META, GOOGL, MSFT, NVDA, TSLA) from 2014 to the present.
b) Analyzes Performance: Calculates daily and annualized returns, volatility, and the correlation matrix.
c) Visualizes Trends: Plots stock price trends.
d) Optimizes Portfolio: Uses an optimization model to maximize returns for a user-defined risk level, ensuring asset weights sum to 100%.
e) Output Results: Displays the optimal portfolio allocation, expected annualized return, and volatility.

The script provides insights into asset allocation, risk management, and portfolio optimization.

TABLE 3.1 Summary of Key Functions and Their Purposes

Function	Purpose
cov_matrix = daily_returns.cov( )	Computes the covariance matrix of daily returns to measure asset co-movement.
portfolio_annualized_performance(weights, mean_returns, cov_matrix)	Calculates the portfolio's annualized return and volatility (risk) given asset weights.
max_return_for_given_risk(mean_returns, cov_matrix, target_risk)	Optimizes the portfolio allocation to maximize return for a given target risk (volatility).
sco.minimize(lambda x: -portfolio_annualized_performance(x, mean_returns, cov_matrix)[1], . . .)	Uses optimization to find the optimal asset weights that maximize return under constraints.
optimal_portfolio = max_return_for_given_risk(mean_returns, cov_matrix, target_risk)	Finds the optimal portfolio that meets the specified risk target.

Script execution and outputs. –

To begin, the first step is to calculate the general characteristics of the stocks that will make up the portfolio. This includes determining the expected return, expected risk (variance or standard deviation), the covariance and the correlation between the assets. These metrics are essential to understanding how each stock contributes to the portfolio's overall performance and risk. By analyzing these characteristics, we can effectively assess diversification opportunities and prepare for the optimization process.

Before this let´s import the necessary Python libraries:

```
# Libraries for the practical exercises 3.1 to 3.5
import pandas as pd
import pandas_datareader.data as web
import numpy as np
import pandas as pd
import yfinance as yf
import matplotlib.pyplot as plt
import scipy.optimize as sco
import statsmodels.api as sm
from datetime import datetime
```

```
# The characteristics of the data are specified
def get_adj_close(symbols, start, end=None):
    data = yf.download(symbols, start=start,
end=end, auto_adjust=False, actions=False, group_
by='ticker',progress=False)
    adj_close = data.xs('Adj Close', level=1, axis=1)
    # Rearrange columns exactly according to ticker list
    adj_close = adj_close[symbols]
    return adj_close

# List of companies
symbols = ['AAPL', 'AMZN', 'META', 'GOOGL','MSFT','NVDA',
'TSLA']
start = '2014-01-01'

prices = get_adj_close(symbols, start)
prices=prices.round(2)
prices
```

After running this code, we obtain the following output:

Ticker	AAPL	AMZN	META	GOOGL	MSFT	NVDA	TSLA
Date							
2014-01-02	17.17	19.90	54.37	27.67	30.89	0.37	10.01
2014-01-03	16.80	19.82	54.23	27.46	30.68	0.37	9.97
2014-01-06	16.89	19.68	56.85	27.77	30.03	0.37	9.80
2014-01-07	16.77	19.90	57.57	28.30	30.27	0.38	9.96
2014-01-08	16.87	20.10	57.87	28.36	29.73	0.39	10.09
...	...	...	...	...	...	...	...
2025-10-27	268.81	226.97	750.82	269.27	531.52	191.49	452.42
2025-10-28	269.00	229.25	751.44	267.47	542.07	201.03	460.55
2025-10-29	269.70	230.30	751.67	274.57	541.55	207.04	461.51
2025-10-30	271.40	222.86	666.47	281.48	525.76	202.89	440.10
2025-10-31	270.37	244.22	648.35	281.19	517.81	202.49	456.56

2977 rows × 7 columns

```
# Let's graphic the share price performance

fig, axes = plt.subplots(nrows=len(symbols), ncols = 1,
figsize = (10,20))
for k, v in enumerate(sorted(symbols),0):
    axes[0].set_title('Adj Close Price Trends')
    axes[k].plot(prices[v], c=np.random.random(3))
    axes[k].legend([v], loc = 0)
```

Output:

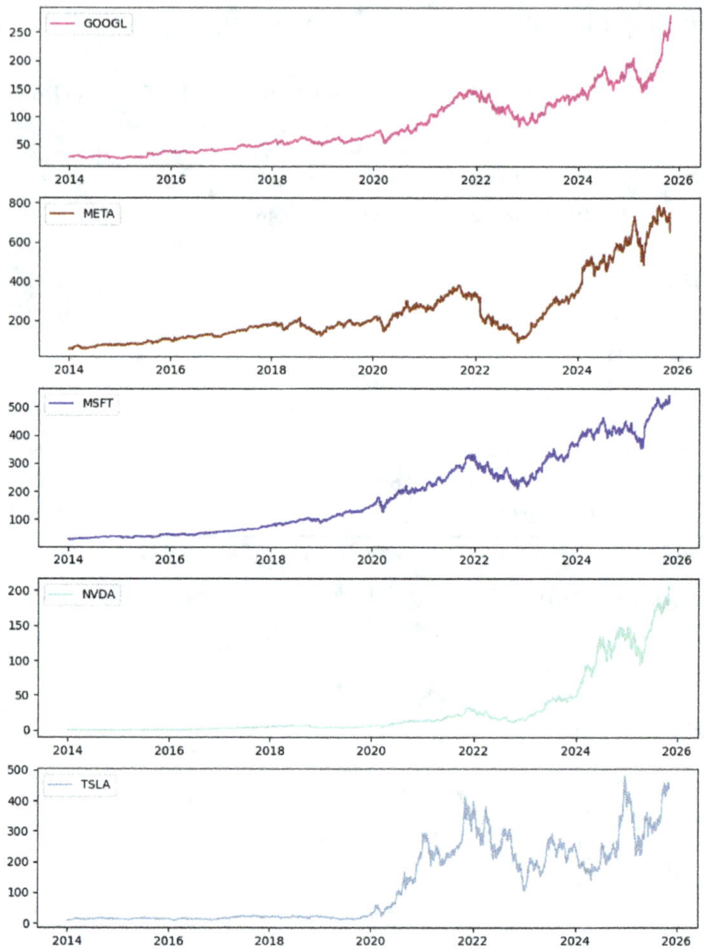


```
# Daily returns are calculated with these prices, starting
from the cells without data.

daily_returns = prices.pct_change().dropna()
daily_returns.columns = symbols

mean_daily_returns = daily_returns.mean(axis=0)
daily_volt=daily_returns.std(axis=0)

# The annualized return and risk are calculated for each
security.

an_volt = daily_volt * np.sqrt(252)
mean_returns = mean_daily_returns * 252
```

```
print('Annualized returns\n')
print(mean_returns.round(3))
print('Annualized volatilities\n')
print(an_volt.round(3))
```

Output:

```
Annualized returns

AAPL     0.274
AMZN     0.267
META     0.281
GOOGL    0.236
MSFT     0.274
NVDA     0.647
TSLA     0.486
dtype: float64

Annualized volatilities

AAPL     0.285
AMZN     0.330
META     0.375
GOOGL    0.282
MSFT     0.264
NVDA     0.477
TSLA     0.572
dtype: float64
```

```
# Let's calculate the correlation matrix

daily_returns.corr().round(2)
```

Output:

	AAPL	AMZN	META	GOOGL	MSFT	NVDA	TSLA
AAPL	1.00	0.53	0.51	0.58	0.65	0.52	0.42
AMZN	0.53	1.00	0.59	0.63	0.62	0.50	0.40
META	0.51	0.59	1.00	0.61	0.57	0.48	0.35
GOOGL	0.58	0.63	0.61	1.00	0.68	0.52	0.39
MSFT	0.65	0.62	0.57	0.68	1.00	0.59	0.40
NVDA	0.52	0.50	0.48	0.52	0.59	1.00	0.41
TSLA	0.42	0.40	0.35	0.39	0.40	0.41	1.00

```
# The covariance matrix is calculated
cov_matrix = daily_returns.cov()

# We provide a specific target level of risk (volatility)
target_risk = float(input("Please enter the target
volatility (e.g., 0.25 for 25%): "))

# We construct the function to calculate portfolio's
annualized performance (volatility and return)
def portfolio_annualized_performance(weights, mean_
returns, cov_matrix):
    returns = np.sum(mean_returns * weights)
    std = np.sqrt(np.dot(weights.T, np.dot(cov_matrix,
    weights))) * np.sqrt(252)
    return std, returns

# We construct the function to maximize portfolio return
given a target risk
def max_return_for_given_risk(mean_returns, cov_matrix,
target_risk):
    num_assets = len(mean_returns)
    args = (mean_returns, cov_matrix)

    # Constraint: weights sum to 1 and portfolio
    volatility equals the target risk
    constraints = ({'type': 'eq', 'fun': lambda x:
    portfolio_annualized_performance(x, mean_returns,
    cov_matrix)[0]- target_risk}, {'type': 'eq', 'fun':
    lambda x: np.sum(x) - 1})

    # Bounds: each weight is between 0 and 1
    bounds = tuple((0, 1) for asset in range(num_assets))

    # Initial guess for the weights (equal distribution)
    initial_weights = num_assets * [1. / num_assets, ]

    # Perform the optimization to maximize return subject
    to constraints
    result = sco.minimize(lambda x: -portfolio_annualized_
    performance(x, mean_returns, cov_matrix)[1],
                          initial_weights, method='SLSQP',
    bounds=bounds, constraints=constraints)
    return result

# We find the optimal portfolio for the given target risk
optimal_portfolio = max_return_for_given_risk(mean_returns,
cov_matrix, target_risk)
optimal_volatility, optimal_return = portfolio_annualized_
performance(optimal_portfolio.x, mean_returns, cov_matrix)

# The optimal portfolio results are displayed
optimal_allocation = pd.DataFrame(optimal_portfolio.x,
```

```
index=adj_close_data.columns, columns=['allocation'])
optimal_allocation.allocation = [round(i * 100, 2) for i
in optimal_allocation.allocation]
optimal_allocation = optimal_allocation.T


print("\nOptimal Portfolio for Target Volatility of
{:.2%}\n".format(target_risk))
print("Annualized Return (%):", round(optimal_return * 100, 3))
print("Annualized Volatility (%):", round(optimal_
volatility * 100, 3))
print("\nAllocation:")
optimal_allocation=optimal_allocation[symbols]
optimal_allocation
```

Output:

```
Please enter the target volatility (e.g., 0.25 for 25%): 0.27

Optimal Portfolio for Target Volatility of 27.00%

Annualized Return (%): 36.07
Annualized Volatility (%): 27.0

Allocation:
```

Ticker	AAPL	AMZN	META	GOOGL	MSFT	NVDA	TSLA
allocation	25.64	2.8	0.0	10.99	33.85	21.42	5.29

3.3.2.1 Construction of the Efficient Frontier Based on Several S&P500 Stocks

Once the characteristics of the assets that will be included in the portfolio have been calculated, we proceed to determine the efficient frontier. The efficient frontier is a key concept in MPT introduced by Harry Markowitz. It represents the set of optimal portfolios that offer the highest expected return for a given level of risk, or, equivalently, the lowest level of risk for a given expected return.

To locate the efficient frontier, we must first establish a feasible set of portfolios. The feasible set, which includes all possible combinations of assets, each combination being a portfolio, is shown in the following graph.

Of this feasible set, the portfolios in the lower plane of the figure are not efficient, since, for the same risks, the portfolios in the upper plane offer higher expected returns. If we were to keep only the upper plane of the figure, we would obtain the efficient frontier, with the first portfolio on the frontier being the minimum variance portfolio.

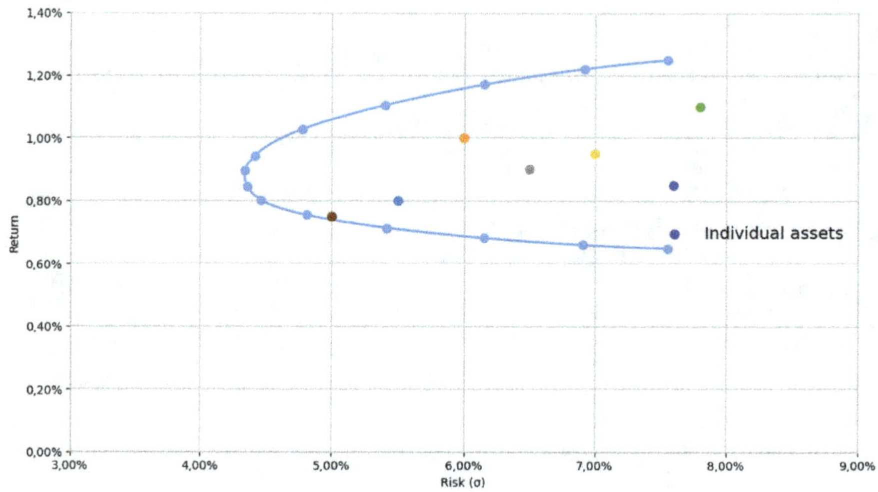

FIGURE 3.2 Feasible Set

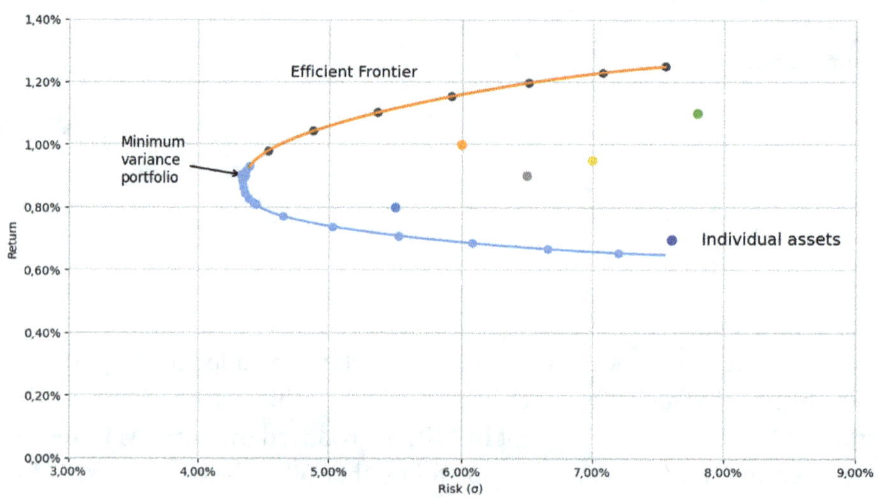

FIGURE 3.3 Efficient Frontier

The investor's choice of portfolio will depend on his or her preferences (profile) in terms of risk-return, expressed by Markowitz through the investor's utility curves.

The efficient frontier helps identify the optimal combination of equities that maximizes return for a given level of risk or minimizes risk for a given level of return. For equity investors, this involves selecting stocks with the best combination of expected returns and volatility (risk).

The efficient frontier acts as a benchmark. If an equity portfolio lies below the efficient frontier, it indicates that the portfolio is suboptimal and could be improved by adjusting the stock selection or weights.

PRACTICAL EXERCISE #3.02 EFFICIENT FRONTIER

Request: Let's construct the efficient frontier with the former companies of the US S&P500 market.

Summary of the script. –

This extended script enhances the portfolio analysis by incorporating Monte Carlo simulations and efficient frontier calculations, allowing for a deeper exploration of optimal investment strategies.

Key Steps of the Code:

a) User Inputs:
   - Number of random portfolios to generate (e.g., 25,000).
   - Risk-free rate for Sharpe ratio calculation (e.g., 2%).

b) Portfolio Performance Calculation:
   - Defines functions to compute annualized return and volatility for given portfolio weights.

c) Random Portfolio Generation:
   - Simulates multiple random portfolios by generating random weight combinations.
   - Calculates return, risk, and Sharpe ratio for each portfolio.

d) Optimal Portfolio Identification:
   - Maximum Sharpe Ratio Portfolio: Portfolio with the highest risk-adjusted return.
   - Minimum Variance Portfolio: Portfolio with the lowest volatility.

e) Efficient Frontier Construction:
   - Uses optimization to determine the minimum volatility for a range of target returns.
   - Plots the efficient frontier, showing optimal portfolios.

f) Results Display:
   - Prints the allocations, annualized return, volatility, and Sharpe ratio for both key portfolios.

g) Visualization:
   - Plots the efficient frontier, marking the maximum Sharpe ratio and minimum variance portfolios.
   - A color-coded scatter plot represents the risk-return profile of the randomly generated portfolios.

This code provides a comprehensive framework for portfolio optimization, helping to identify the best investment allocations based on risk-return tradeoffs using the efficient frontier and the capital market line (CML) approach.

TABLE 3.2 Summary of Key Functions and Their Purposes

Function	Purpose
portfolio_annualized_performance	Calculates annualized return and volatility of a portfolio.
generate_random_portfolios	Generates portfolios with random weights and calculates performance.
minimize_volatility	Finds the minimum volatility portfolio for a given return.
max_sharpe_idx / min_vol_idx	Identifies key portfolios (max Sharpe, min volatility).
Efficient Frontier Calculation	Constructs an efficient frontier by optimizing portfolios.
Plotting Function	Visualizes the efficient frontier and key portfolios.

Script execution and outputs. –

```
# We provide the number of portfolios to be generated
num_portfolios = float(input("Please enter the number of
portfolios to be generated (e.g., 25000): "))
num_portfolios = int(num_portfolios)
Please enter the number of portfolios to be generated
(e.g., 25000): 25000

# We provide the risk free rate
risk_free_rate = float(input("Please enter the risk free
rate (e.g., 0.01 for 1%): "))
Please enter the risk free rate (e.g., 0.01 for 1%): 0.02

# We construct a Portfolio Performance Function

def portfolio_annualized_performance(weights, mean_
returns, cov_matrix):
    returns = np.sum(mean_returns * weights)
    std = np.sqrt(np.dot(weights.T, np.dot(cov_matrix,
    weights))) * np.sqrt(252)
    return std, returns

# We generate Random Portfolios
def generate_random_portfolios(num_portfolios, mean_
returns, cov_matrix, risk_free_rate):
    results = np.zeros((3, num_portfolios))
    weights_record = []
    for i in range(num_portfolios):
        weights = np.random.random(len(symbols))
        weights /= np.sum(weights)
        weights_record.append(weights)
        portfolio_std_dev, portfolio_return = portfolio_
        annualized_performance(weights, mean_returns, cov_
        matrix)
        results[0, i] = portfolio_std_dev
        results[1, i] = portfolio_return
        results[2, i] = (portfolio_return - risk_free_rate) /
        portfolio_std_dev
    return results, weights_record
```

```
# We construct a function to minimize for Efficient Frontier

def minimize_volatility(mean_returns, cov_matrix, target_
return):
    num_assets = len(mean_returns)
    args = (mean_returns, cov_matrix)

    constraints = ({'type': 'eq', 'fun': lambda x: portfolio_
    annualized_performance(x, mean_returns, cov_matrix)[1] -
    target_return},
                   {'type': 'eq', 'fun': lambda x:
                   np.sum(x) - 1})

    bounds = tuple((0, 1) for asset in range(num_assets))
    result = sco.minimize(lambda x: portfolio_annualized_
    performance(x, mean_returns, cov_matrix)[0],
                          num_assets * [1. / num_assets],
    method='SLSQP', bounds=bounds, constraints=constraints)

    return result

# We generate Portfolios and identify Key Portfolios
results, weights = generate_random_portfolios(num_
portfolios, mean_returns, cov_matrix, risk_free_rate)

# We identify the Maximum Sharpe Ratio Portfolio, which is
the portfolio of maximum slope in the efficient frontier:

max_sharpe_idx = np.argmax(results[2])
sdp, rp = results[0, max_sharpe_idx], results[1, max_
sharpe_idx]
sharpe_ratio = (rp - risk_free_rate) / sdp
max_sharpe_allocation = pd.DataFrame(weights[max_sharpe_idx],
index=symbols, columns=['allocation'])
max_sharpe_allocation.allocation = [round(i*100,2) for i
in max_sharpe_allocation.allocation]

# We identify the Minimum Variance Portfolio, which is the
first portfolio of the efficient frontier:

min_vol_idx = np.argmin(results[0])
sdp_min, rp_min = results[0, min_vol_idx], results[1,
min_vol_idx]
min_vol_allocation = pd.DataFrame(weights[min_vol_idx],
index=symbols, columns=['allocation'])
min_vol_allocation.allocation = [round(i*100,2) for i in
min_vol_allocation.allocation]

# We calculate the Efficient Frontier (Starting from the MVP)

target_returns = np.linspace(rp_min, max(mean_returns), 100)
efficient_volatilities = []
efficient_returns = []
```

```
for target_return in target_returns:
    optimized_result = minimize_volatility(mean_returns,
    cov_matrix, target_return)
    efficient_volatilities.append(optimized_result.fun)
    efficient_returns.append(target_return)
efficient_volatilities = np.array(efficient_volatilities)
efficient_returns = np.array(efficient_returns)


# We display Portfolio Characteristics:

print("\033[1m Maximum Sharpe Ratio Portfolio
Allocation\033[0m\n ")
print("Annualized Return:", round(rp*100, 2))
print("Annualized Volatility:", round(sdp*100, 2))
print("Sharpe Ratio:", round(sharpe_ratio, 2))
print(max_sharpe_allocation.T)

print("\n\033[1m Minimum Variance Portfolio
Allocation\033[0m\n")
print("Annualized Return:", round(rp_min*100, 2))
print("Annualized Volatility:", round(sdp_min*100, 2))
print(min_vol_allocation.T)



# We plot the Efficient Frontier

plt.figure(figsize=(8, 6))
plt.grid(True)
plt.scatter(results[0, :], results[1, :], c=results[2, :],
cmap='YlGnBu', marker='o', s=10, alpha=0.3)
plt.colorbar()
plt.plot(efficient_volatilities, efficient_returns, linestyle='-',
color='black', linewidth=2, label='Efficient Frontier')
plt.scatter(sdp, rp, marker='o', color='r', s=100,
label='Maximum Sharpe ratio Portfolio')
plt.scatter(sdp_min, rp_min, marker='o', color='b', s=100,
label='Minimum Variance Portfolio')
plt.title('EFFICIENT FRONTIER')
plt.xlabel('annualized volatility')
plt.ylabel('annualized returns')
plt.legend(labelspacing=0.8)
plt.show()
```

Output:

```
Maximum Sharpe Ratio Portfolio Allocation

Annualized Return: 50.17
Annualized Volatility: 35.59
Sharpe Ratio: 1.35
```

```
                AAPL  AMZN  META  GOOGL   MSFT    NVDA    TSLA
allocation      6.12  5.73  1.02   6.83  12.34   53.74   14.22

Minimum Variance Portfolio Allocation

Annualized Return: 26.68
Annualized Volatility: 24.2
                AAPL  AMZN   META  GOOGL MSFT  NVDA  TSLA
allocation      30.1 11.96  5.19  23.6  28.37 0.46  0.33
```

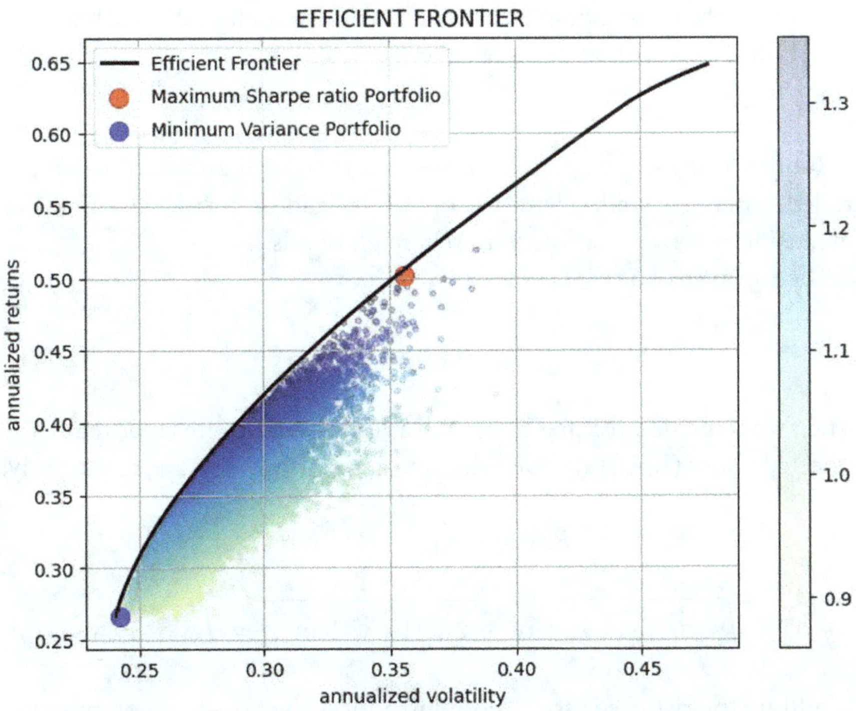

3.3.3 The Incorporation of Risk-Free Assets

What happens if risk-free investments (a traditional example is 10-year sovereign bonds) are included in portfolios? Presumably, investors who are totally risk averse would opt for a less risky combination of risky assets and sovereign bonds.

Therefore, a more sophisticated model than the one initially offered by Markowitz is required, in which the risk-free return on new investments can be calibrated to the risk of the market portfolio.

James Tobin (1958), revising the Keynesian theory of liquidity preferences, developed a model built on Markowitz's efficiency and perfect capital market assumptions and underpinning Irving Fisher's (1930) separation theorem.

> The principle of separation into two funds or Tobin's theorem was later reformulated by the work of W. F. Sharpe (1964) and J. Lintner (1965), since Tobin's explicit aim was not to provide a model of financial risk management, but to provide a sound basis for liquidity preference theory. Tobin's original model did not envisage a monetary asset at a risk-free interest rate, but rather cash without remuneration.
>
> *(Ruiz et al., 2000)*

Tobin shows that in a perfect market where risky financial securities are traded, assets are traded with the option to lend or borrow at a risk-free rate, using risk-free assets such as sovereign bonds.

The variance of a risk-free asset is:

$$\sigma_{rf} = 0$$

When we combine a risk-free asset with a risky asset (or with a portfolio), the expected return ($E(R_p)$) and the risk of the new portfolio (σ_p) are, respectively:

$$E(R_p) = w_i E(R_i) + (1 - w_i) R_f$$

$$\sigma_p = \sqrt{w_i^2 \sigma_i^2 + (1 - w_i)^2 \sigma_{rf}^2 + 2w_i(1 - w_i)\mathrm{cov}_{i,rf}} = \sqrt{w_i^2 \sigma_i^2} = w_i \sigma_i$$

By adding the risk-free asset, Tobin introduces the possibility of investing (lending) or borrowing at the risk-free interest rate, i.e., if:

- $wR_f = 1\text{-}w_i > 0$, means that it is invested in a risk-free asset or lends at the interest rate R_f, and we would be dealing with a lending portfolio.
- $wR_f = 1\text{-}w_i < 0$, means borrowing at the interest rate R_f to invest it in a risky portfolio (such as the market portfolio), and this would be a borrowing portfolio.

Since both the return and risk of this portfolio are linear combinations, the graph representing the risk and return of the portfolio is a straight line joining the two assets. This straight line is called the transformation line:

$$E(R_p) = R_f + \frac{E(R_i) - R_f}{\sigma_i} \times \sigma_p$$

Any point on the transformation line can be reached by investing a part of the portfolio in the risky asset w_i, and the rest $(1 - w_i)$, in the riskless asset. This line of investment possibilities dominates all the possibilities of the efficient frontier:

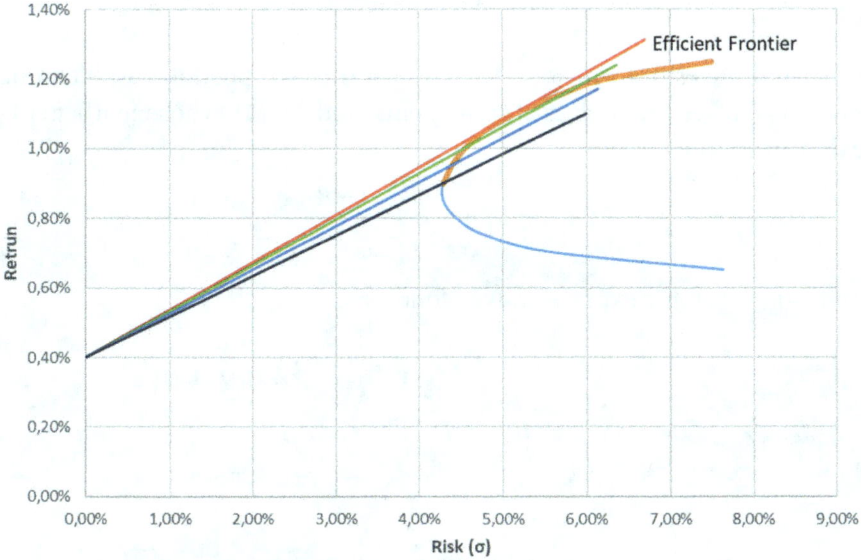

FIGURE 3.4 Transformation Lines

Although the investor can now combine any of the efficient frontier portfolios with the risk-free asset, only one of the efficient frontier portfolios, portfolio C, achieves the maximum return for any level of risk.

By investing in the right proportions in R_f and C, each investor will achieve his or her chosen level of risk. In other words, the main consequence of this analysis is striking: all investors will own a portfolio C regardless of their risk-return preferences and will achieve the desired level of risk by lending or borrowing at the risk-free interest rate, R_f.

If we now assume that investors have homogeneous expectations, i.e. they all have the same expected return and risk estimates for all risky assets, the Transformation line becomes the capital market Line (CML) and the tangent portfolio becomes the market portfolio (MP). Now all investors have the same expectations and consequently have the same efficient frontier.

The market portfolio includes all risky assets: if an asset were not in the portfolio in which everyone wants to invest, then its demand would disappear, and it would have no value. The market portfolio is a fully diversified portfolio, where the specific and unique risk of each asset disappears.

This MP is located at the point of tangency between the efficient frontier and the CML, i.e., this portfolio would have the maximum slope:

$$\text{Máx}\frac{E(R_i)-R_f}{\sigma_i}$$

so that all investors will want to invest in this MP portfolio and lend or borrow to place themselves at some point on the CML whose mathematical expression is:

$$E\left(R_p\right)=R_\text{f}+\frac{E\left(R_{MP}\right)-R_\text{f}}{\sigma_{MP}}\times\sigma_p$$

and whose graphic expression is as follows:

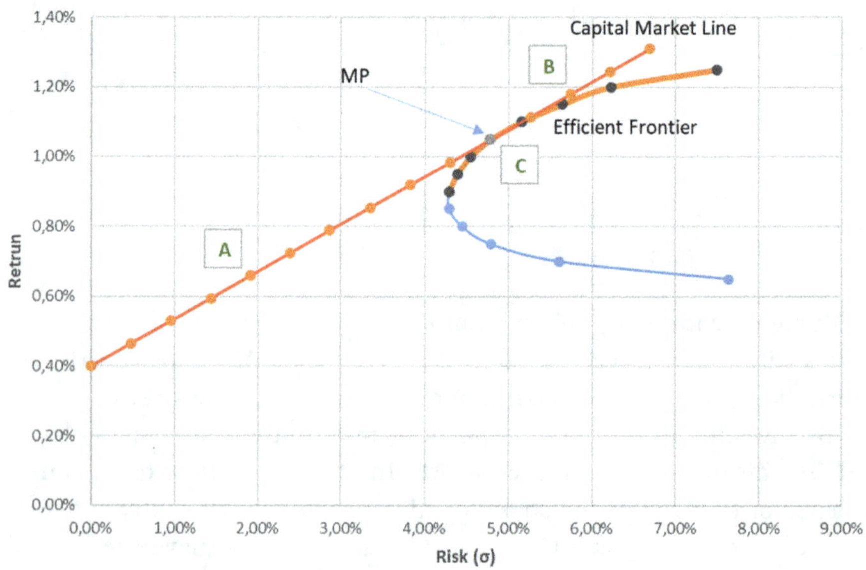

FIGURE 3.5 Capital Market Line

where position A is a lending portfolio and position B is a borrowing portfolio. Position C is a position fully invested in the market portfolio. The particular point chosen will depend on the investor's degree of risk aversion (utility curve).

PRACTICAL EXERCISE #3.03 CAPITAL MARKET LINE

Request: Let us construct the capital market line from the above efficient frontier.

Summary of the script. –

The code given is an implementation of the capital market line concept in portfolio management, which includes the following key steps:

a) Portfolio Return and Allocation Calculation:
   - Computes the expected return of a portfolio lying on the CML
   - Determines the weights of the market portfolio and the risk-free asset in the target portfolio
   - Calculates the allocation to risky assets based on the maximum Sharpe ratio portfolio.

b) Portfolio Type Determination:
   - Classifies the portfolio as either a lending portfolio (if the weight in the market portfolio is less than 100%) or a borrowing portfolio (if greater than 100%).

c) Displaying Portfolio Characteristics:
   - Prints key statistics of the target portfolio, such as:
     i) Target risk (percentage)
     ii) Expected return (percentage)
     iii) Weights in market portfolio and risk-free asset

d) Efficient Frontier Visualization:
   - Plots the efficient frontier using scatter plots and lines:
     i) Displays efficient portfolios based on simulated returns and volatilities.
     ii) Highlights the maximum Sharpe ratio portfolio and the minimum variance portfolio.

e) Capital Market Line (CML) Plot:
   - Constructs and plots the CML using the risk-free rate and Sharpe ratio.
   - Overlays the target portfolio on the CML to show its position relative to the efficient frontier.

f) Graph Formatting and Presentation:
   - The final plot contains labeled axes, a legend, and titles, ensuring clarity in visualization.

Overall, the code provides a comprehensive implementation of the CML framework, allowing for the assessment of an optimal portfolio's allocation and visualization within the efficient frontier.

TABLE 3.3 Summary of Key Functions and Their Purposes

Function/Calculation	Purpose
cml_return = risk_free_rate + sharpe_ratio * target_risk	Calculates the expected return of the portfolio on the capital market line.
weight_market_portfolio = target_risk / sdp	Determines the weight of the market portfolio for a given target risk.
weight_risk_free = 1 – weight_market_portfolio	Computes the proportion of the risk-free asset in the portfolio.
target_portfolio_allocation = weight_market_portfolio * max_sharpe_allocation['allocation'] / 100	Calculates the optimal asset allocation for the target risk portfolio.

Script execution and outputs. –

```
# Additional Code for Incorporating CML

# We calculate portfolio return and weights in market
portfolio and risk-free asset

cml_return = risk_free_rate + sharpe_ratio * target_risk
weight_market_portfolio = target_risk / sdp
weight_risk_free = 1 - weight_market_portfolio

# We calculate the portfolio characteristics for the
target risk

target_portfolio_allocation = weight_market_portfolio *
max_sharpe_allocation['allocation'] / 100


# We determine if it's a lending or borrowing portfolio

if weight_market_portfolio < 1:
    portfolio_type = "Lending Portfolio"
else:
    portfolio_type = "Borrowing Portfolio"


# We display the characteristics of the portfolio with the
target risk

print(portfolio_type)
print("Target Risk (%):", round(target_risk*100, 2))
print("Return (%):", round(cml_return*100, 2))
print("Weight in Market Portfolio (%):", round(weight_
market_portfolio*100, 2))
print("Weight in Risk-Free Asset (%):", round(weight_risk_
free*100, 2))
```

Output:

```
Lending Portfolio
Target Risk (%): 27.0
Return (%): 38.54
Weight in Market Portfolio (%): 75.87
Weight in Risk-Free Asset (%): 24.13
```

```
# We plot Efficient Frontier

plt.figure(figsize=(8, 6))
plt.grid(True)
plt.scatter(results[0, :], results[1, :], c=results[2, :],
cmap='YlGnBu', marker='o', s=10, alpha=0.3)
plt.colorbar()
plt.plot(efficient_volatilities, efficient_returns,
linestyle='-', color='black', linewidth=2, label='Efficient
Frontier')
plt.scatter(sdp, rp, marker='o', color='r', s=100,
label='Maximum Sharpe ratio Portfolio')
plt.scatter(sdp_min, rp_min, marker='o', color='b', s=100,
label='Minimum Variance Portfolio')
plt.title('EFFICIENT FRONTIER')
plt.xlabel('annualized volatility')
plt.ylabel('annualized returns')
plt.legend(labelspacing=0.8)

# We plot CML

cml_x = np.linspace(0, max(results[0, :]) * 1.5, 100)
cml_y = risk_free_rate + sharpe_ratio * cml_x
plt.plot(cml_x, cml_y, linestyle='-', color='brown',
label='Capital Market Line')

# Plot Tobin Portfolio at Target Risk

plt.scatter(target_risk, cml_return, marker='o',
color='g', s=100, label=f'{portfolio_type}')

plt.title('CAPITAL MARKET LINE (CML)')
plt.xlabel('annualized volatility')
plt.ylabel('annualized returns')
plt.legend(labelspacing=0.8)
plt.show()
```

Output:

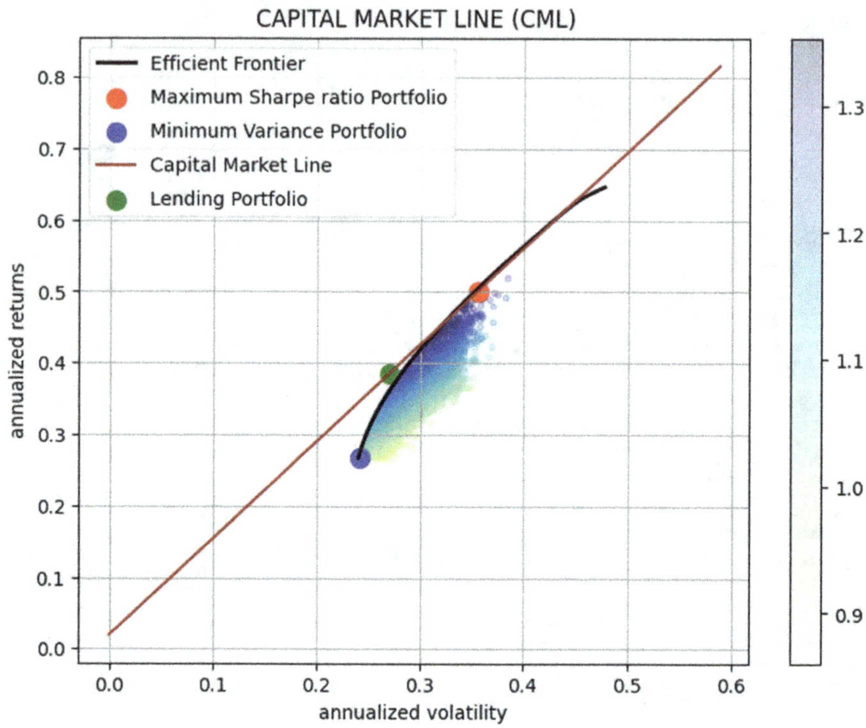

3.3.4 The CAPM Model

The purpose of diversification is to reduce the overall risk (standard deviation) of a portfolio. Due to correlations of less than unity, when we add stocks to a portfolio, the risk is reduced. How many stocks should we include to arrive at a risk-free portfolio? No matter how many stocks we add, there is always an unavoidable risk that does not disappear with diversification.

The most efficiently diversified portfolio is the market portfolio. Because you cannot have a more efficiently diversified portfolio than the market portfolio (maximum Sharpe ratio), the risk associated with this portfolio is unavoidable, or systematic. That is, the only risk remaining after efficient diversification is systematic risk in the sense that it affects all tradable financial assets in a particular market. Therefore, systematic risk is the risk that is not eliminated by diversification; it is the risk caused by macroeconomic variables, the risk that remains in the market portfolio.

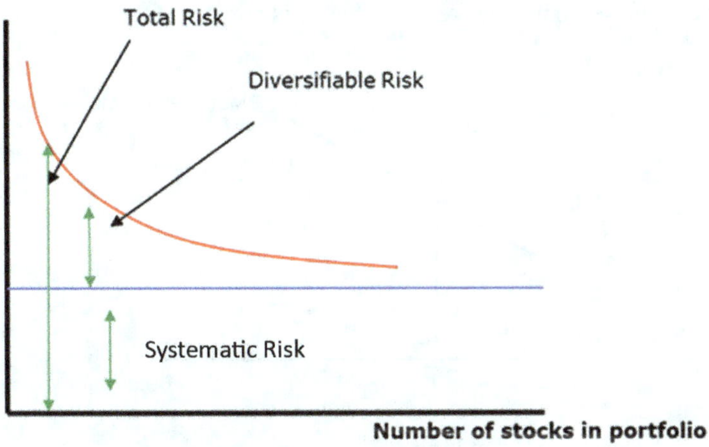

FIGURE 3.6 Systematic Risk

And here appears Sharpe's model, which extends Markowitz and Tobin's analysis of optimal portfolio selection to a capital market equilibrium model, dealing only with systematic risk and, as a result, offering a demand-side model of the capital market equilibrium (Febrero, 1991).

The first model used that dealt with systematic risk was the one developed almost simultaneously by Sharpe (1964) and Treynor (1961) and later extended by Mossin (1966), Lintner (1965) and Black et al. (1972). This model, called the capital asset pricing model (CAPM), shows that in an efficient market the rate of return of any financial asset with risk is a function of its covariance with the rate of return of the market portfolio, i.e. the portfolio that contains each and every asset in the market in a certain proportion. In other words, the risk premium of an asset is equal to its beta multiplied by the risk premium of the market portfolio. The beta measures the degree of co-variability between the expected return of the asset (E(Ri)) and the expected return of the market portfolio ($E(R_M)$):

$$E(R_i) = R_f + \beta_i \left(E(R_M) - R_f\right)$$

where

$$\beta_i = \frac{\mathrm{cov}_{i,M}}{\sigma_M^2}$$

From here the security market line (SML) is constructed:

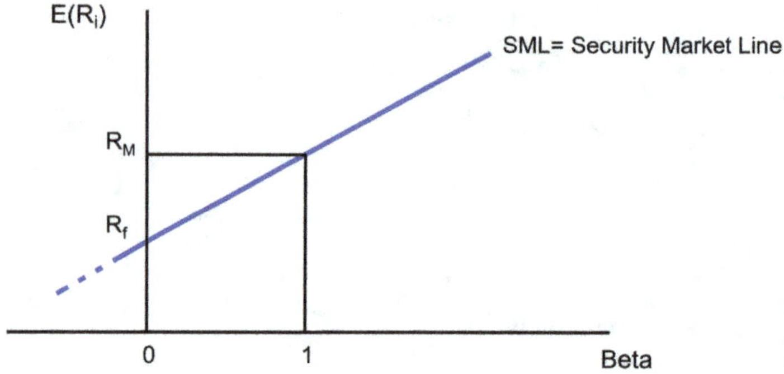

FIGURE 3.7 Security Market Line

This model makes it possible to diagnose whether a financial asset is overvalued or undervalued by the market.

An important advantage of beta is that the beta of a portfolio is the weighted average of the betas of the assets that make up the portfolio. If a portfolio has n assets:

$$\beta_p = w_1\beta_1 + w_2\beta_2 + \ldots + w_n\beta_n$$

where w_i is the portfolio weight of asset i.

Assume the following SML around which different securities with their expected returns are placed:

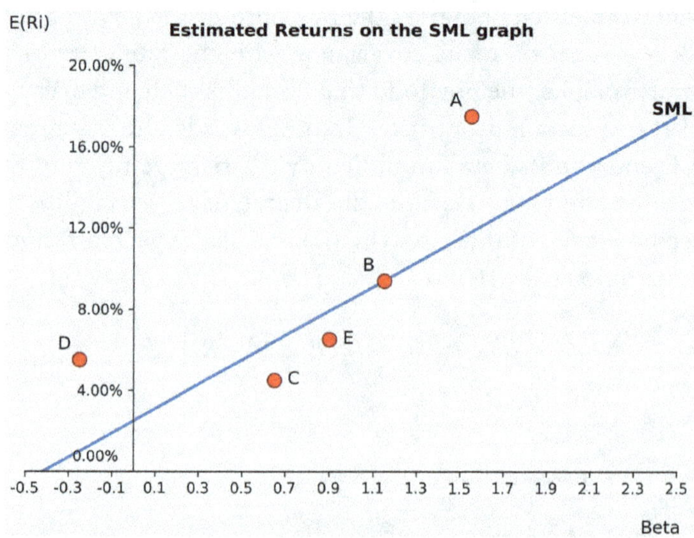

FIGURE 3.8 Estimated Returns and SML

Stocks A and B have a higher systematic risk than the market (aggressive stocks); therefore, they should provide returns commensurate with their level of risk. Stock C has a lower risk than the market (defensive), and we will expect a lower return. E has a systematic risk equal to the market, so the return we require from it is equal to that of the market. Finally, D is a rare case, due to its negative beta, which means the asset tends to move in the opposite direction of the overall market; when the market goes up, the asset tends to go down, and vice versa. Gold is often an example of this.

In equilibrium, all assets and all portfolios should be valued so that their required returns are consistent with their levels of systematic risk and therefore graphically above the security market line. Any asset above the SML should be considered undervalued because it implies that the return we have estimated that asset will deliver is higher than its beta (see A and D shares). Conversely, assets with estimated returns below the SML should be considered overvalued (see stocks C and E).

PRACTICAL EXERCISE #3.04 SECURITY MARKET LINE

Request: Let us construct the security market line with the former companies of the US market

Summary of the script. –

This Python script performs portfolio analysis and visualization based on the capital asset pricing model, focusing on a set of selected technology stocks and the S&P 500 index as the market benchmark. The process involves data retrieval, return calculations, beta estimations, required return calculations, and visualization of the security market line. The key steps are outlined below:

a) Function for Data Collection and Preparation
   - Define a list of stock tickers and the S&P 500 index.
   - Retrieve adjusted closing prices from Yahoo Finance.
   - Calculate daily and annualized returns for stocks and the market.

b) Beta Calculation
   - Prompt the user to enter the number of historical days to analyze.
   - Filter the data for the specified period.
   - Use linear regression to estimate beta values for each stock.

c) CAPM-Based Required Return Calculation
   - Prompt the user to input the risk-free rate.
   - Apply the CAPM formula to determine the required return for each stock.

d) Valuation Analysis
   - Compare expected returns (historical) with required returns (CAPM).
   - Categorize stocks as undervalued, overvalued, or fairly valued.

e) Portfolio Simulation
   - Prompt the user to enter the number of portfolios to simulate.
   - Generate random portfolio weight allocations.
   - Calculate the portfolio-level beta and return.

f) Security Market Line (SML) Visualization
   - Plot the SML to compare individual stocks and simulated portfolios.
   - Include market index and risk-free rate in the plot.
   - Annotate each stock on the chart.

g) Results Display
   - Print expected vs. required returns.
   - Show portfolio valuation insights.
   - Present the SML chart for visual interpretation.

This script provides a hands-on analysis of stock performance within a portfolio context, helping users assess asset valuation using CAPM principles, simulate portfolios, and visualize investment opportunities through the SML framework.

TABLE 3.4 Summary of Key Functions and Their Purposes

Function	Purpose
portfolio_annualized_performance(weights, CAPMreturn, beta)	Computes portfolio-level return and beta given specific weights.
random_portfolios(num_portfolios, CAPMreturn, beta)	Generates random portfolios, calculating risk-return characteristics.
Simulated_SML(CAPMreturn_array, beta_array, num_portfolios)	Creates the security market line plot and overlays portfolios and individual securities.

Script execution and outputs. –

```
# List of companies and function that downloads adjusted
prices from Yahoo Finance for a list of stocks and a
market index,
symbols = ['AAPL', 'AMZN', 'META', 'GOOGL','MSFT','NVDA',
'TSLA']
start = '2014-01-01'
prices = get_adj_close(symbols, start)
symbol = ['^GSPC']
start = '2014-01-01'
index = get_adj_close(symbol, start)
index = index.rename(columns={'^GSPC': 'S&P500'})
```

```
# Calculates daily and annualized returns for both the
portfolio and the market.
```

```
def get_portfolio_data(prices, index):
    # Combine share prices and index
    adj_close_data = prices.join(index, how='inner')

    # Daily returns
    portfolio_daily_returns = prices.pct_change(fill_
    method=None).dropna()
    market_daily_returns = index['S&P500'].pct_change(fill_
    method=None).dropna()

    # Average annual returns (252 trading days)
    portfolio_mean_returns = portfolio_daily_
    returns.mean() * 252
    market_mean_return = market_daily_returns.mean() * 252

    return adj_close_data, portfolio_daily_returns, market_
    daily_returns, portfolio_mean_returns, market_mean_return


# Apply the function to the list of stocks
symbols = ['AAPL', 'AMZN', 'META', 'GOOGL', 'MSFT',
'NVDA', 'TSLA']
start = '2014-01-01'

prices = get_adj_close(symbols, start)
index = get_adj_close(['^GSPC'],
start).rename(columns={'^GSPC': 'S&P500'})

adj_close_data, portfolio_daily_returns, market_daily_
returns, portfolio_mean_returns, market_mean_return = \
    get_portfolio_data(prices, index)

print("\nMarket annualized return:", round(market_mean_
return, 4))
print("\nStock annualized returns:")
print(portfolio_mean_returns.round(4))
```

Output:

```
Market annualized return: 0.127

Stock annualized returns:
Ticker
AAPL     0.2740
AMZN     0.2666
META     0.2809
GOOGL    0.2362
MSFT     0.2736
NVDA     0.6444
TSLA     0.4833
dtype: float64
```

```
# We define the start and end dates for the period you want
to analyze

days_before = float(input("Please enter the number of
previous days (e.g., 50):"))
end_date=adj_close_data.index.max()
start_date = end_date - pd.DateOffset(days=days_before)
start_date = pd.to_datetime(start_date,format='%Y%m%d')
end_date = pd.to_datetime(end_date,format='%Y%m%d')
filtered_data = adj_close_data.loc[start_date:end_date]
num_observations = len(filtered_data)
print('Start date:', start_date)
print('End date:', end_date)
print("Trading sessions:", num_observations)
```

Output:

```
Please enter the number of previous days (e.g., 50):365
Start date: 2024-10-31 00:00:00
End date: 2025-10-31 00:00:00
Trading sessions: 251
```

```
# Beta is calculated on a specific period basis

# We filter the daily returns data for the specified date
range

portfolio_filtered = portfolio_daily_returns.loc[start_
date:end_date]
portfolio_filtered=portfolio_filtered.reindex(columns=symbols)
market_filtered = market_daily_returns.loc[start_date:end_date]

# We calculate the beta for each asset within the selected
date range

X = market_filtered
y = portfolio_filtered


X1 = sm.add_constant(X)
model = sm.OLS(y, X1)
reg = model.fit()
beta = reg.params[1:]  # Extract the beta coefficients
beta.columns = (symbols)

# We display the calculated betas
print('Betas')
beta.round(2)
```

Output:

```
Betas

       AAPL  AMZN  META  GOOGL  MSFT  NVDA  TSLA
S&P500 1.29  1.39  1.44   1.06  0.96  1.92  2.43
```

When you estimate a stock's beta (its sensitivity to market movements), you do it by running a linear regression of the stock's returns against market returns. However, not all regressions give a strong relationship – sometimes the R^2 (coefficient of determination) is low, meaning the market doesn't explain much of that stock's behavior.

For unreliable betas, it adjusts the value toward the market beta (which is 1) using this formula:

$$\beta_i = 0{,}667\beta_e + 0{,}333\beta_M$$

This is a Blume-type adjustment, commonly used in finance to make extreme betas more realistic – high betas are adjusted down, and low betas are adjusted up.

```
# Let's calculate R² for every stock and correct
stock beta if R² < 0.5  following Blume-type
adjustment =====================

# Calculate R² for each asset
r2_values = {}
for t in symbols:
    yi = y[t].dropna()
    yhat_i = reg.fittedvalues[t].reindex(yi.index)
    resid_i = (yi - yhat_i).dropna()

    yi_aligned = yi.reindex(resid_i.index)
    ssr = np.sum(resid_i**2)
    sst = np.sum((yi_aligned - yi_aligned.mean())**2)
    r2 = np.nan if sst == 0 else (1 - ssr / sst)
    r2_values[t] = r2

r2_series = pd.Series(r2_values).reindex(symbols)
print("\n\033[1mR² per asset:\033[0m\n")
print(r2_series)

# Apply modified beta only if R² < 0.5
w = 0.667
beta_market = 1.0
```

```
# Convert beta (DataFrame) to Series for easy operation
if isinstance(beta, pd.DataFrame):
    beta_series = beta.iloc[0].astype(float)
else:
    beta_series = pd.Series(beta, index=symbol, dtype=float)

# Create a copy for the final version
beta_final = beta_series.copy()

# Apply correction only to assets with R² < 0.5
for t in symbols:
    if r2_series[t] < 0.5:
        beta_final[t] = w * beta_series[t] + (1 - w) *
        beta_market

print("\n\033[1mFinal beta (correcting only those with R² <
0.5):\033[0m\n")
print(beta_final)
```

Output:

```
R² per asset:

AAPL     0.559672
AMZN     0.556235
META     0.506872
GOOGL    0.376467
MSFT     0.532010
NVDA     0.537327
TSLA     0.461524
dtype: float64

Final beta (correcting only those with R² < 0.5):

AAPL     1.289208
AMZN     1.394105
META     1.440959
GOOGL    1.039008
MSFT     0.959749
NVDA     1.917910
TSLA     1.955699
Name: S&P500, dtype: float64
```

```
# The required profitability of each security is defined:
# Ask for the risk free rate
risk_free_rate = float(input("Please enter the risk free
rate (e.g., 0.01 for 1%): "))
```

```
CAPMreturn=risk_free_rate+beta_final.T*(market_mean_return-
risk_free_rate)
CAPMreturn=CAPMreturn.round(2)
CAPMreturn=CAPMreturn.T
print('\n')
print('\033[1mRequired returns:\033[0m\n')
print(CAPMreturn)
Please enter the risk free rate (e.g., 0.01 for 1%): 0.02
```

Output:

```
Required returns:
AAPL      0.157905
AMZN      0.169126
META      0.174138
GOOGL     0.131142
MSFT      0.122663
NVDA      0.225157
TSLA      0.229199
Name: S&P500, dtype: float64
```

```
# Transpose both dataframes to make tickers rows (indexes)
Expected_Returns = portfolio_mean_returns.T
Required_Returns = CAPMreturn.T

# If there is an extra index (such as ^GSPC), we remove it.
Required_Returns = Required_Returns.reset_index(drop=True)
Required_Returns.index = Expected_Returns.index

# Now we join both dataframes by the index (the tickers)
combined_df = pd.concat([Expected_Returns*100, Required_
Returns*100], axis=1)

# We rename the columns for clarity
combined_df.columns = ['Expected return (%)', 'Required
return (%)']

# Add a new column to indicate whether it is undervalued,
overvalued or fairly valued.
combined_df['valuation'] = combined_df.apply(
    lambda row: 'Undervalued' if row['Required return (%)'] <
    row['Expected return (%)'] else
                'Overvalued' if row['Required return (%)']
                 > row['Expected return (%)'] else
                'Fairly Valued', axis=1)

# Display the combined dataframe
combined_df.round(2)
```

Output:

	Expected return (%)	Required return (%)	Valuation
Ticker			
AAPL	27.40	15.79	Undervalued
AMZN	26.66	16.91	Undervalued
META	28.09	17.41	Undervalued
GOOGL	23.62	13.11	Undervalued
MSFT	27.36	12.27	Undervalued
NVDA	64.44	22.52	Undervalued
TSLA	48.63	22.92	Undervalued

```
# The function that reflects the performance of the portfolios
is defined:

def portfolio_annualized_performance(weights, CAPMreturn,
beta):
    returnsp = np.sum(CAPMreturn*weights )
    betap = np.sum(beta*weights)
    return betap, returnsp

# The number of portfolios to be created is determined:
num_portfolios = int(input("Please enter the number of
portfolios to simulate (e.g., 25000 for 25,000):"))
```

```
Please enter the number of portfolios to simulate (e.g., 25000
for 25,000):25000
```

```
# Portfolios are randomly created by attributing their
profitability and risk:


def random_portfolios(num_portfolios, CAPMreturn, beta_final):
    results = np.zeros((3,num_portfolios))
    weights_list = []
    for i in range(num_portfolios):
        weights = np.random.random(len(symbols))
        weights /= np.sum(weights)
        weights_list.append(weights)
        portfolio_beta, portfolio_return = portfolio_
annualized_performance(weights, CAPMreturn, beta)
        results[0,i] = portfolio_beta
        results[1,i] = portfolio_return

    return results, weights_list
# The results tables of betas and returns are converted
into matrices:
```

```
CAPMreturn_array=np.array(CAPMreturn)
beta_array=np.array(beta_final)
portfolio_mean_returns_array=np.array(portfolio_mean_returns)

# The role of the SML is defined on the basis of the
portfolios created, incorporating the individual securities:

def Simulated_SML(CAPMreturn_array, beta_array,
num_portfolios):
    results, weights = random_portfolios(num_portfolios,
    CAPMreturn_array, beta_array)
    betas = [x/10 for x in range(30)]
    assetReturns =[risk_free_rate+x*(market_mean_return-
    risk_free_rate) for x in betas]

    plt.figure(figsize=(11, 6))
    plt.grid(True)
    plt.scatter(results[0,:],results [1,:], marker='o',
    s=10, alpha=0.3)

    plt.scatter(beta_array,CAPMreturn_array,marker='o',col
    or='r',s=100,edgecolors='k')
    plt.scatter(beta,portfolio_mean_returns_
    array,marker='o', color='y', s=100,edgecolors='k')
    plt.scatter(1,market_mean_return,marker='o',color='b',
    s=100, label='Market Index',edgecolors='k')
    plt.scatter(0, risk_free_rate, marker='o',color='k',s=100,
    label='Risk free asset')
    plt.plot(betas,assetReturns, label='SML')
    plt.legend(loc='center left', bbox_to_anchor=(-0.3,
    0.5), frameon=False)

     # Annotate each ticker on the plot
    for i in range(len(symbols)):
        plt.annotate(symbols[i], (beta_array.T[i], CAPMreturn_
        array.T[i]), xytext=(5,5), textcoords='offset points',
        fontsize=6, color='black')
         plt.annotate(symbols[i], (beta_array.T[i],
         portfolio_mean_returns_array.T[i]), xytext=(5,5),
         textcoords='offset points', fontsize=8,
         color='black')

    plt.title('Simulated Security Market Line')
    plt.xlabel('beta')
    plt.ylabel('returns (%)')

    plt.legend(labelspacing=0.8)
    plt.show()

# Results are shown

Simulated_SML(CAPMreturn_array, beta_array, num_portfolios)
```

Output:

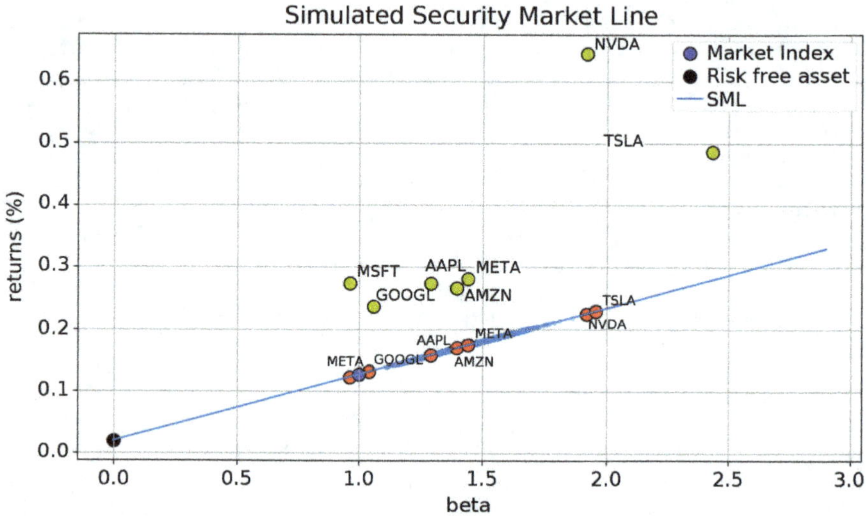

PRACTICAL EXERCISE #3.05 CAPM PORTFOLIO

Request: Let's find a CAPM Portfolio for a target beta

Summary of the script. –

The given code is an implementation of the capital asset pricing model and the security market line concepts for a portfolio of selected technology stocks. The main components of the code are as follows:

- Data Acquisition: Pulls stock price data from Yahoo Finance.
- Returns Calculation: Computes daily and annualized returns for stocks and the market.
- Beta Estimation: Uses regression to calculate stock betas.
- CAPM Application: Determines required returns based on the risk-free rate.
- Valuation: Classifies stocks based on expected vs. required returns.
- Portfolio Simulation: Generates random portfolios to assess performance.
- SML Visualization: Plots the security market line and portfolio positions.

This code provides a comprehensive CAPM-based analysis, including portfolio risk assessment and performance evaluation through the visualization of the SML.

TABLE 3.5 Summary of Key Functions and Their Purposes

Function/Calculation	Purpose
pl.LpProblem("CAPM_Weights", pl.LpMaximize)	Sets up the linear programming problem for portfolio optimization.
pl.lpSum([portfolio_mean_returns_series[ticker_indexes[i]] * stocks_vars[i] for i in sorted(tickers)])	Defines the objective function to maximize portfolio return.
prob += pl.lpSum([stocks_vars[i] for i in sorted(tickers)]) == 1	Ensures that the sum of portfolio weights equals 1 (full allocation).
prob += pl.lpSum([stocks_vars[i] * betastocks[i] for i in sorted(tickers)]) - BetaTarget == 0.0	Constrains the portfolio beta to the investor's target beta.
prob.writeLP("WeightsPortfolioCAPM.lp")	Writes the optimization problem to an .lp file for review.
prob.solve( )	Solves the optimization problem to determine the optimal weights.
pl.value(prob.objective)	Extracts the expected portfolio return from the optimization result.

Script execution and outputs. –

```
import pulp as pl
# It is a Python library used for modeling and
# solving optimization problems using linear programming
sorted(tickers)
```

Output:

```
['AAPL', 'AMZN', 'GOOGL', 'META', 'MSFT', 'NVDA', 'TSLA']
```

```
# The betas are needed in dictionary format for the optimization
function.
# To do this: # First, the betas are passed to matrix format,
# then to list format, and finally to dictionary format:
beta_final=beta_final.round(2)
beta2=np.array(beta_final)
beta2=beta2.T
beta2=beta2.tolist()
betastocks=[]
for i in range (len(symbols)):
    betastocks.append(beta2[i])
betastocks=dict(zip(sorted(symbols),betastocks))
```

```
# In order to set the target beta, it is necessary to know
# the range of betas of the securities that make up the
portfolio:
print ("\033[1mRange of Betas\033[0m")
print ("Maximum Beta=",max(beta2))
print ("Minimum Beta=",min(beta2))
```

Output:

```
Range of Betas
Maximum Beta= 1.96
Minimum Beta= 0.96
```

```
# The beta that fits the investor's profile is established:
BetaTarget = float(input("Please enter the beta seeked
(e.g., 1.5):"))
Please enter the beta seeked (e.g., 1.5):1.5

#This code is setting up a linear programming problem for
portfolio optimization.
# It creates a mapping from stock tickers to their
indexes, computes a weighted sum of stock returns (where
the weights are decision variables),
# and adds this sum to a linear programming problem, as
part of the objective function.

# --- Ensure series are labeled by tickers (robust even if
they already are) ---
portfolio_mean_returns_series = pd.Series(portfolio_mean_
returns_series, index=symbols)
betastocks = pd.Series(betastocks, index=symbols)

# Consistent ordering
sorted_tickers = sorted(symbols)

# Reindex to that order (avoids any mismatch)
mu = portfolio_mean_returns_series.reindex(sorted_
tickers)
beta = betastocks.reindex(sorted_tickers)

# --- Define LP: maximize expected return ---
prob = pl.LpProblem("PortfolioOptimization", pl.LpMaximize)

# Decision variables: weights per ticker (long-only;
adjust bounds as needed)
stocks_vars = pl.LpVariable.dicts("w", sorted_tickers,
lowBound=0.0, upBound=1.0)

# Objective: sum_i mu_i * w_i
prob += pl.lpSum(mu[t] * stocks_vars[t] for t in sorted_
tickers)
```

```
# Constraints
# 1) Full investment
prob += pl.lpSum(stocks_vars[t] for t in sorted_tickers) == 1.0

# 2) Target beta
prob += pl.lpSum(beta[t] * stocks_vars[t] for t in sorted_
tickers) == float(BetaTarget)

# An .lp file is created to summarize all the optimization:

prob.writeLP("WeightsPortfolioCAPM.lp")
```

Output:

```
[w_AAPL, w_AMZN, w_GOOGL, w_META, w_MSFT, w_NVDA, w_TSLA]
```

```
# The entire optimization approach is presented:
print(prob)
```

Output:

```
PortfolioOptimization:


MAXIMIZE
0.27396059088944574*w_AAPL + 0.2665667072868041 5*w_AMZN +
0.2362197297819244 6*w_GOOGL + 0.2809156887860389 5*w_META +
0.273629907172268 6*w_MSFT + 0.644379909536967*w_NVDA +
0.4862716548554984*w_TSLA + 0.0
SUBJECT TO
_C1: w_AAPL + w_AMZN + w_GOOGL + w_META + w_MSFT + w_NVDA + w_TSLA = 1

_C2: 1.29 w_AAPL + 1.39 w_AMZN + 1.44 w_GOOGL + 1.04 w_META +
0.96 w_MSFT + 1.92 w_NVDA + 1.96 w_TSLA = 1.5

VARIABLES
w_AAPL <= 1 Continuous
w_AMZN <= 1 Continuous
w_GOOGL <= 1 Continuous
w_META <= 1 Continuous
w_MSFT <= 1 Continuous
w_NVDA <= 1 Continuous
w_TSLA <= 1 Continuous
```

```
# We proceed to solve the optimization:

prob.solve() # This line executes the optimization problem
and returns the status code of the solution; 1 indicates
that an optimal solution was found successfully; 0 means
the solver did not find an optimal solution
```

Output:

```
1
```

```
# The status of the optimization is indicated:

print ("Status:", pl.LpStatus[prob.status])
Status: Optimal
# The results are printed:

print("\033[1mAsset Allocation (%)\033[0m")
print("_________________")
for v in prob.variables():
    print (v.name, "=", round(v.varValue*100,2))
print("\n")

print("\033[1mPortfolio Performance\033[0m")
print("______________________")
print("Beta =", BetaTarget)
print ("Expected Return (%)=", round(pl.value(prob.objective)*
100,2))
CAPMreturnTarget=risk_free_rate+BetaTarget*(market_mean_
return-risk_free_rate)
print("Required Return (%)=", round(CAPMreturnTarget*100,2))
```

Output:

```
Asset Allocation (%)
_________________
w_AAPL = 0.0
w_AMZN = 0.0
w_GOOGL = 0.0
w_META = 0.0
w_MSFT = 43.75
w_NVDA = 56.25
w_TSLA = 0.0

Portfolio Performance
______________________
Beta = 1.5
Expected Return (%)= 48.22
Required Return (%)= 18.05
```

Criticism of the CAPM model. –

The CAPM is a model permanently exposed to the critical opinion of professionals and researchers. They have tried to replicate the model in the reality of the markets, for different time periods and financial assets, providing extensive empirical evidence, although not conclusive, and establishing a division between supporters and detractors. The main element of the model that has been the object of much criticism is beta and its instability, largely due to the model's assumptions – especially when it is calculated using historical data (Fernández & Carabias, 2015). The unrealistic nature of a risk-free rate (Fama & French, 2004) at which one can lend or borrow is also criticized.

3.3.5 Alternatives to the CAPM Model

One of the models that tries to complement the CAPM is what is known as Fisher Black's version (1972), or zero-beta model, in which a portfolio with zero beta is used instead of the risk-free asset used in Sharpe's model (1964). This version of Black's model presents the original model without the assumption of the possibility of unlimited lending or borrowing at the risk-free rate. Black's model replaces the risk-free investment rate with short sales of risky assets.

$$\mathrm{E}(\mathrm{R}_\mathrm{i}) = E(R_{0M}) + \beta_{iM} * (\mathrm{E}(\mathrm{R}_\mathrm{M}) - E(R_{0M}))$$

This model states that the expected return of a financial asset with zero beta ($E(R_{0M})$) must be less than the expected market return for the premium to positive. Black et al. (1972) in his study concludes that a financial asset at whose rate of return investors can lend and borrow indefinitely is not required. Consequently, Black also considers beta as an appropriate measure of systematic investment risk and the linear nature of the risk-return trade-off is maintained. The model is also criticized by Fama and French (2004) as the assumption that short sales are unrestricted is just as unrealistic as the existence of a risk-free investment rate for lending and borrowing.

The I-CAPM (intertemporal CAPM) or continuous-time CAPM valuation model was created by Robert Merton (1973), who developed a model that considers more sources of risk (macroeconomic factors) when optimizing consumption over a period of time:

$$E(R_i) = R_f + \beta_{i,M}(E(R_M) - R_f) + \sum_{k=1}^{N} \beta_{i,k}(E(R_k) - R_f)$$

Where

$$\sum_{k=1}^{N} \beta_{i,k}(E(R_k) - R_f)$$

includes all macroeconomic factors (GDP, interest rates, corporate debt, etc.). I-CAPM assumes that financial asset returns follow a normal distribution over multiple time periods, and that all future consumption will be realized with stock returns

The arbitrage pricing theory or arbitrage pricing model (APT) was introduced by Ross (1976) as an alternative to the CAPM model. The APT can be more general than the CAPM because it allows for multiple risk factors. Unlike the CAPM, the APT does not require the identification of the market portfolio or the framework of a market in equilibrium. Unlike the I-CAPM, the first factor is not explicitly identified with the CAPM market model. In its most general form the APT provides an approximate relationship between the expected return on an asset and a specific number of unidentified factors. APT assumes that financial asset returns are generated by market and industry factors, although it does not state what these other factors are. The APT is based on the idea that all those portfolios that can be selected under no-risk conditions, on average, cannot generate returns. The APT states that a risk-free arbitrage portfolio can be obtained by eliminating both systematic and unsystematic risk.

With the work of Rubinstein (1976), Lucas (1978) and Breeden (1979), the consumption capital asset pricing model (C-CAPM) or consumption-based CAPM appeared. This model incorporates an element specific to investors: the determination of the amount of wealth earmarked for investment and the amount of wealth reserved for consumption. According to this model:

$$E(R_i) = R_f + \beta_{i,C}\left(E(R_M) - R_f\right)$$

where $\beta_{i,C}$ determines the sensitivity of the expected return on the security with respect to changes in consumption needs. This beta is called the consumption beta. However, not all consumers in an economy can be considered active investors in the capital markets and, therefore, the relationship between consumption and the expected return on financial assets is not realistic or representative.

Fama and French (1992) conducted an empirical investigation studying the beta of the initial CAPM model, concluding that this variable does not fully explain the profitability of financial assets. In a subsequent investigation (Fama & French, 1993), they search for factors that significantly explain expected stock returns, using a sample of stocks from the US market (NYSE, AMEX, and NASDAQ) in the period from July 1963 to December 1991. They conclude that variables related to company size and value most significantly explained stock returns.

The Carhart four-factor model (Carhart, 1997) is an extension of the Fama and French three-factor model and was introduced by Mark M. Carhart in 1997 in his influential article "On Persistence in Mutual Fund Performance" published in *The Journal of Finance*. Mark M. Carhart introduced the fourth factor, momentum, to address one of the most persistent anomalies in financial markets. The momentum effect was documented by Narasimhan Jegadeesh and Sheridan Titman in 1993 (Jegadeesh & Titman, 1993), who showed that stocks that had performed well over the past 3 to 12 months tended to continue to outperform in the short term.

In 2015 and as a continuation of the three factor model, Fama and French developed a new asset valuation model, the five factor model. The new model includes size, capitalization ratio, operating profitability of the business and corporate investment patterns in assets, in addition to market risk.

These three last models will be seen in the section "Factor Investing."

3.3.6 Measures of Management Quality

Any method that measures the quality of a portfolio's performance must combine the risk-return trade-off. It is common practice to compare the performance of a portfolio management with the performance achieved by an unmanaged portfolio with the same risk, i.e. the risk-adjusted market portfolio would become the target (benchmark) to compare with.

As Roll (1977) comments, if the target is misspecified (benchmark error) this model cannot be used to assess management performance. A miscalculated market portfolio will have two effects: first, the beta will be incorrect; second, the TML found will also be incorrect because it passes through the wrong market portfolio. In general, the errors tend to overestimate portfolio management because the approximation to the market portfolio used is not as efficient as the true market portfolio. Despite all this, and due to its widespread use and simplicity of calculation, there are some measures of management based on the CAPM.

The so-called Jensen's alpha is one of them (known simply as management alpha). Let it be the return of a portfolio according to the CAPM:

$$E\left(R_p\right)=R_f+\beta_p\left(E\left(R_M\right)-R_f\right)$$

and let R_p' be the return obtained by the manager for that portfolio, then alpha is calculated as R_p':

$$\alpha = R_p' - \left(R_f + \beta_p\left(E\left(R_M\right) - R_f\right)\right)$$

As we can see, alpha tells us the excess (or shortfall) of return obtained over what could be expected according to the systematic risk. A positive alpha indicates that the manager has outperformed and added value. The higher the alpha, the more value contributed by the manager. Negative alpha indicates that not even the return required by the CAPM has been achieved, due to systematic risk. The manager has destroyed value. The more negative the alpha, the worse the management.

Exercise: Two investors claim to be very good at selecting assets. Investor 1 chooses portfolio 1 which has a beta of 1.5; investor 2 chooses portfolio 2 whose beta is 1. After one year it turned out that R1=19% and R2=16%. Which investor do you think selected better – give a reason – if RM was 14% and Rf was 6%? Answer: investor 2 selected better, since the alpha is higher.

$$\begin{aligned}\alpha_1 &= R_p' - \left(R_{rf} + \beta_p\left(E\left(R_M\right) - R_{rf}\right)\right) = 19\% - \left(6\% + 1{,}5 \times \left(14\% - 6\%\right)\right) \\ &= 19\% - 18\% = 1\% \\ \alpha_2 &= 16\% - \left(6\% + 1 \times \left(14\% - 6\%\right)\right) = 16\% - 14\% = 2\%\end{aligned}$$

The Treynor ratio is also based on beta; it relates the excess return over the risk-free return earned by a portfolio to the beta of that portfolio:

$$T = \frac{R_p - R_f}{\beta_p}$$

This ratio is a measure of the portfolio's return per unit of systematic risk. Since risk is measured as beta, the ratio assumes that the portfolio is fully diversified.

For the market portfolio the Treynor ratio is the slope of the SML, or the market risk premium:

$$T = \frac{R_M - R_f}{\beta_M} = \frac{R_M - R_f}{1} = R_M - R_f$$

Portfolios with a ratio above the market are those that are above the SML and are worth investing in. The Sharpe ratio is very similar to the Treynor measure, but considers the relevant risk to be the total risk:

$$S = \frac{R_p - R_f}{\sigma_p}$$

It measures the portfolio's return on the risk-free interest rate per unit of risk. The higher the Sharpe ratio, the better the portfolio has been managed. Note that the Sharpe ratio is the slope of the capital market line.

When a portfolio is perfectly diversified, the two ratios will give the same result, since the relevant measure of risk will be beta; but for poorly diversified portfolios, the results will vary, and it will be more correct to use the Sharpe ratio.

3.3.7 The Efficient Markets Hypothesis

The efficient markets hypothesis (EMH), proposed by economist Eugene Fama in the 1960s (Fama, 1970, 1991), is a fundamental theory in the field of finance that suggests that the prices of financial assets, such as stocks, always reflect all the information available in the market (Malkiel, 1999, 2003). This means that it is virtually impossible to consistently "beat the market" through stock selection or technical analysis, as any opportunity for extraordinary gains would already have been taken advantage of and reflected in the stock price.

3.3.7.1 Types of Market Efficiency

The EMH comes in three forms, each of which depends on the type of information believed to be reflected in the prices:

- Weak efficiency: In a weakly efficient market, stock prices reflect all available historical information, such as past prices and volumes. According to this form, it is not possible to predict future stock prices solely by analyzing historical data (such as technical analysis). Fama introduced this to explore if markets "learn" from their own history.

- Semi-strong efficiency: In a semi-strong efficient market, stock prices reflect not only historical information, but also all publicly available information. This includes financial reports, news and any other publicly available information. Under this assumption, neither technical analysis nor fundamental analysis (which analyzes public financial information) can offer a competitive advantage. Fama tests the market's ability to process and react quickly to new information.

- Strong efficiency: In a strong efficient market, stock prices reflect all information, both public and private (including information not available to the general public). This means that even insider investors cannot consistently earn above-average returns. This extreme form examines if any advantage, even private or insider information, can lead to consistent above-market returns. It sets the theoretical boundary for market efficiency.

Fama's categorization acknowledges that market efficiency operates on a spectrum, with varying degrees of accessibility and integration of information. By breaking down efficiency into these forms, he provided a structured way to analyze and test the concept empirically, helping to advance our understanding of how information influences asset prices in real-world markets.

3.3.7.2 Implications of the EMH

EMH has several important implications for investors and portfolio management:

- Impossibility of extraordinary profits: Since all relevant information is already embedded in asset prices, abnormal profits are not possible without taking on additional risk.
- The randomness of prices: According to the EMH, changes in asset prices are essentially random and follow a "random walk," meaning that they cannot be accurately predicted over the long term.
- Passive vs. active management: If markets are efficient, passive management (investing in index funds that follow the market) is a more effective and lower-cost strategy than active management (trying to pick stocks or manage portfolios to outperform the market).

3.3.7.3 Criticism and Controversy

Despite its influence, the efficient markets hypothesis has faced significant criticism and sparked considerable debate (Jaffe, 1974; Finnerty, 1976; Grossman & Stiglitz, 1980; Seyhun, 1986; Malkiel, 2005) due to observed market behaviors and anomalies that challenge its core assumptions:

- Market Anomalies: Empirical evidence highlights several anomalies that seem to contradict the EMH, such as:

 - The January Effect, where stock prices tend to rise more in January than in other months.
 - The Value Effect, which suggests that value stocks (those with low price-to-earnings or price-to-book ratios) often outperform growth stocks.
 - The Size Effect, where smaller-cap stocks historically deliver higher risk-adjusted returns than larger-cap stocks. These patterns suggest the existence of predictable price movements, which would not occur in a fully efficient market.

- Irrational Investor Behavior: Critics argue that investors do not always act rationally as assumed by the EMH. Emotional responses, herd behavior, and speculative bubbles (e.g., the dot-com bubble) demonstrate periods when markets deviate significantly from efficiency. Similarly, market panics (e.g., the 2008 financial crisis) reveal instances where prices fail to reflect intrinsic value accurately.
- Behavioral Finance: This field has emerged as a major critique of the EMH, emphasizing that cognitive biases, such as overconfidence, loss aversion, and confirmation bias, influence decision-making. Behavioral finance argues that these biases lead to systematic deviations from rationality, creating inefficiencies in market prices that persist over time.

These criticisms have led to ongoing research and debate (Fama, 1998), with some suggesting that markets are "efficient enough" for practical purposes, while others advocate for alternative models that incorporate behavioral insights and adaptive dynamics to better explain real-world market behavior.

3.3.7.4 Conclusion

The efficient markets hypothesis remains a cornerstone of financial theory, profoundly shaping how economists, academics, and investors approach financial markets. By asserting that market prices incorporate all available information, EMH has provided a framework for understanding the behavior of asset prices and the limits of arbitrage opportunities.

Although the hypothesis is still a subject of intense debate, particularly in the context of behavioral finance and market anomalies, its influence is undeniable. It has driven the development of key financial concepts such as modern portfolio theory, which emphasizes risk and return trade-offs, as well as advanced methods of asset valuation and investment management strategies, including passive indexing and efficient portfolio construction.

The EMH has also prompted critical thinking and empirical testing, leading to a deeper exploration of market dynamics. While critics point to instances of irrational behavior, bubbles, and inefficiencies as evidence against the hypothesis, proponents argue that these deviations are exceptions rather than the rule.

In practice, the EMH has encouraged investors to focus on diversification, risk management, and long-term investment horizons, influencing the rise of passive investment vehicles such as index funds and ETFs. Despite its limitations, the EMH remains a foundational theory that continues to guide both academic research and practical investment strategies.

3.4 VALUE AT RISK OF A PORTFOLIO

3.4.1 Introduction to Value at Risk (VaR)

Value at risk (VaR) is one of the most widely used tools in risk management, providing a quantitative measure of potential losses within a portfolio. Its primary function is to estimate the maximum expected loss over a specified time period for a given confidence level. This makes it a critical tool for financial institutions, investment managers, and regulatory bodies aiming to assess and control financial risk.

At its core, VaR answers the question: "What is the maximum amount I could lose, within a certain level of confidence, over a defined time horizon?" For instance, if a portfolio has a daily VaR of €1 million at a 95% confidence level, it means that there is only a 5% probability that the portfolio will lose more than €1 million in a single day. Conversely, there is a 95% probability that losses will not exceed this amount.

VaR is extensively used across various domains in finance, including:

- Risk Measurement and Management: Institutions use VaR to identify and manage risks in portfolios, set risk limits, and allocate capital effectively.
- Regulatory Compliance: Regulatory frameworks, such as Basel III, require financial institutions to calculate and report their VaR to ensure they maintain sufficient capital reserves.

- Stress Testing and Scenario Analysis: While VaR provides a baseline risk measure, it is often complemented by stress tests to evaluate the impact of extreme market events.

VaR can be calculated using different approaches, each with its own advantages and limitations:

a) Historical Simulation:
   - This method relies on historical data to estimate potential losses. It assumes that past market movements are indicative of future risks.
   - *Pros*: Simple to implement and requires no assumptions about the distribution of returns.
   - *Cons*: May not account for future market conditions or extreme events do not present in historical data.

b) Variance-Covariance (Parametric) Method:
   - This approach assumes that portfolio returns follow a normal distribution and uses the mean and standard deviation of returns to calculate potential losses.
   - *Pros*: Computationally efficient and straightforward for portfolios with linear instruments.
   - *Cons*: May be inaccurate for portfolios with non-linear instruments (e.g., options) or when returns deviate significantly from normality.

c) Monte Carlo Simulation:
   - This method generates a large number of hypothetical scenarios for portfolio returns based on assumed distributions and models.
   - *Pros*: Highly flexible and capable of capturing complex portfolio characteristics.
   - *Cons*: Computationally intensive and reliant on the accuracy of the input models and assumptions.

When deciding which value at risk model to use, several important factors come into play. The choice of the model often depends on the nature of the portfolio, the availability of data, the specific needs of the organization, and practical constraints such as computational resources.

First, the composition of the portfolio is a critical consideration. For portfolios composed of linear instruments like stocks and bonds, the variance-covariance method is often a practical choice due to its simplicity and efficiency. However, for portfolios that include complex or non-linear instruments, such as derivatives or structured products, Monte Carlo simulation is typically better suited. Its flexibility allows for a more accurate representation of the portfolio's behavior under different market conditions.

The availability and quality of data also play a significant role. If rich historical data is available and the portfolio's assets exhibit stable historical patterns, the historical simulation method can provide reliable insights. However, if the available data is limited or may not accurately reflect future risks, Monte Carlo simulation, with its ability to model hypothetical scenarios, becomes a more robust option.

Another key factor is the organization's risk tolerance and the level of precision required. For routine risk reporting or scenarios where computational speed is essential, the variance-covariance method offers a quick and straightforward solution. On the other hand, if the focus is on understanding extreme events or tail risks, Monte Carlo simulation's ability to simulate a wide range of scenarios makes it invaluable.

Computational resources are another practical consideration. While the variance-covariance method is highly efficient and ideal for organizations with limited computational capabilities, Monte Carlo simulation requires significant processing power and expertise, making it more suitable for institutions with advanced technological infrastructure.

Finally, regulatory and reporting requirements often influence the choice of VaR model. Financial regulators, such as those following Basel III guidelines, may specify certain methods or confidence levels for risk calculations. In such cases, the chosen model must align with these external mandates.

Ultimately, selecting the right VaR model involves balancing these factors to meet the specific needs of the portfolio and the organization. In many cases, institutions may opt to use multiple models simultaneously to cross-check results and ensure a comprehensive understanding of risk exposure. By carefully weighing the portfolio's characteristics, data availability, precision needs, and resource constraints, risk managers can choose the model that best aligns with their goals.

TABLE 3.6 VaR Model Summary Table

Model	When to Use	Strengths	Limitations
Historical Simulation	Stable portfolios with rich historical data	Simple, no assumptions about distribution	Ignores unprecedented risks
Variance-Covariance	Linear portfolios, time-critical reporting	Fast, suitable for large datasets	Assumes normality, struggles with non-linear instruments
Monte Carlo Simulation	Complex portfolios with non-linear instruments	Flexible, models tail risks well	Computationally expensive

Despite its popularity, VaR has some notable limitations:

- Tail Risk Ignorance: VaR does not provide information about the potential severity of losses beyond the confidence level (e.g., what happens in the worst 5% of cases?).
- Assumption Dependency: The accuracy of VaR depends on the assumptions underlying the chosen method, such as the normality of returns or the relevance of historical data.
- Non-Additivity: VaR is not always additive across portfolios, which can complicate risk aggregation in large institutions.

In summary, VaR is a powerful and versatile tool for risk management that provides a clear and interpretable metric for potential losses. However, its use should be complemented with other risk measures, such as conditional VaR (CVaR) or stress testing, to ensure a comprehensive understanding of risk exposure.

3.4.2 Historical Simulation VaR

The historical simulation VaR uses historical data to analyze changes in market risk factors, applying these changes to current values to create simulated distributions of profits and losses. This approach does not rely on any predefined assumptions about the shape of the distributions, instead deriving them directly from actual historical figures.

The historical simulation approach calculates VaR by leveraging historical data to simulate how the portfolio would have behaved in the past under actual market conditions. The method involves these key steps:

a) Collecting Historical Data:

- Gather historical prices or returns for all assets in the portfolio over a defined time horizon.

- Calculate the portfolio's historical returns using the asset weights.

b) Constructing the Portfolio Return Distribution: Combine individual asset returns into a portfolio return for each historical period:

$$R_p^{(t)} = \sum_{i=1}^{n} w_i R_i^{(t)}$$

where:

- $R_p^{(t)}$: Portfolio return at time *t*.
- w_i: Weight of asset *i* in the portfolio.
- $R_i^{(t)}$: Historical return of asset *i* at time *t*.

c) Sorting Returns: Sort the historical portfolio returns from worst to best.

d) Identifying the VaR: The VaR at a confidence level α is the return corresponding to the (1−α)-th percentile of the sorted return distribution:

$$VaR_\alpha = \text{Percentile}_{(1-\alpha)} R_p^{(t)}$$

For example, at 95% confidence, the VaR is the 5th percentile of the return distribution.

3.4.3 Parametric VaR (Variance Approach)

This approach is grounded in the assumption that portfolio returns follow a normal distribution, making it computationally efficient and relatively straightforward to implement. The process begins with an understanding of the portfolio's characteristics, including its expected return, variance, and covariance of asset returns. These metrics help quantify the portfolio's overall risk and determine the potential losses, and follow these steps:

a) Determine the Portfolio's Risk Metrics: First, calculate the portfolio's mean return (μ_p) and standard deviation (σ_p), which are key inputs for the parametric VaR formula. For a portfolio with n assets, the mean return is given by:

$$\mu_p = \sum_{i=1}^{n} w_i \mu_i$$

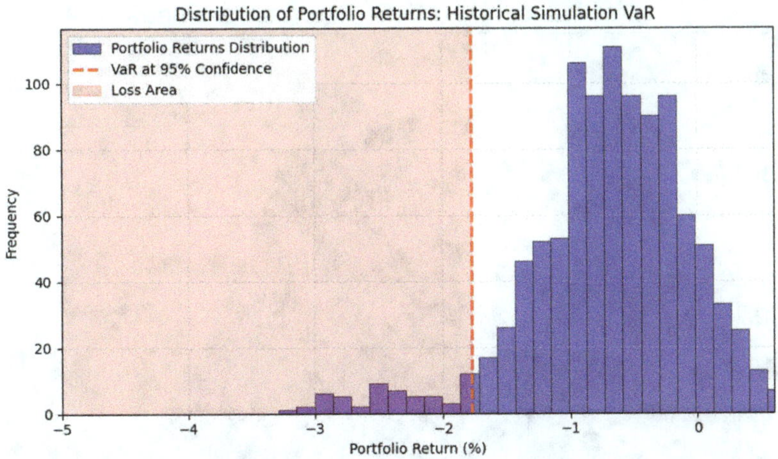

FIGURE 3.9 Historical Simulation VaR

Here, w_i represents the weight of asset *i*, and μ_i is the expected return of asset *i*.

The standard deviation, which measures the portfolio's risk, is derived from the variance:

$$\sigma_p^2 = \sum_{i=1}^{n}\sum_{j=1}^{n} w_i w_j \sigma_{ij}$$

where σ_{ij} is the covariance between asset *i* and asset *j*.

b) Select a Confidence Level:

- Choose a confidence level, typically 95% or 99%, depending on the level of risk tolerance.
- Identify the corresponding Z-score from the standard normal distribution:
  - At 95% confidence, the Z-score is −1.645.
  - At 99% confidence, the Z-score is −2.33.

c) Apply the Parametric VaR Formula:

$$\text{VaR}_\alpha = Z_\alpha \cdot \sigma_p$$

d) Interpret the VaR: The result represents the maximum expected loss at the chosen confidence level over a specified time horizon.

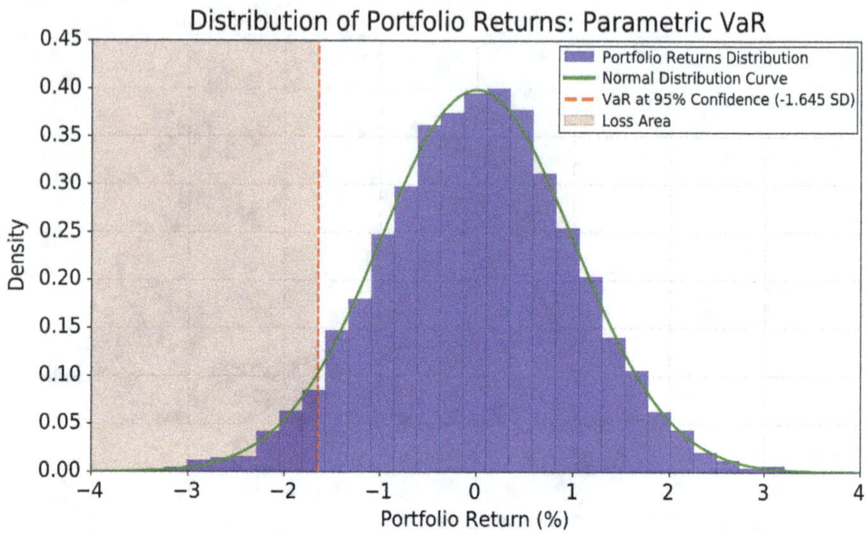

FIGURE 3.10 Parametric VaR

3.4.4 Monte Carlo Simulation VaR

Monte Carlo VaR is a more flexible approach that does not assume a specific distribution of returns. Returns follow a specified distribution (e.g., normal, t-distribution, or others). It uses simulation to generate a large number of potential outcomes for portfolio returns based on historical data or other models. VaR is calculated as the return at the desired percentile of the simulated portfolio return distribution:

$$\text{VaR}_\alpha = \text{Percentile}_{(1-\alpha)}\ (\text{Simulated Portfolio Returns})$$

a) Define Key Inputs

   Before starting the simulation, determine the following:

   - Portfolio Composition: Define the weights of the assets in the portfolio.
   - Asset Return Parameters:
     - Mean returns (μ_i).
     - Covariance matrix (Σ) to model relationships between assets.

- Student's *t* Distribution Parameters:
  - Degrees of freedom (v): Controls the tail thickness (smaller values = fatter tails).
  - Scale parameter: Derived from the covariance matrix.
- Confidence Level (α): Typically 95% or 99%.
- Number of Simulations (N): The number of random scenarios to generate.

b) Simulate Random Returns Using the Student's *t* Distribution

i) Generate Multivariate Random Variables:

- Use the Student's *t* distribution with degrees of freedom (v) to model random returns.
- For a portfolio of *n* assets, generate *N* random vectors

$$R_i^{(k)} \sim t_\nu\left(\mu_i, \Sigma\right)$$

where:

- $R_i^{(k)}$: Simulated return of asset i in the k-th scenario.
- t_v: Multivariate Student's *t* distribution with:
- v: Degrees of freedom, controlling the thickness of the tails.
- μ_i: Mean return of asset ii.
- Σ: Covariance matrix capturing the relationships between asset returns.

ii) Transform Random Variables: Use the Cholesky decomposition of the covariance matrix (Σ) to introduce correlations between assets.

c) Calculate Portfolio Returns for Each Scenario: Combine the simulated asset returns into a portfolio return for each of the N scenarios:

$$R_p^{(k)} = \sum_{i=1}^{n} w_i R_i^{(k)}$$

where:

- w_i: Weight of asset i in the portfolio.
- $R_i^{(k)}$: Simulated return of asset i in the k-th scenario.

d) Build the Portfolio Return Distribution

- After simulating NNN scenarios, you have a distribution of portfolio returns $\left\{R_p^{(1)}, R_p^{(2)}, \ldots, R_p^{(N)}\right\}$
- Sort the returns in ascending order to analyze the distribution.

e) Calculate VaR: Identify the percentile corresponding to the $(1-\alpha)$ confidence level. For example: At 95% confidence, take the 5th percentile:

$$\text{VaR}_{95\%} = \text{Percentile}_{(1-\alpha)}\,(\text{Rp})$$

f) Interpret the VaR: The result represents the maximum expected loss at the chosen confidence level over the specified time horizon.

3.4.5 Conclusion

VaR models are valuable tools in risk management, each with its own strengths and weaknesses. The choice between them depends on the portfolio's characteristics and the specific needs of the risk manager. Understanding the assumptions and limitations of each method is crucial for effective risk assessment and management.

PRACTICAL EXERCISE #3.06 HISTORICAL SIMULATION VAR

Request: Let's calculate a portfolio historical simulation daily VaR given some features

Summary of the script. –

This code calculates the value at risk for an equally weighted stock portfolio using historical simulation based on daily returns of selected stocks. Steps:

a) Data Collection and Preprocessing
- Retrieves adjusted closing prices for seven technology stocks (AAPL, AMZN, META, GOOGL, MSFT, NVDA, TSLA) from Yahoo Finance, starting from January 1, 2021.
- Computes daily percentage returns and removes missing values.

b) Portfolio Construction
- Assumes an equal-weighted portfolio, distributing investment equally across all assets.
- Calculates the portfolio's daily returns by applying weights to individual stock returns.

c) VaR Calculación Methodology
   - A confidence level of 95% is set.
   - Portfolio daily returns are sorted in ascending order to identify extreme losses.
   - The 5th percentile of sorted returns is extracted to estimate potential worst-case loss.
   - The VaR is expressed in dollar terms assuming a total portfolio value of $1,000,000.

d) Output and Interpretation
   - The estimated VaR value is printed, representing the potential maximum loss at the specified confidence level.

This code provides a simple and effective implementation of historical VaR, allowing users to quantify portfolio risk based on past market performance.

TABLE 3.7 Summary of Key Functions and Their Purposes

Function/Calculation	Purpose
data.xs('Adj Close', level=1, axis=1)	Extracts the adjusted closing prices from the multi-level DataFrame.
weights = np.array([1.0 / num_assets] * num_assets)	Defines an equally weighted portfolio allocation.
portfolio_returns = daily_returns.dot(weights)	Calculates the total portfolio returns by multiplying asset returns with their respective weights.
np.sort(portfolio_returns)	Sorts portfolio returns in ascending order to assess potential worst-case losses.
np.percentile(sorted_returns, var_percentile)	Computes the value at risk as the (1-confidence level) percentile of sorted returns.
portfolio_value * -VaR	Converts the calculated VaR into dollar terms based on the total portfolio value.

Script execution and outputs. –

```
# Import libraries

import yfinance as yf
import numpy as np
import pandas as pd
#Download historical data

symbols = ['AAPL', 'AMZN', 'META', 'GOOGL', 'MSFT', 'NVDA',
'TSLA']
start = '2021-01-01'
```

```
end = None  # This will download data up to the present
data = yf.download(symbols, start=start, end=end,
group_by='symbols', progress=False, auto_adjust=False,
actions=False)

# Extract adjusted close prices

adj_close_data = data.xs('Adj Close', level=1, axis=1,)
adj_close_data= adj_close_data[symbols]

#Calculate daily returns for each asset

daily_returns = adj_close_data.pct_change(fill_
method=None).dropna()
daily_returns = daily_returns.reindex(columns=symbols)

# Define portfolio weights (e.g., equal-weighted portfolio)

num_assets = len(symbols)  # Calculate the number of
assets in the portfolio
weights = np.array([1.0 / num_assets] * num_assets)  #
Equally weighted portfolio

# Calculate portfolio returns: Multiply each day's returns
by the corresponding asset weights and sum them to get
portfolio returns
portfolio_returns = daily_returns.dot(weights)

# Set the confidence level (e.g., 95% confidence level)

confidence_level = 0.95

# Sort the portfolio returns to identify worst-case losses

sorted_returns = np.sort(portfolio_returns)

# Calculate the VaR: VaR is the value at the (1-confidence_level)
percentile of the sorted returns

var_percentile = (1 - confidence_level) * 100
VaR = np.percentile(sorted_returns, var_percentile)

# Calculate VaR in dollar terms based on the portfolio's
total value
portfolio_value = 1_000_000  # Example portfolio value of
$1 million
VaR_value = portfolio_value * -VaR  # VaR value (negative
because it's a loss)
# Print the results

print(f"Historical Simulation VaR ({confidence_level*100}%
confidence level): ${VaR_value:,.2f}")
```

Output:

```
Historical Simulation VaR (95.0% confidence level): $31,890.92
```

PRACTICAL EXERCISE #3.07 PARAMETRIC VAR

Request: Let's calculate a portfolio parametric VaR given some features Summary of the script. –

This code estimates the parametric value at risk for an investment portfolio using statistical methods based on user inputs.

The code provides a robust approach to risk assessment through the following features:

a) User-Defined Flexibility:
The user can customize key parameters such as confidence level, investment value, and time horizon, allowing for scenario-based analysis.
b) Statistical Accuracy:
Utilizing the standard normal distribution, the calculation ensures accurate and reliable VaR estimation under normal market conditions.
c) Time Horizon Adjustability:
The inclusion of different period lengths (daily, monthly, biannual, annually) helps tailor the risk calculation to various investment strategies and reporting needs.
d) Ease of Interpretation:
The results are formatted and displayed in a clear and concise manner, making them accessible for risk managers and investors without advanced statistical knowledge.

This code serves as a practical tool for estimating potential portfolio losses, helping investors and financial professionals assess risk exposure across different timeframes.

TABLE 3.8 Summary of Key Functions and Their Purposes

Function/Calculation	Purpose
confidence_level = float(input(...))	Takes user input for the confidence level in percentage form (e.g., 95 for 95%).
norm.ppf(confidence_level)	Computes the Z-score corresponding to the given confidence level.
var_parametric = z_score * volatility * portfolio_value	Calculates the parametric value at risk.
formatted_var_parametric = "${:,.2f}".format(abs(var_parametric))	Formats the calculated VaR in a human-readable currency format.
formatted_volatility="{:,.2f}%".format(abs(volatility*100))	Formats the volatility as a percentage for display.

Script execution and outputs. –

```
# Parametric VaR

import numpy as np
from scipy.stats import norm

# Input data
confidence_level = float(input("Enter the confidence level
(e.g., 0.95 for 95%): "))
portfolio_value = float(input("Enter the amount invested
(e.g., 1000000 for 1,000,000): "))
annual_volatility = float(input("Enter the annual
volatility (e.g., 0.25 for 25%): "))
period_length = str(input("Enter the period length (e.g.,
daily, monthly, biannual, or annually):"))

# Calculate the Z-score for the given confidence level
z_score = norm.ppf(confidence_level)

# Determine the volatility based on the period length
if period_length.lower() == 'daily':
    volatility = annual_volatility / np.sqrt(252)
elif period_length.lower() == 'monthly':
    volatility = annual_volatility / np.sqrt(12)
elif period_length.lower() == 'biannual':
    volatility = annual_volatility / np.sqrt(2)
elif period_length.lower() == 'annually':
    volatility = annual_volatility
else:
    raise ValueError("Period length must be 'daily',
    'monthly', 'biannual', or 'annually'")

# Calculate the Parametric VaR
var_parametric = z_score * volatility * portfolio_value
# Format and print the result
formatted_var_parametric = "${:,.2f}".format(abs(var_
parametric))
formatted_volatility="{:,.2f}%".format(abs(volatility*100))
print('Z-score:',round(z_score,3))
print('Volatility:', formatted_volatility)
print('Period length:',period_length )
print('Parametric VaR=', formatted_var_parametric)
```

Output:

```
Enter the confidence level (e.g., 0.95 for 95%): 0.95
Enter the amount invested (e.g., 1000000 for 1,000,000): 1000000
Enter the annual volatility (e.g., 0.25 for 25%): 0.27
Enter the period length (e.g., daily, monthly, biannual, or
annually):daily
Z-score: 1.645
Volatility: 1.70%
```

```
Period length: daily
Parametric VaR= $27,976.33
```

PRACTICAL EXERCISE #3.08 MONTE CARLO VAR

Request: Let's calculate a portfolio Monte Carlo VaR given some features

Summary of the script. –

This code estimates the Monte Carlo value at risk for an investment portfolio by simulating potential future losses based on user-defined inputs.

This code provides a comprehensive risk assessment tool with the following features:

a) Flexibility:
   Users can specify different investment values, confidence levels, and periods, allowing scenario-based analysis.
b) Monte Carlo Approach:
   Unlike traditional VaR methods, this approach leverages stochastic simulations, capturing a wide range of potential market outcomes.
c) Time Horizon Customization:
   Allows the user to adjust risk calculations for different periods (daily, monthly, biannual, annual), making it adaptable to various investment strategies.
d) Realistic Risk Estimation:
   Simulated returns account for the randomness of market movements, providing a probabilistic distribution of possible losses.

This code serves as a practical tool for investors and risk managers to estimate portfolio losses under simulated market conditions, offering insights into potential financial risks.

TABLE 3.9 Summary of Key Functions and Their Purposes

Function/Calculation	Purpose
calculate_var_monte_carlo(num_simulations, confidence_level, portfolio_value, annual_volatility, period_length)	Computes the value at risk using Monte Carlo simulation.
norm.ppf(confidence_level)	Calculates the Z-score for the given confidence level.
np.random.normal(0, volatility, num_simulations)	Generates random returns based on normal distribution using given volatility.
portfolio_value * (1 + random_returns)	Simulates potential future portfolio values based on returns.
losses = portfolio_value - simulated_portfolio_values	Calculates potential losses by comparing initial and simulated values.
np.percentile(losses, (1 - confidence_level / 100) * 100)	Computes the percentile loss corresponding to the confidence level.

Script execution and outputs. –

```
import numpy as np
from scipy.stats import norm

# Function to calculate VaR using Monte Carlo simulation
with user inputs
def calculate_var_monte_carlo(num_simulations, confidence_
level, portfolio_value, annual_volatility, period_length):
    # Calculate the Z-score for the given confidence level
    z_score = norm.ppf(confidence_level)

    # Determine the volatility based on the period length
    if period_length.lower() == 'daily':
        volatility = annual_volatility / np.sqrt(252)
    elif period_length.lower() == 'monthly':
        volatility = annual_volatility / np.sqrt(12)
    elif period_length.lower() == 'biannual':
        volatility = annual_volatility / np.sqrt(2)
    elif period_length.lower() == 'annually':
        volatility = annual_volatility
    else:
        raise ValueError("Period length must be 'daily',
        'monthly', or 'annually'")

    # Generate random returns based on the chosen period's
    volatility
    random_returns = np.random.normal(0, volatility,
    num_simulations)

    # Simulate portfolio values
    simulated_portfolio_values = portfolio_value * (1 +
    random_returns)
    # Calculate the potential losses
    losses = portfolio_value - simulated_portfolio_values

    # Calculate the VaR at the specified confidence level
    var_monte_carlo = np.percentile(losses, (1 - confidence_
    level / 100) * 100)

    # Report VaR as an absolute value
    formatted_var_monte_carlo = "${:,.2f}".format(abs(v
    ar_monte_carlo))

    return formatted_var_monte_carlo, z_score

# Input data
num_simulations = int(input("Enter the number of
simulations (e.g., 10000 for 10,000): "))
confidence_level = float(input("Enter the confidence level
(e.g., 0.95 for 95%): "))
```

```
portfolio_value = float(input("Enter the amount invested
(e.g., 1000000 for 1,000,000): "))
annual_volatility = float(input("Enter the annual
volatility (e.g., 0.25 for 25%): "))
period_length = str(input("Enter the period length (e.g.,
daily, monthly, biannual, or annually):"))

# Calculate VaR
var_result, calculated_z_score = calculate_var_monte_
carlo(num_simulations, confidence_level, portfolio_value,
annual_volatility, period_length)

# Format and print the result

print('Z-score:',round(calculated_z_score,3))
formatted_volatility="{:,.2f}%".format(abs(annual_
volatility*100))
print('Annual Volatility:', formatted_volatility)
print('Period length:',period_length )
print('Monte Carlo VaR=', var_result)
```

Output:

```
Enter the number of simulations (e.g., 10000 for 10,000): 10000
Enter the confidence level (e.g., 0.95 for 95%): 0.95
Enter the amount invested (e.g., 1000000 for 1,000,000): 1000000
Enter the annual volatility (e.g., 0.25 for 25%): 0.27
Enter the period length (e.g., daily, monthly, biannual, or
annually):daily
Z-score: 1.645
Annual Volatility: 27.00%
Period length: daily
Monte Carlo VaR= $40,894.10
```

3.5 MONTE CARLO SIMULATION FOR THE VALUE OF A PORTFOLIO

Monte Carlo simulation is a powerful tool for portfolio management, since it allows modeling and analyzing the future behavior of a portfolio under different market conditions, considering the uncertainty and risk inherent to investments.

An effective and commonly used approach is, in effect, to combine Markowitz portfolio optimization with Monte Carlo simulation. In this way, you can first construct an optimal portfolio based on modern portfolio theory (Markowitz) and then use Monte Carlo to evaluate how that portfolio might behave under different future scenarios.

Steps to build the portfolio and perform the Monte Carlo simulation:

1. Calculate the statistics of the assets:
   - Gather the historical returns of the two assets.
   - Calculate the expected return and volatility (standard deviation) of each asset.
   - Calculate the correlation matrix between the assets.
2. Markowitz optimization:
   - Uses the expected returns, volatilities and correlation matrix to find the optimal weightings of the assets in the portfolio that minimize volatility for a given expected return or maximize return for a given level of risk (efficient frontier).
3. Monte Carlo Simulation:

- Uses the portfolio statistics (expected return and volatility) to generate multiple simulated trajectories of the portfolio value. Analyzes the distribution of the final portfolio values to understand the risk and expected return under different scenarios.

Distributions to follow for the simulation (among others):

1. *Normal distribution*: also known as the Gaussian distribution, is a symmetric probability distribution described by its mean (mu, μ) and standard deviation (sigma, σ). It has the famous "bell" shape and is widely used in statistics and probability. In finance, daily, weekly or monthly returns on assets (such as stocks, bonds, etc.) are often modelled using a normal distribution. This implies that returns are symmetrically distributed around a mean (the expected return) with a certain standard deviation (volatility). The assumption of normality in returns facilitates the calculation of risk and return metrics, such as value at risk or Sharpe ratio.

   Limitations: Although the normal distribution is easy to use and has mathematical properties that simplify many calculations, its limitations can lead to an underestimation of risk and an inadequate assessment of performance in the context of portfolio management. These limitations include the underestimation of extreme events, the inability to capture asymmetries in returns, the assumption of time independence and constant correlations, and the lack of realism in modeling assets with price limits.

2. *Log-normal distribution*: While asset returns are usually modelled with a normal distribution, asset prices are best modelled with a log-normal distribution.This is because prices cannot be negative and tend to grow exponentially over time, which is best captured by log-normality.A log-normal price implies that the logarithm of prices follows a normal distribution. The log-normal distribution has a longer tail to the right, which better reflects the risk of significant increases in the price of an asset, while avoiding the possibility of negative prices.Log-normality is consistent with observed market behaviour, where prices tend to grow and where losses are limited but gains can be theoretically unlimited.

   Limitations: Although the log-normal distribution is a useful tool in portfolio management, especially for modeling asset prices that cannot be negative, it has important limitations that include underestimation of extreme events (financial crisis or "black swan" events), fixed skewness, dependence on log transformations, parameter sensitivity, and difficulties in capturing correlations and diversification in complex portfolios.

3. *Student's t distribution*: The Student's *t* distribution is often used to model data with heavier tails compared to the normal distribution, making it more appropriate for capturing extreme events or outliers in financial data. It is defined by its degrees of freedom, which control the thickness of the tails: fewer degrees of freedom result in thicker tails. In finance, it is particularly useful for modeling returns that exhibit fat tails and for stress testing portfolios under extreme conditions. Unlike the normal distribution, the Student´s *t* distribution is more flexible in capturing the probability of large deviations from the mean, making it a preferred choice in scenarios with higher uncertainty or risk.

   Limitations: The Student´s *t* distribution, while more realistic for modeling heavy-tailed data, also has its drawbacks. These include sensitivity to the choice of degrees of freedom, which can significantly affect results, and less straightforward parameter estimation compared to the normal distribution. Additionally, it may still fail to capture skewness or other asymmetric features often observed in financial returns.

In most portfolio management models, such as Markowitz portfolio theory, asset returns are assumed to be normally distributed. This allows for simplified risk and return calculations; however, for assessing future portfolio value or extreme price risk (as in Monte Carlo simulation), it is more appropriate to model asset prices with a log-normal distribution. This better reflects the multiplicative nature of price growth and its asymmetric behaviour. In more complex financial contexts, where extreme events are expected to occur or where correlations between assets vary over time, it is preferable to use distributions with heavier tails or more sophisticated models that can capture these dynamics more accurately.

PRACTICAL EXERCISE #3.09 MONTE CARLO SIMULATION (WITH NORMAL DISTRIBUTION)

Request: We are going to perform a Monte Carlo simulation of the value of a portfolio with the following characteristics:

- Initial value = $1,000,000.00
- Expected daily return = 0.001451
- Daily volatility = 0.01701
- Simulation period = 252 days (one trading year)
- Number of simulations = 10,000
- Distribution to follow: Normal

Summary of the script. –

This code simulates the future value of an investment portfolio using the Monte Carlo method, considering expected returns and volatility over a one-year trading horizon.

The code provides a comprehensive risk assessment and forecasting framework with the following features:

a) Realistic Portfolio Simulations:
It captures the uncertainty and variability of returns over time using a stochastic process based on historical data.
b) Scenario Analysis:
Allows investors to visualize potential best- and worst-case portfolio outcomes, providing insights into risk exposure and return potential.
c) Risk Management Tool:
The analysis of percentiles provides a measure of downside risk (e.g., the 5th percentile), which can be used to estimate value at risk.

d) Visual Insights:
Graphical representations of both individual paths and the final value distribution help stakeholders better understand the potential outcomes.

This Monte Carlo simulation approach is a powerful tool for investment decision-making, offering probabilistic estimates of future portfolio performance under uncertain market conditions.

TABLE 3.10 Summary of Key Functions and Their Purposes

Function/Calculation	Purpose
future_values = np.zeros((simulations, days))	Initializes a matrix to store portfolio value simulations over time.
np.random.normal(expected_return, volatility, simulations)	Generates random daily returns based on normal distribution with given mean and volatility.
future_values[:, t] = future_values [:, t − 1] * (1 + z)	Simulates portfolio value evolution using generated daily returns.
np.mean(final_value)	Computes the mean (expected) final portfolio value.
np.std(final_value)	Calculates the standard deviation of the simulated portfolio values.
np.percentile(final_value, [5, 50, 95])	Extracts key percentiles (5%, 50%, and 95%) from the distribution.

Script execution and outputs. –

```
import numpy as np
import matplotlib.pyplot as plt

# Input parameters
initial_value = 1000000  # Initial portfolio value
expected_return = 0.001451  # Daily expected return
volatility = 0.01701  # Daily standard deviation
days = 252  # Number of days in the time horizon (one
trading year)
simulations = 10000  # Number of simulations

# Create a matrix for storing simulation results
future_values = np.zeros((simulations, days))

# Fill in the first column with the initial price
future_values[:, 0] = initial_value
```

```
# Generate simulations
for t in range(1, days):
    # Generate random daily returns
    z = np.random.normal(expected_return, volatility,
    simulations)
    # Calculate the share price for the following day
    future_values[:, t] = future_values[:, t - 1] * (1 + z)

# Plotting some simulated trajectories
plt.figure(figsize=(10, 6))
plt.plot(future_values.T, lw=1, alpha=0.1)
plt.title('Monte Carlo simulations for the value of a
portfolio')
plt.xlabel('Days')
plt.ylabel('Portfolio Value')
plt.show()

# Analyze results
final_value = future_values[:, -1]
plt.figure(figsize=(10, 6))
plt.hist(final_value, bins=50, alpha=0.75)
plt.title('Simulated Final Value Distribution')
plt.xlabel('Portfolio Value')
plt.ylabel('Frequency')
plt.show()

# Statistics
mean_final = np.mean(final_value)
std_final = np.std(final_value)
percentiles = np.percentile(final_value, [5, 50, 95])

# Print results with thousands separators and two decimal
places
print(f"Final average value: ${mean_final:,.2f}")
print(f"Standard deviation of final value: ${std_final:,.2f}")
print(f"Percentile 5%: ${percentiles[0]:,.2f}")
print(f"Percentile 50% (Median): ${percentiles[1]:,.2f}")
print(f"Percentile 95%: ${percentiles[2]:,.2f}")
```

Output:

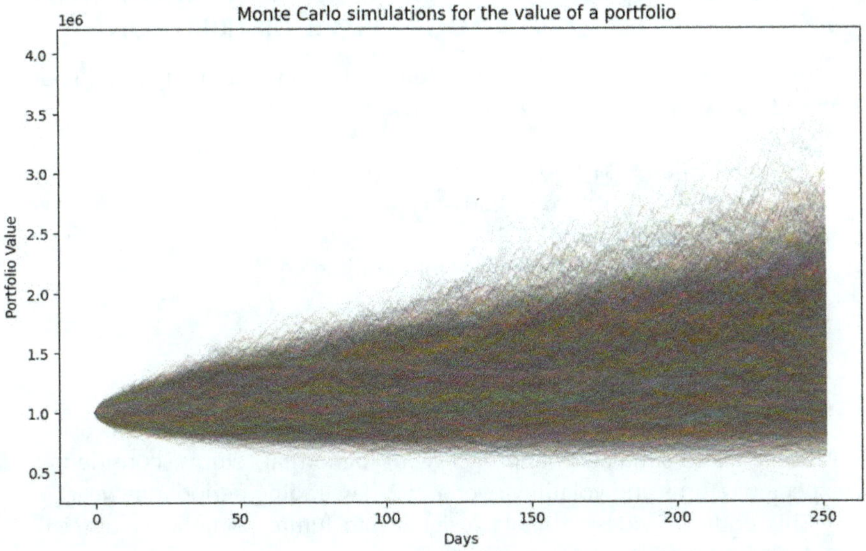

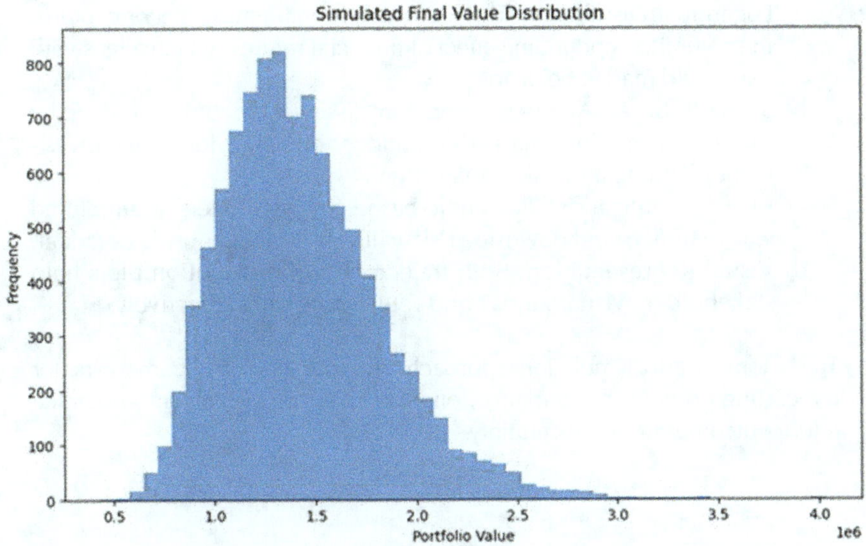


```
Final average value: $1,438,748.94
Standard deviation of final value: $392,511.90
Percentile 5%: $892,128.13
Percentile 50% (Median): $1,386,327.26
Percentile 95%: $2,152,368.31
```

PRACTICAL EXERCISE #3.10 MONTE CARLO SIMULATION (WITH LOG-NORMAL DISTRIBUTION)

Request: We are going to perform a Monte Carlo simulation of the value of a portfolio with the following characteristics:

- Initial value = $1,000,000.00
- Expected daily return = 0.001451
- Daily volatility = 0.01701
- Simulation period = 252 days (one trading year)
- Number of simulations = 10,000
- Distribution to follow: Log-Normal

Summary of the Script. –

This code simulates the future value of an investment portfolio using a Monte Carlo simulation approach with lognormal returns, considering expected returns and volatility over a 252-day trading period (one year).

This code provides valuable insights into future portfolio value estimates with the following features:

a) Lognormal Distribution: The use of lognormal returns better captures the natural compounding effect of financial returns, which aligns with real-world market behavior.
b) Scenario-Based Analysis: Users can assess potential outcomes by simulating multiple market conditions, allowing for better investment planning and risk management.
c) Risk Quantification: Percentile-based analysis offers a structured way to understand downside risk (value at risk) and upside potential.
d) Visual Representation: Both trajectory and distribution plots help stakeholders visualize risk and return dynamics effectively.

This Monte Carlo simulation approach provides a robust framework for forecasting portfolio performance, offering investors insights into potential future outcomes under uncertainty.

TABLE 3.11 Summary of Key Functions and Their Purposes

Function/Calculation	Purpose
future_values = np.zeros((simulations, days))	Initializes a matrix to store portfolio value simulations over time.
np.random.lognormal(mean=mu, sigma=sigma, size=simulations)	Generates random daily returns based on a lognormal distribution.
future_values[:, t] = future_values[:, t – 1] * z	Simulates portfolio value evolution using generated lognormal returns.
np.mean(final_value)	Computes the mean (expected) final portfolio value.
np.std(final_value)	Calculates the standard deviation of the simulated portfolio values.
np.percentile(final_value, [5, 50, 95])	Extracts the 5th, 50th (median), and 95th percentiles of final values.

Script execution and outputs. –

```
import numpy as np
import matplotlib.pyplot as plt

# Parameters
initial_value = 1_000_000  # Initial portfolio value
mu = 0.001451  # Mean of log returns
sigma = 0.01701  # Volatility
days = 252  # Number of days to simulate
simulations = 10000  # Number of simulations

# Initialize the matrix to store simulation results
future_values = np.zeros((simulations, days))

# Set the initial portfolio value for all simulations
future_values[:, 0] = initial_value

# Perform the simulation
for t in range(1, days):
    # Generate daily lognormal returns
    z = np.random.lognormal(mean=mu, sigma=sigma,
    size=simulations)
    # Calculate the portfolio value for the next day
    future_values[:, t] = future_values[:, t - 1] * z

# Plotting some simulated trajectories
plt.figure(figsize=(10, 6))
plt.plot(future_values.T, lw=1, alpha=0.1)
plt.title('Monte Carlo simulations for the value of a
portfolio')
plt.xlabel('Days')
```

```
plt.ylabel('Portfolio Value')
plt.show()

# Analyze results
final_value = future_values[:, -1]
plt.figure(figsize=(10, 6))
plt.hist(final_value, bins=50, alpha=0.75)
plt.title('Simulated Final Value Distribution')
plt.xlabel('Portfolio Value')
plt.ylabel('Frequency')
plt.show()

# Statistics
mean_final = np.mean(final_value)
std_final = np.std(final_value)
percentiles = np.percentile(final_value, [5, 50, 95])

# Print results with thousands separators and two decimal
places
print(f"Final average value: ${mean_final:,.2f}")
print(f"Standard deviation of final value: ${std_
final:,.2f}")
print(f"Percentile 5%: ${percentiles[0]:,.2f}")
print(f"Percentile 50% (Median): ${percentiles[1]:,.2f}")
print(f"Percentile 95%: ${percentiles[2]:,.2f}")
```

Output:

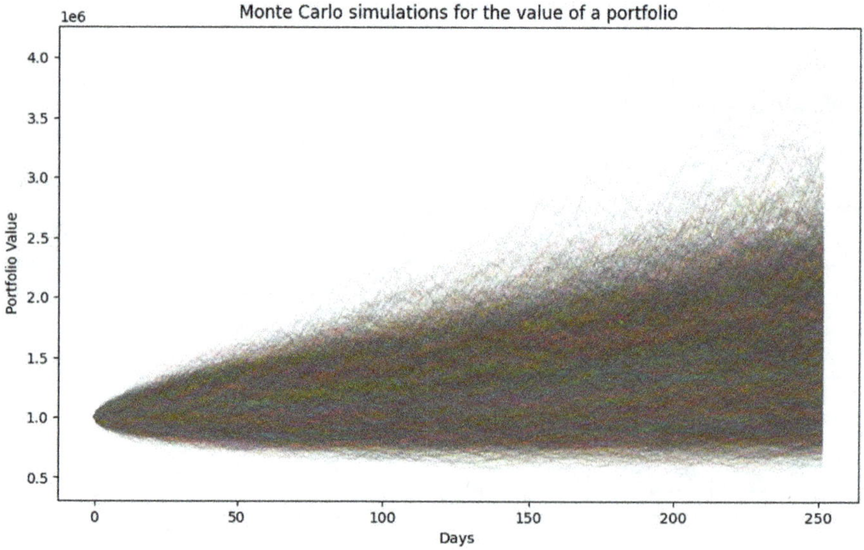

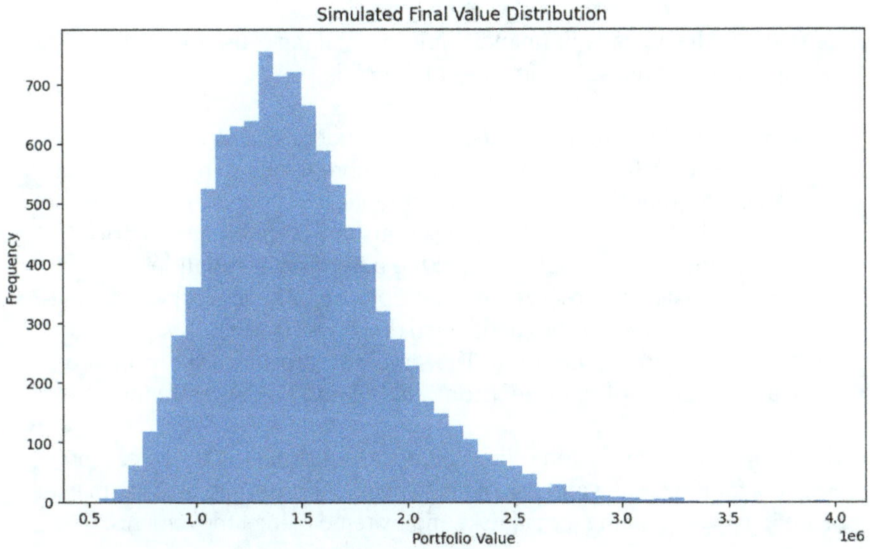


```
Final average value: $1,491,564.80
Standard deviation of final value: $408,162.01
Percentile 5%: $922,686.05
Percentile 50% (Median): $1,436,854.89
Percentile 95%: $2,237,497.03
```

PRACTICAL EXERCISE #3.11 MONTE CARLO SIMULATION (WITH STUDENT´S *T* DISTRIBUTION)

Request: We are going to perform a Monte Carlo simulation of the value of a portfolio with the following characteristics:

- Initial value = $1,000,000.00
- Annualized mean return = 7%
- Annualized volatility = 15%
- Simulation period = 252 days (one trading year)
- Number of simulations = 10,000
- Degrees of freedom: 5
- Distribution to follow: Student´s *t*

Summary of the script. –

This code performs a Monte Carlo simulation to estimate the future value of an investment portfolio over a specified period, using the Student´s *t* distribution for modeling daily returns. The Student´s *t* distribution accounts for potential heavy tails in financial returns, making it useful for modeling extreme market events. Key features of the code:

a) Fat-Tailed Distribution Modeling: The Student's *t* distribution accounts for extreme events, which are more frequent in financial markets compared to a normal distribution.
b) Scenario-Based Analysis: Allows users to test different scenarios by adjusting volatility, returns, and the number of simulations.
c) Risk Management Insights: Provides a probabilistic view of potential outcomes, helping investors understand downside risks (e.g., 5% percentile).
d) Graphical Representation: The simulation results are visualized using plots for better decision-making and risk assessment.

This Monte Carlo simulation using a Student's *t* distribution provides a powerful tool for forecasting and risk management, offering more realistic market modeling by accounting for tail risks and extreme market movements.

TABLE 3.12 Summary of Key Functions and Their Purposes

Function/Calculation	Purpose
monte_carlo_tstudent_simulation(. . .)	Simulates the portfolio value using Monte Carlo with Student's t distribution.
np.random.standard_t(degrees_of_freedom, size=simulations) * daily_sigma + daily_mu	Generates daily portfolio returns using the Student's t distribution.
future_values[:, t] = future_values [:, t – 1] * (1 + z)	Computes portfolio values for subsequent days based on simulated returns.
np.mean(final_value)	Computes the average final portfolio value.
np.std(final_value)	Calculates the standard deviation of simulated portfolio values.
np.percentile(final_value, [5, 50, 95])	Extracts the 5th, 50th (median), and 95th percentiles of final values.

Script execution and outputs. –

```
import numpy as np
import matplotlib.pyplot as plt

def monte_carlo_tstudent_simulation(initial_value, mu,
sigma, days, simulations, degrees_of_freedom):
    """
    Simulate the portfolio value using Monte Carlo method
    with Student's t distribution.
```

```
    Parameters:
    initial_value (float): Initial portfolio value.
    mu (float): Mean of log returns (annualized).
    sigma (float): Volatility (standard deviation, annualized).
    days (int): Number of trading days to simulate.
    simulations (int): Number of simulations.
    degrees_of_freedom (int): Degrees of freedom for the
    Student´s t distribution.

    Returns:
    None: Displays graphs and prints statistics.
    """

    # Convert annualized mean and volatility to daily
    values
    daily_mu = mu / 252
    daily_sigma = sigma / np.sqrt(252)

    # Initialize the matrix to store simulation results
    future_values = np.zeros((simulations, days))

    # Set the initial portfolio value for all simulations
    future_values[:, 0] = initial_value

    # Perform the simulation
    for t in range(1, days):
        # Generate daily returns from Student´s t
        distribution
        z = np.random.standard_t(degrees_of_freedom,
        size=simulations) * daily_sigma + daily_mu
        # Calculate the portfolio value for the next day
        future_values[:, t] = future_values[:, t - 1] * (1 + z)

    # Plotting some simulated trajectories
    plt.figure(figsize=(10, 6))
    plt.plot(future_values.T, lw=1, alpha=0.1)
    plt.title('Monte Carlo simulations for the value of a
    portfolio (Student´s t distribution)')
    plt.xlabel('Days')
    plt.ylabel('Portfolio Value')
    plt.grid(True)  # Adding grid for better visualization
    plt.show()

    # Analyze results
    final_value = future_values[:, -1]

    # Plot distribution of the final portfolio values
    plt.figure(figsize=(10, 6))
    plt.hist(final_value, bins=50, alpha=0.75)
    plt.title('Simulated Final Value Distribution
    (Student´s t distribution)')
    plt.xlabel('Portfolio Value')
    plt.ylabel('Frequency')
```

```
    plt.grid(True)  # Adding grid for better visualization
    plt.show()

    # Statistics
    mean_final = np.mean(final_value)
    std_final = np.std(final_value)
    percentiles = np.percentile(final_value, [5, 50, 95])

    # Print results with thousands separators and two
    decimal places
    print(f"Final average value: ${mean_final:,.2f}")
    print(f"Standard deviation of final value: ${std_
    final:,.2f}")
    print(f"Percentile 5%: ${percentiles[0]:,.2f}")
    print(f"Percentile 50% (Median): ${percentiles[1]:,.2f}")
    print(f"Percentile 95%: ${percentiles[2]:,.2f}")

# Example usage
monte_carlo_tstudent_simulation(
    initial_value=1000000,
    mu=0.07,  # Annualized mean return (7%)
    sigma=0.15,  # Annualized volatility (15%)
    days=252,  # Simulating for one year (252 trading days)
    simulations=10000,
    degrees_of_freedom=5  # Degrees of freedom for the
    Student's t distribution
)
```

Output:

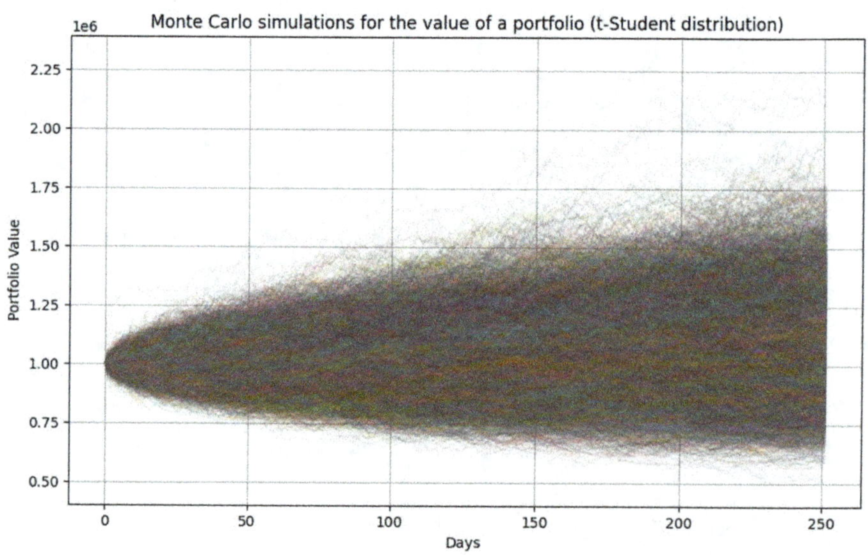

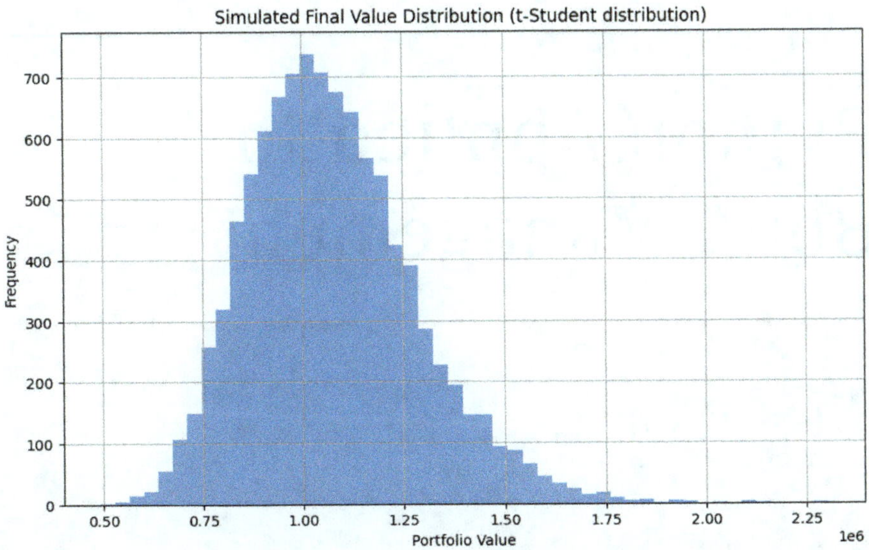


```
Final average value: $1,071,872.40
Standard deviation of final value: $208,092.39
Percentile 5%: $765,610.06
Percentile 50% (Median): $1,052,179.72
Percentile 95%: $1,446,748.63
```

CHAPTER 4

Python Applied to Bond Management

4.1 CHAPTER OVERVIEW

This chapter presents a practical and structured guide to managing fixed-income portfolios using Python. It begins by explaining how Python enhances traditional bond analysis through tools for pricing, yield curve construction, and optimization. The chapter covers core bond concepts such as valuation, duration, convexity, and zero-coupon rates and then applies them through Python code to compute key metrics like IRR and sensitivity to interest rates. It introduces portfolio strategies – including bullet, barbell, ladder, immunization, and cash flow matching – each supported by real-world Python implementations that automate portfolio construction and evaluation. The chapter emphasizes aligning investment choices with risk, return, and liability objectives, offering readers both financial theory and hands-on coding skills to manage bond portfolios effectively

4.2 PYTHON APPLIED TO BOND MANAGEMENT

In the fixed-income market, bond management is a critical discipline that requires precision, analytical rigor, and a deep understanding of interest rate dynamics. Bonds, being one of the fundamental instruments in financial markets, offer a relatively stable investment option, providing regular income through interest payments. Effective bond management ensures that these instruments not only preserve capital but also meet specific

DOI: 10.1201/9781003781394-4

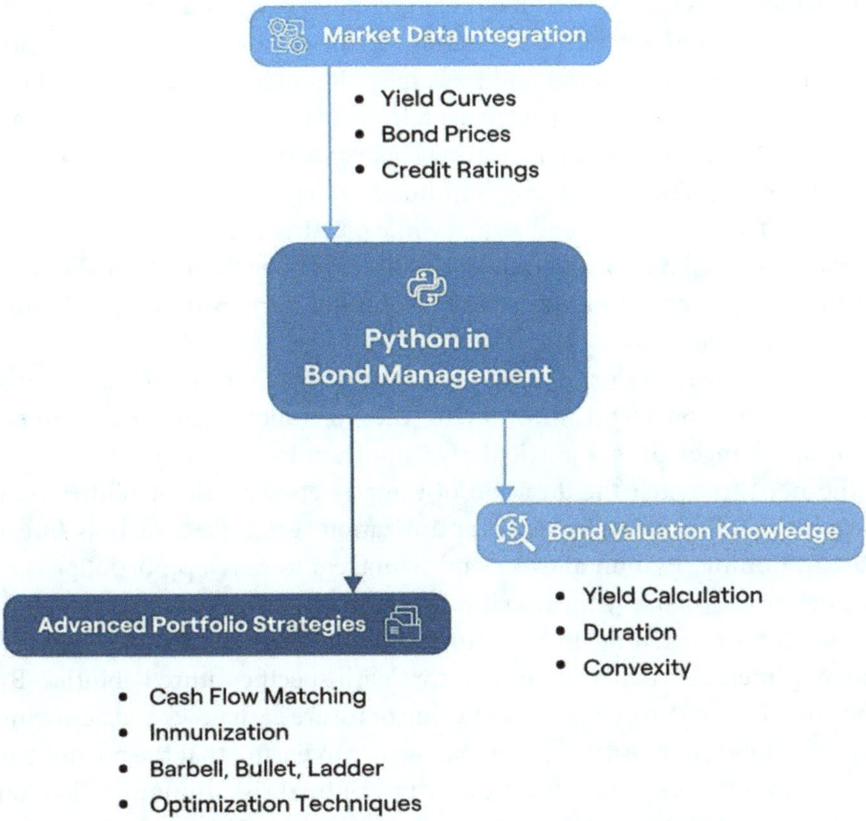

FIGURE 4.1 Python in Bond Management: Integration and Strategies

investment objectives, such as generating steady income, maintaining liquidity, or achieving targeted returns with controlled risk.

Python, a versatile and powerful programming language, has become an essential tool in bond management, offering a range of functionalities that streamline complex calculations, optimize portfolios, and enhance decision-making processes. This introduction explores the application of Python in bond management, highlighting its role in optimizing portfolios, managing duration and convexity, and addressing cash flow matching and immunization strategies.

Bond management involves the selection and management of a portfolio of bonds to meet specific financial objectives. These objectives might include maximizing yield, minimizing risk, or matching the cash flows of liabilities.

To achieve these goals, portfolio managers must navigate a landscape characterized by interest rate fluctuations, credit risk, and market liquidity. Python's extensive libraries and tools make it an ideal choice for handling the complexities of bond management, from analysing yield curves and calculating bond prices to implementing sophisticated optimization models.

One of the central challenges in bond management is optimizing the portfolio to balance risk and return while meeting specific investment criteria. Python plays a pivotal role in this process by enabling the implementation of optimization models that account for various factors, including yield, duration, convexity, and credit risk.

For instance, Python can be used to construct portfolios that meet a desired duration target, minimizing the portfolio's sensitivity to interest rate changes. This is particularly important for institutional investors who need to match the duration of their assets with the liabilities they are intended to fund. By using optimization techniques, such as linear programming, Python allows bond managers to develop portfolios that achieve this balance while maximizing returns.

Cash flow matching and immunization are critical strategies in bond management, particularly for investors with specific future liabilities. By accurately calculating the present value of future cash flows and adjusting the portfolio composition, bond managers can ensure that the portfolio is structured to meet future liabilities with minimal risk. Immunization, on the other hand, involves structuring a bond portfolio in such a way that its value is protected from interest rate fluctuations. Python's optimization libraries allow bond managers to construct immunized portfolios by carefully selecting bonds with appropriate durations and convexities. This ensures that the portfolio's value remains stable, even in the face of changing interest rates, providing a safeguard against market volatility.

4.3 BOND VALUATION

This section provides a comprehensive foundation for understanding and analysing fixed-income instruments. It begins with a clear definition of bonds, highlighting their key features - such as face value, coupon rate, and maturity - which determine their income profile and risk-return dynamics. Various bond types are categorized by issuer, structure, and purpose, including green and catastrophe bonds, each serving distinct financial or social goals. The section then delves into the mechanics of zero-coupon bonds and spot rates, which are essential for constructing yield curves and valuing future cash flows. It explains the yield curve's role as a barometer of economic expectations, outlines its shapes and underlying theories, and introduces bond pricing based on spot rates. Duration and modified duration are presented as measures of interest rate sensitivity, while convexity refines this analysis by accounting for non-linear price movements. The section concludes with a practical Python exercise that calculates a bond's price, yield, duration, and convexity using swap-derived zero-coupon curves – offering readers both conceptual clarity and a hands-on tool for real-world bond analysis.

4.3.1 Bond Definition

A bond is a fixed-income financial instrument that represents a loan made by an investor to a borrower (typically corporate or governmental). A bond can be thought of as an IOU between the lender and borrower that includes the details of the loan and its payments.

4.3.1.1 Key Features of Bonds

Understanding the key features of bonds is essential for evaluating their suitability in investment strategies (Fabozzi, 2007). These features define how bonds function, their associated risks, and their potential returns. From determining the periodic income received to assessing how market factors influence bond prices, each characteristic plays a critical role in shaping the bond's value and appeal to investors.

The main attributes of bonds, such as their face value, coupon rate, and maturity, provide a foundation for analysing their performance under various market conditions:

a) Principal: The amount of money that the bond issuer agrees to repay the bondholder at the maturity date. It is also known as the face value or par value of the bond.

b) Coupon Rate: The interest rate that the bond issuer will pay on the face value of the bond, expressed as a percentage. It represents the periodic interest payments that the bondholder will receive.

c) Coupon Dates: The specific dates on which the bond issuer will make interest payments to the bondholder. These payments are usually made semi-annually or annually.

d) Maturity Date: The date on which the bond will mature and the bond issuer will pay the bondholder the face value of the bond.

e) Issuer: The entity that issues the bond. Issuers can be corporations, municipalities, governments, or other organizations.

f) Day-Count Convention: The day-count convention is used to determine how interest accrues over time. Among the most common conventions are 30/360, 30/365, actual/360, actual/365, and actual/actual.

4.3.1.2 Types of Bonds

The classification of bonds is based on several factors, such as the issuer, structure, and purpose. Governments, corporations, and municipal entities are among the most common issuers, while bond structures can include fixed-rate, floating-rate, and zero-coupon varieties. Each type of bond serves a specific financial goal, whether it's funding public infrastructure, corporate expansion, or managing cash flows.

According to the issuers:

a) Government Bonds: Issued by national or local governments and are often considered low-risk investments. Examples include U.S. Treasury bonds, notes, and bills.

b) Corporate Bonds: Issued by companies to raise capital for various purposes, such as expanding operations, funding research and development, or refinancing debt.

The most common types of bonds based on their structure include:

a) Fixed-Rate Bonds: These bonds pay a fixed interest rate throughout their lifetime, providing predictable income streams and stability in cash flow.

b) Floating-Rate Bonds (FRNs): These bonds have variable interest rates that reset periodically based on a benchmark rate, such as EURIBOR or SOFR. They offer protection against rising interest rates.

c) Zero-Coupon Bonds: These bonds do not pay periodic interest. Instead, they are issued at a discount to their face value and mature at par, making them appealing for investors seeking long-term growth.

d) Inflation-Linked Bonds: Designed to protect against inflation, the principal or interest payments of these bonds adjust based on changes in inflation indexes, such as the Consumer Price Index (CPI).

e) Callable Bonds: These bonds give the issuer the right to redeem the bond before maturity, typically when interest rates decline, allowing them to refinance at lower rates.

f) Puttable Bonds: These bonds give the bondholder the right to sell the bond back to the issuer before maturity, offering additional flexibility and risk mitigation.

g) Convertible Bonds: These bonds can be converted into a predetermined number of the issuer's equity shares, providing a combination of debt and equity features.

h) Perpetual Bonds: These bonds have no fixed maturity date and pay interest indefinitely, making them similar to equity in certain respects.

i) Amortizing Bonds: These bonds pay back the principal gradually over time through regular payments, reducing credit risk as the loan balance decreases.

Each bond structure serves specific needs, whether it's managing interest rate risk, protecting against inflation, or blending debt with equity exposure. By understanding these structures, investors can make more informed decisions and tailor their portfolios to achieve their financial objectives.

Bonds can also be classified based on their purpose, which refers to the specific financial objectives of the bond issuer or the targeted use of funds raised through bond issuance. Understanding the purpose behind a bond helps investors assess the associated risks, potential returns, and alignment with their own financial or ethical goals.

a) Green Bonds: Issued specifically to fund environmentally friendly and sustainable projects. Comparable to the issuer's traditional bonds but often appeals to socially responsible investors.

b) Social Bonds: Issued to fund projects with positive social outcomes, such as affordable housing, healthcare, or education. Reflects the issuer's creditworthiness and alignment with social impact goals.

c) Development Bonds: Issued by governments or international organizations to fund economic development in underdeveloped or emerging markets, combat poverty, build infrastructure, and stimulate economic growth.

d) War Bonds: Issued during wartime to fund military operations and defence efforts. Mobilize public savings for national defence.

e) Catastrophe Bonds (Cat Bonds): Issued to transfer the risk of catastrophic events (e.g., natural disasters) to bondholders. Provide funds to insurance companies in the event of disasters like earthquakes or hurricanes.

f) Infrastructure Bonds: Issued to finance large-scale infrastructure projects such as highways, airports, or utilities.

g) Securitization bonds: bonds created by pooling together financial assets (like mortgages, car loans, or credit card debt) and turning them into tradable securities.

By categorizing bonds according to their purpose, investors can align their choices with their financial objectives, ethical values, or risk tolerance. This perspective helps evaluate not just the returns but also the broader impact of their investments.

4.3.1.3 How Bonds Work

When you purchase a bond, you are lending money to the issuer in exchange for periodic interest payments and the return of the bond's face value when it matures. The interest payments are typically made at fixed intervals (e.g., semi-annually), and the face value is repaid on the maturity date. For example, if you buy a €1,000 bond with a maturity of 10 years, the issuer will pay you €50 per year (5% of €1,000) for 10 years, and at the end of the 10 years, you will receive the €1,000 face value of the bond.

4.3.1.4 Advantages of Investing in Bonds

The advantages of bonds stem from their predictable cash flows, lower risk profile, and unique features tailored to different investment objectives. Whether it's a government issuing bonds to finance infrastructure or an individual seeking steady returns, bonds play a vital role in meeting financial goals. The main advantages are:

a) Stable Income: Bonds provide a predictable income stream through regular interest payments.

b) Diversification: Including bonds in your investment portfolio can help diversify and reduce overall risk.

c) Capital Preservation: Bonds are generally less volatile than stocks and can help preserve capital.

4.3.1.5 Risks of Investing in Bonds

While bonds are often considered a safer investment compared to equities, they are not without risks. Investing in bonds involves exposure to various financial, economic, and market-related uncertainties that can affect their value, income, and overall performance. Understanding these risks is crucial for investors to make informed decisions and properly manage their portfolios. The main risks are:

a) Interest Rate Risk: Bond prices inversely correlate with interest rates. When interest rates rise, bond prices fall, and vice versa.

b) Credit Risk: The risk that the bond issuer may default on interest payments or the repayment of the principal.

c) Inflation Risk: The risk that inflation will erode the purchasing power of the bond's future cash flows.

d) Liquidity Risk: The risk that you may not be able to sell the bond easily at its fair market value.

e) Cash-Flow Risk: Floating-rate bonds are exposed to the risk that future cash flows may increase or decrease due to changes in interest rates.

By understanding these characteristics and types of bonds, investors can make informed decisions about incorporating bonds into their investment portfolios.

4.3.2 Bond Characteristics

4.3.2.1 Zero Coupon Rate

A zero-coupon rate, also known as a spot rate, is the yield on a zero-coupon bond. A zero-coupon bond does not pay periodic interest (coupons) but is sold at a discount to its face value and pays the face value at maturity. The zero-coupon rate represents the annualized return on such a bond.

4.3.2.1.1 Characteristics of Zero-Coupon Bonds Zero-coupon bonds are a unique type of fixed-income security that differs from traditional bonds in their structure and cash flow characteristics. Understanding these features will help investors evaluate whether zero-coupon bonds are a suitable addition to their investment portfolios, particularly for strategies like matching future cash flow needs or taking advantage of interest rate movements.

a) No Periodic Interest Payments: Zero-coupon bonds do not make regular interest payments. Instead, the interest is compounded and paid in full at maturity.

b) Sold at a Discount: These bonds are sold at a price lower than their face value. The difference between the purchase price and the face value represents the interest earned by the investor.

c) Maturity: The bondholder receives the face value of the bond at the maturity date.

4.3.2.1.2 Calculation of Zero-Coupon Rate The zero-coupon rate can be derived from the price of the zero-coupon bond. The formula to calculate the zero-coupon rate (spot rate) is:

$$P = \frac{F}{(1+r)^n}$$

where:

- P is the current price of the zero-coupon bond.
- F is the face value of the bond.
- r is the zero-coupon rate (spot rate).
- n is the number of periods until maturity.

Rearranging to solve for the zero-coupon rate (r):

$$r=\left(\frac{F}{P}\right)^{\frac{1}{n}}-1$$

4.3.2.1.3 Applications of Zero-Coupon Rates Zero-coupon rates play a vital role in the field of fixed-income finance and financial modelling. These rates represent the yield on zero-coupon bonds for a specific maturity, and they provide a foundational tool for valuing bonds and other financial instruments. Unlike coupon-bearing bonds, zero-coupon rates reflect the pure time value of money, making them instrumental in stripping away the effects of periodic interest payments. These are the main applications:

a) Yield Curve Construction: Zero-coupon rates are used to construct the yield curve, which is a graphical representation of interest rates for different maturities.

b) Discount Factors: Zero-coupon rates are used to calculate discount factors, which are used to discount future cash flows to their present value.

c) Pricing Bonds and Derivatives: Zero-coupon rates are essential in the valuation of bonds and financial derivatives.

4.3.2.1.4 Advantages and Disadvantages In finance, every investment, strategy, or financial instrument comes with its own set of advantages and disadvantages.

Advantages

- Predictability: Investors know exactly how much they will receive at maturity.
- No Reinvestment Risk: Since there are no periodic interest payments, investors do not face reinvestment risk.

Disadvantages

- Price Volatility: Zero-coupon bonds can be more volatile in price compared to coupon-bearing bonds.
- Taxation: In some jurisdictions, the imputed interest on zero-coupon bonds may be taxable annually, even though no cash is received until maturity.

By understanding zero-coupon rates, investors can better assess the value and yield of zero-coupon bonds and make more informed investment decisions.

4.3.2.2 Yield Curve

The yield curve is a graphical representation of the interest rates on debt for a range of maturities. It shows the relationship between the interest rate (or cost of borrowing) and the time to maturity of the debt for a given borrower in a given currency. The yield curve is typically used to predict changes in economic output and growth.

4.3.2.2.1 Types of Yield Curves Understanding the different types of yield curves is essential for investors, analysts, and policymakers, as each shape provides unique insights into the market's outlook (Fabozzi, 2010). The most common types of yield curves include:

a) Normal Yield Curve: This curve slopes upward, indicating that longer-term debt instruments have a higher yield compared to short-term debt instruments. This is the most common shape and suggests that the economy is expected to grow in the future.

b) Inverted Yield Curve: This curve slopes downward, indicating that shorter-term debt instruments have a higher yield compared to longer-term debt instruments. An inverted yield curve can be a predictor of economic recession.

c) Flat Yield Curve: This curve is relatively flat, indicating that there is little difference in yield between short-term and long-term debt instruments. A flat yield curve can indicate economic transition or uncertainty.

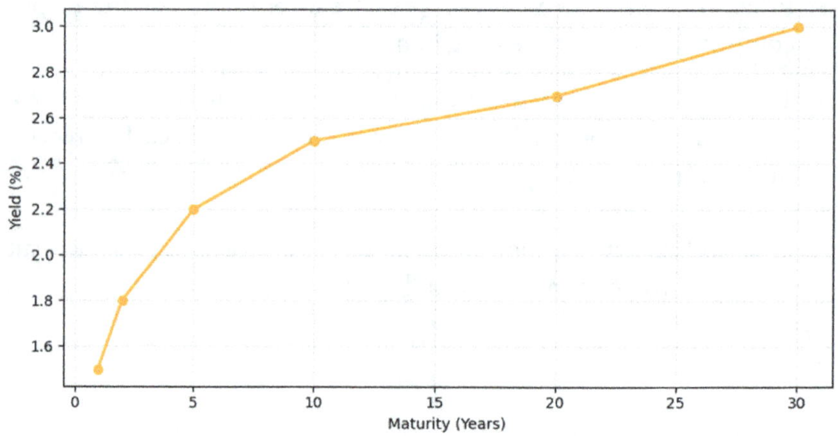

FIGURE 4.2 Normal Yield Curve

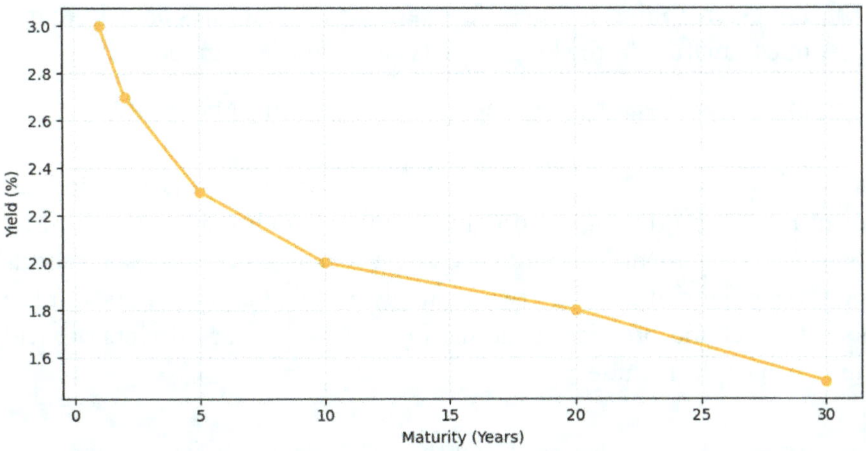

FIGURE 4.3 Inverted Yield Curve

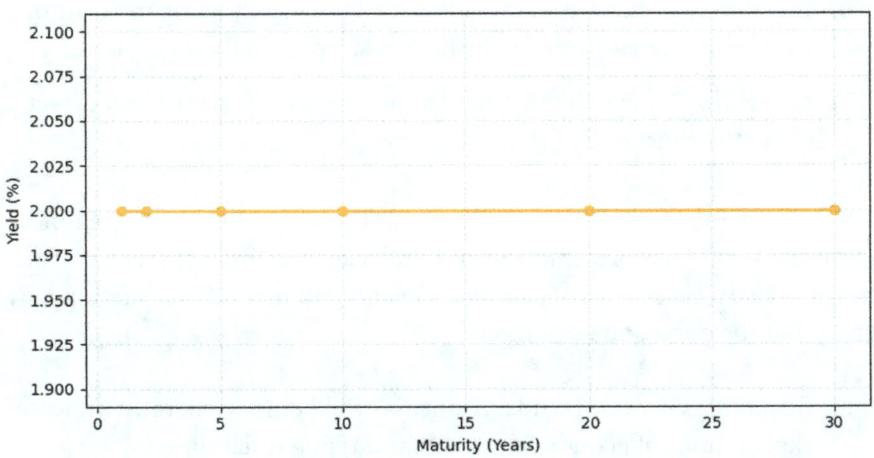

FIGURE 4.4 Flat Yield Curve

4.3.2.2.2 Components of the Yield Curve The yield curve plays a pivotal role in understanding interest rates and economic trends. To interpret the yield curve effectively, it is essential to understand its key components, which provide insights into market dynamics and investor expectations.

The components of the yield curve include:

a) Short-Term Interest Rates: These are the interest rates on debt that is due to mature in the short term, typically less than a year.

b) Long-Term Interest Rates: These are the interest rates on debt that is due to mature in the long term, typically more than ten years.

c) Maturity: This is the time at which the debt must be repaid.

4.3.2.2.3 Factors Affecting the Yield Curve The yield curve is a key indicator of market sentiment, economic conditions, and monetary policy. Its shape and movements are influenced by a variety of factors, each reflecting the complex interplay between supply and demand dynamics in the bond market and broader economic forces. The primary drivers of yield curve behaviour include:

a) Economic Conditions: Growth expectations, inflation expectations, and monetary policy can all influence the shape of the yield curve.

b) Inflation Expectations: If investors expect higher inflation in the future, long-term interest rates will be higher, steepening the yield curve.

c) Monetary Policy: Central banks' policies on interest rates directly affect the short end of the yield curve.

4.3.2.2.4 Interpretation of the Yield Curve The yield curve serves as more than just a visual representation of bond yields across different maturities; it is also a barometer of economic health and market expectations. By analysing the curve, one can infer:

a) Economic Growth Trends: A normal yield curve generally indicates expectations of economic growth and rising inflation.

b) Recession Risk: An inverted yield curve is often seen as a predictor of economic recession.

c) Interest Rate Expectations: The shape and movement of the yield curve reflect investor predictions about future interest rate changes, influenced by central bank policies, inflation, and market dynamics.

4.3.2.2.5 Yield Curve Theories Several theories have been developed to explain its behaviour. These yield curve theories provide frameworks for interpreting the curve's shape and what it signals about market expectations, investor behaviour, and economic conditions. The three primary theories explaining the yield curve are:

a) Expectations Theory: This theory suggests that long-term interest rates are a reflection of expected future short-term interest rates.

b) Liquidity Preference Theory: This theory posits that investors demand a premium for holding longer-term debt due to increased risk, leading to a normally upward-sloping yield curve.

c) Market Segmentation Theory: This theory suggests that the yield curve shape is determined by supply and demand for funds in different maturity segments.

These theories provide a foundation for analysing the yield curve, each offering unique insights into the forces shaping its structure.

4.3.2.3 Price

To calculate the price of a bond using zero-coupon interest rates (also known as spot rates) extracted from the yield curve, we need to discount each future cash flow of the bond using the corresponding spot rate.

The price of a bond is the sum of the present values of all its future cash flows, discounted at the corresponding spot rates. The general formula is:

$$P=\sum_{t=1}^{T} C_t / (1+y)^t$$

where:

- P is the current price of the bond.
- C_t is the cash flow at time t (including coupon payments and the face value at maturity).
- y is the yield to maturity.
- t is the number of periods until the cash flow.
- T is the total number of periods until the bond's maturity.

They cannot be solved algebraically in a simple manner, so an iterative method or numerical algorithm is generally used. In Python, the *numpy_financial.irr* function can be used to calculate the y of a series of cash flows.

4.3.2.4 Macaulay Duration and Modified Duration

Bond duration is a measure of the sensitivity of a bond's price to changes in interest rates. It indicates how much the price of a bond is expected to fluctuate when there is a change in interest rates. The most common measures of duration are Macaulay duration and modified duration.

Macaulay duration is the weighted average time until cash flows are received, and it is expressed in years. The formula for Macaulay duration is:

$$Macaulay\ Duration = \frac{\sum_{t=1}^{T} \frac{t \cdot C_t}{(1+y)^t}}{P}$$

where:

- t is the time period.
- C_t is the cash flow at time t.
- y is the yield to maturity.
- P is the current price of the bond.
- T is the total number of periods until the bond's maturity.

Modified duration adjusts Macaulay duration to account for changes in yield to maturity. It provides a direct measure of the sensitivity of a bond's price to interest rate changes. The formula for modified duration is:

$$Modified\ Duration = (Macaulay\ Duration) / (1+y)$$

where: y is the yield to maturity.

Interpretation

- Higher Duration: Bonds with higher duration are more sensitive to changes in interest rates. For instance, if a bond has a modified duration of 5, a 1% increase in interest rates will result in an approximate 5% decrease in the bond's price.
- Lower Duration: Bonds with lower duration are less sensitive to interest rate changes.

Applications

- Interest Rate Risk Management: Investors use duration to assess and manage the interest rate risk of their bond portfolios.

- Investment Strategies: Duration helps in constructing bond portfolios that match the investor's risk tolerance and investment horizon.

By understanding bond duration, investors can make more informed decisions about their fixed-income investments and better manage the risks associated with interest rate fluctuations.

Modified duration is a key metric used in fixed-income analysis to estimate how sensitive a bond's price is to changes in interest rates (yield). It quantifies the relationship between bond prices and yields, helping investors and portfolio managers assess and manage interest rate risk. The price-yield relationship is inverse: when yields rise, bond prices fall, and vice versa. Modified duration provides a measure of this sensitivity by estimating the percentage change in the bond's price for a 1% (or 100 basis points) change in yield.

The sensitivity formula measures the sensitivity of a bond's price to interest rate changes.

$$\Delta P \approx -D_M \cdot \Delta y \cdot P$$

where:

- ΔP: Change in bond price.
- D_M: Modified duration.
- Δy: Change in yield (expressed as a decimal).
- P: Initial bond price.

4.3.2.5 Discrete Convexity

Duration assumes that there is a linear relationship between changes in yield and changes in price. However, the relationship between the relative change in the price of a bond and the yield to maturity is not linear.

However, the relationship between bond price and yield is actually curved, that is, it is not linear. The use of the modified duration to estimate bond price changes will result in the following errors when interest rate changes are large in magnitude:

- Underestimate of price increase when the yield falls
- Overestimate of price decrease when the yield rises

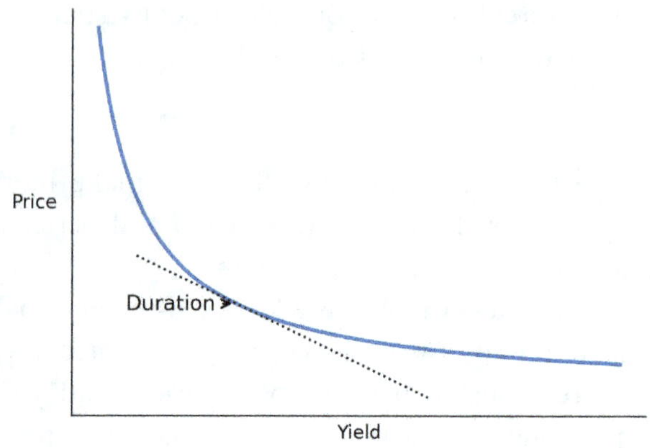

FIGURE 4.5 Duration

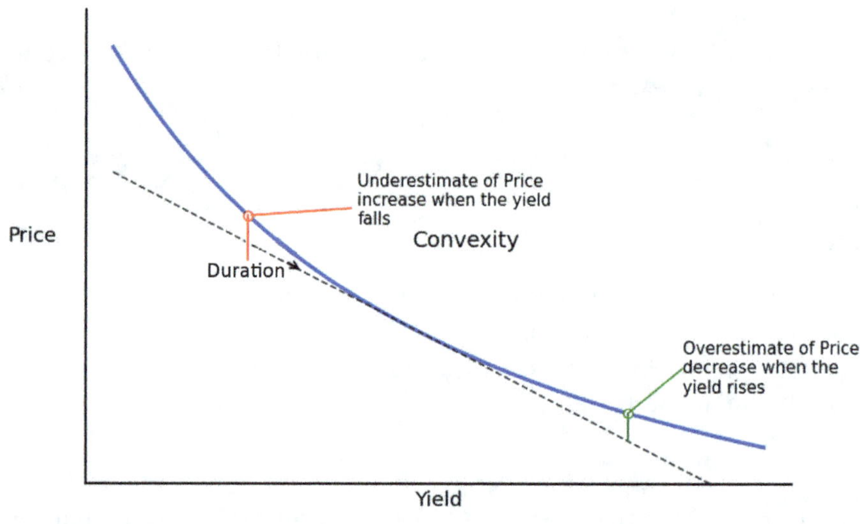

FIGURE 4.6 Convexity

For more significant changes in interest rates, convexity becomes important, as the relationship between bond price and yield is actually curved, not linear. Convexity captures the non-linear price sensitivity to yield changes, which becomes more pronounced with larger interest rate shifts. Including convexity accounts for this curvature and gives a more precise estimate.

The convexity of a bond is a measure of the sensitivity of the bond's duration to changes in interest rates. It is used to measure the curvature in the relationship between bond prices and interest rates. The formula for the convexity of a bond is expressed as follows:

$$\text{Convexity} = \frac{1}{P}\sum_{t=1}^{T}\frac{C_t \cdot t(t+1)}{(1+y)^{t+2}}$$

where:

- P is the current price of the bond.
- C_t is the cash flow at time t (coupon or principal payment).
- y is the yield to maturity of the bond.
- T is the total number of periods until the bond's maturity.

Adding convexity makes the price-interest rate sensitivity formula more accurate, particularly for long-term bonds or bonds with more embedded options. The sensitivity formula incorporating convexity is:

$$\frac{\Delta P}{P} \approx -D_M \cdot \Delta y + \frac{1}{2} C \cdot (\Delta y)^2$$

In summary, convexity quantifies the sensitivity of a bond's duration to changes in interest rates, providing a measure of the curvature of the bond price-yield relationship.

PRACTICAL EXERCISE #4.01 BOND CHARACTERISTICS

Request: We are going to calculate the main characteristics of a bond with the following features:

- Face value = 1000€
- Maturity = 10 years
- Bond coupon rate = 2%
- Bond spread over the interbank zero-coupon curve = 50 basis points

Summary of the script. –

This code implements a comprehensive bond valuation model using interbank zero-coupon rates, derived from interest rate swap (IRS) rates. It calculates key bond metrics such as price, yield, duration, and convexity, providing insights into bond valuation and risk characteristics.

The code provides a comprehensive approach to bond valuation with several key features:

a) Zero Coupon Curve Construction:
   - Uses swap rates to build a zero coupon curve through iterative discounting.
   - Enables accurate pricing of bonds by discounting future cash flows.
b) Comprehensive Bond Analysis:
   - Calculates bond price, yield (IRR), duration, modified duration, and convexity.
   - Provides insights into interest rate sensitivity and risk assessment.
c) Graphical Visualization:
   - Plots the swap rate curve against the zero coupon curve for comparison.
   - Helps visualize bond pricing trends and cash flow distributions.
d) Customizable Inputs:
   - Allows users to analyse different bond scenarios by adjusting face value, maturity, coupon rate, and credit spreads.
   - Useful for pricing corporate and government bonds under varying market conditions.
e) Formatted Output:
   - Presents bond valuation metrics in a structured and readable table.
   - Facilitates interpretation for both technical and non-technical users.

These features make the code a valuable tool for fixed-income analysis and risk management.

TABLE 4.1 Summary of Key Functions and Their Purposes

Function/Calculation	Purpose
pd.concat([IRSwaps,ZCCIntbank], axis=1)	Combines swap rates and zero-coupon rates for comparison.
def bond_characteristics_calculation(...)	Calculates key bond metrics such as price, IRR, duration, and convexity.
ZCRates = 1 + (Tipos.ZCRate.T / 100) + (SWsprd / 10000)	Adjusts zero-coupon rates for bond spread.
BondPrice = (SUMvacoupons + VAFaceVal).round(2)	Computes the bond price by summing discounted cash flows.
npf.irr(BondCF) * 100	Calculates the internal rate of return (IRR) of the bond.
Duration = (SUMACFDur + (VAFace * mty)) / BondPrice	Computes the bond's Macaulay duration.
ModConvx = AbsConvx / BondPrice	Calculates bond convexity.

Script execution and outputs. –

4.3.2.5.1 Importing the Necessary Libraries

```
import pandas as pd
import numpy as np
import numpy_financial as npf
import matplotlib.pyplot as plt
from tabulate import tabulate
```

4.3.2.5.2 Obtaining the Yield Curve from the IRS Curve From this method we obtain the zero coupon curve that is actually being used in the interbank market, since the assets used for its calculation, 12-month deposit and 2- to 10-year swaps, are assets of this market.

The best way to understand this curve is to see it on a numerical example: Let's start with the following quotes:

TABLE 4.2 Interest Rates Swaps

Deposits	12 Months	4.00%
IRS	2 years	4.50%
IRS	3 years	4.70%
IRS	4 years	4.90%
IRS	5 years	5.00%
IRS	6 years	5.12%
IRS	7 years	5.25%
IRS	8 years	5.28%
IRS	9 years	5.32%
IRS	10 years	5.35%

1-year zero coupon rate:

The 1-year zero coupon rate for the interbank market is already given by the rate of the Deposit: 4.0%.

2-year zero coupon rate:

The 2-year SWAP rate (4.50%) represents the fixed part of a contractual relationship in which one of the parties will deliver to the other this fixed rate in exchange for the variable rate (Míbor/Euribor/ . . .) that exists on each payment date. In other words, the cash flows of the fixed part could be represented by the following graph:

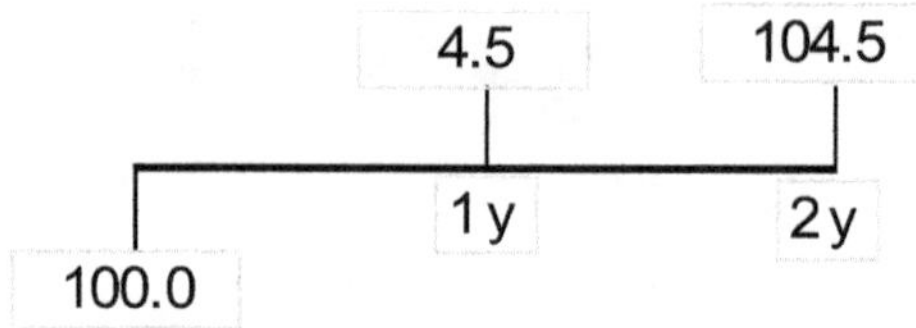

Since we already know the 1-year rate (4.0%), we could calculate the present value of the first flow:

$$\frac{4.5}{(1+0.04)^1} = 4.327$$

Thus, we could easily transform the above graph into that of a 2-year zero coupon:

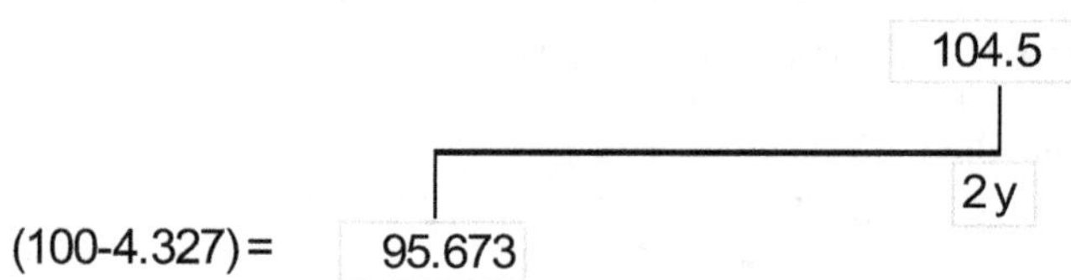

Therefore, the 2-year zero coupon rate would be the one resulting from the following equality:

$$95.673x(1+i_2)^2 = 104.5$$

$$i_2 = 4.511\%$$

3-year zero coupon rate:

The process for its calculation would be very similar, using now the rates calculated for 1 and 2 years. As we did previously with the 2-year IRS, the fixed part of the 3-year SWAP could be represented as follows:

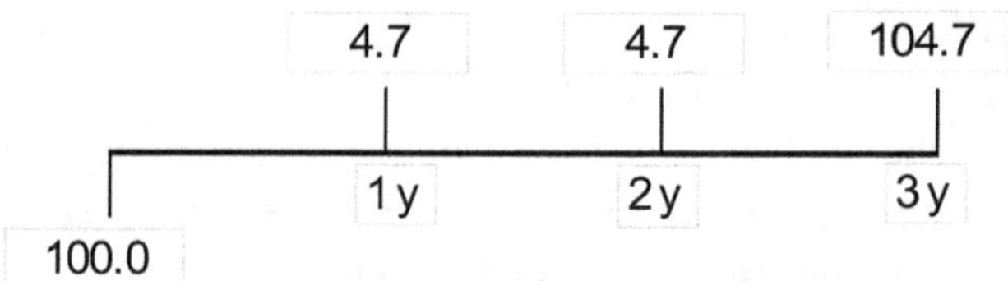

We can calculate the present value of the cash flows corresponding to the first and second year:

$$\frac{4.7}{(1+0.04)^1} = 4.519$$

$$\frac{4.7}{(1+0.04511)^1} = 4.303$$

Thus, we would be left with a 3-year zero coupon:

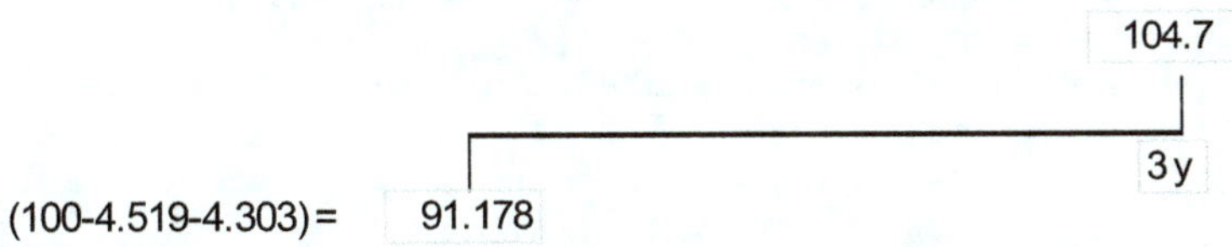

The 3-year zero coupon rate would be:

$$91.178x(1+i_3)^3 = 104.7$$

$$i_3 = 4.717\%$$

This calculation could continue to be repeated for the different timeframes.

Now this process is coded.

```
#Downloading IRS Curve from a file

infile=pd.ExcelFile("EURIBORIRS.xlsx")
IRSwaps=infile.parse('Hoja1')

#IRS file filtering

IRSwaps=IRSwaps[['Term','Ask']]
IRSwaps=IRSwaps.rename(columns={'Ask':'SWRate'})
IRSwaps.index+=1

# Zero coupon interest rates in the interbank market are
constructed from IRS rates.

ZCC=[] # A matrix is created to collect the zero coupon
interest rates.
i1=IRSwaps.SWRate[1]/100 # The 1-year zero coupon rate is
matched to the 1-year IRS rate.
```

```
ZCC.append(i1)

for x in range(2,21): # The zero coupon rates for years 2
to 20 are calculated.

    maturity=x # Rates will be calculated by maturity.
    Coupon=[] # The matrix that will collect the coupons
    is created.
    for n in range(maturity-1): # The coupons of all
maturities are selected except for the last year.

        Maturities=list(range(maturity)) # A maturity list
        is created
        coupon=(IRSwaps.SWRate[maturity])/((1+ZCC[n])**(Ma
        turities[n+1]))
        # Coupons are updated to the zero coupon rates
        generated up to that time.
        Coupon.append(coupon) # The updated coupons are
        added to the coupon matrix.
        VACoupon=np.sum(Coupon) # The total value of the
        updated coupons is calculated

        Current_Price=100-(VACoupon) # To find the price
        at source, the present value of the coupons is
        subtracted from the nominal value.

        Last_CashFlow=100+IRSwaps.SWRate[maturity] # The
        last cash flow of the bond is calculated, which is
        the nominal plus the coupon.

        i1=((Last_CashFlow/Current_Price)**(1/maturity))-1
        #The zero coupon rate is calculated for this
        maturity.

    ZCC.append(i1) # The zero coupon rate is added to
    those already calculated for previous periods.


ZCC=[round(b*100,5) for b in ZCC] # Rates are rounded
ZCC=pd.DataFrame(ZCC)

# The comparison between swap rates and interbank zero-
coupon rates is displayed.

ZCCIntbank=pd.DataFrame(ZCC)
ZCCIntbank=ZCCIntbank.rename(columns={0:'ZCRate'})
ZCCIntbank.index+=1
Rates=pd.concat([IRSwaps,ZCCIntbank], axis=1)
Rates
```

Output:

	Term	SWRate	ZCRate
1	1Y	2.115	2.11500
2	2Y	2.136	2.13622
3	3Y	2.212	2.21385
4	4Y	2.291	2.29520
5	5Y	2.366	2.37313
6	6Y	2.434	2.44442
7	7Y	2.499	2.51330
8	8Y	2.561	2.57976
9	9Y	2.619	2.64262
10	10Y	2.672	2.70069
11	11Y	2.721	2.75498
12	12Y	2.764	2.80302
13	13Y	2.801	2.84463
14	14Y	2.833	2.88082
15	15Y	2.859	2.91018
16	16Y	2.880	2.93375
17	17Y	2.895	2.95005
18	18Y	2.907	2.96283
19	19Y	2.915	2.97064
20	20Y	2.920	2.97468

```
# Both curves are plotted graphically

plt.figure(figsize=(12, 8))
plt.grid(True)
plt.scatter(Rates['Term'], Rates['ZCRate'] ,marker='o',col
or='r',s=50, label='Zero Coupon Rates')
plt.plot(Rates['Term'], Rates['ZCRate'] ,linestyle='-',
color='black', label='Zero Coupon Curve')
plt.scatter(Rates['Term'], Rates['SWRate'] ,marker='o',col
or='b',s=50, label='Swaps Rates')
plt.plot(Rates['Term'], Rates['SWRate'] ,linestyle='-',
color='grey', label='Swaps Curve')
plt.title('ZERO COUPON CURVE versus SWAPS CURVE')
plt.xlabel('YEARS')
plt.ylabel('RATES (%)')
plt.legend(labelspacing=0.8)
```

Output:

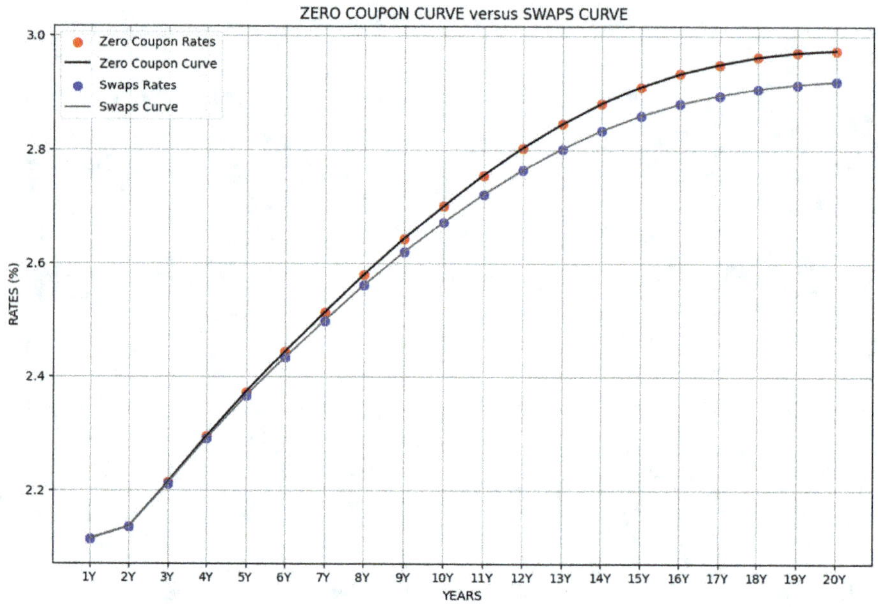

Once the yield curve is known, we are in a position to calculate the characteristics of the bond.

4.3.2.5.3 Obtaining the Bond Characteristics

```
# We define the bond characteristics function

def bond_characteristics_calculation(face_value, mty,
coupons, SWsprd):

    # Calculation of discount factor

    ZCRates = 1 + (Rates.ZCRate.T / 100) + (SWsprd / 10000)


    # Calculation of the present value of all cash flows

    coupon=(coupons/100)*face_value
    coupons_record = np.array([coupon] * mty)

    # Generation of maturities

    n = np.arange(1, mty + 1)
```

```
# Value of each coupon discounted at the discount
factor raised at maturity

VAcoupons = coupons_record/(ZCRates.values
[0:mty].T ** n)
SUMvacoupons = np.sum(VAcoupons) # Sum of all coupons
at current value



# Calculation of the present value of the nominal
value

VAFaceVal = face_value / (ZCRates.values[(mty -
1):mty] ** mty)


# Bond price calculation

BondPrice = (SUMvacoupons + VAFaceVal)
.round(2)
BondPrice = BondPrice.item()


# Establishing the cash flows of the Bond

BondCF=list(coupons_record[0:mty - 1])
BondCF.append(face_value+(coupon))
BondCF.insert(0, -BondPrice)

# Transforming cash flows to normal floats
BondCF = [float(x) for x in BondCF]


# Calculating the bond's IRR from its cash flows.

BondIRR = npf.irr(BondCF) * 100

# Calculating the MacAuley duration of the bond

Maturities = np.arange(1, mty)
VAFace = (face_value + coupon) / (ZCRates.values[(mty
- 1):mty] ** mty)
CFDur = [(a * b) for a, b in zip(VAcoupons,
Maturities)]
SUMACFDur = np.sum(CFDur)
Duration = (SUMACFDur + (VAFace * mty)) / BondPrice
Duration = Duration.item()
ModifiedDuration = Duration / (1 + (BondIRR / 100))
```

```
    # Calculate convexity

    t = np.arange(1, mty)
    VAcoupons2 = coupons_record[1:mty + 1] / ((1 +
    (BondIRR / 100)) ** (t + 2))
    Maturities2 = [i * (i + 1) for i in range(1, mty)]
    CFConvx = [(a * b) for a, b in zip(VAcoupons2,
    Maturities2)]
    VAFaceConvx = (face_value + coupon) / ((1 + (BondIRR /
    100)) ** (mty + 2))
    VAFaceConvx = VAFaceConvx * mty * (mty + 1)
    AbsConvx = np.sum(CFConvx) + VAFaceConvx
    ModConvx = AbsConvx / BondPrice
    ModConvx = ModConvx.item()

    # Creating a results dictionary

    results = {
        'Metric': ['Face Value (€)', 'Bond Price (€)',
        'Bond Maturity (years)', 'Coupon (€)','Coupon rate
        (%)','Bond IRR (%)', 'Duration (years)', 'Modified
        Duration', 'Discrete Convexity', 'Bond Cash-
        Flows'],
        'Value': [round(face_value,2), BondPrice,
len(Maturities)+1, coupon, coupons, round(BondIRR,2),
round(Duration,2), round(ModifiedDuration,2),
round(ModConvx,2), BondCF]
    }


    # Converting dictionary to a DataFrame

    results_df = pd.DataFrame(results)

    return results_df

def printing_in_bold_type(df):
    bold_end = '\033[1m'
    table = tabulate(df, headers='keys', tablefmt='tsv')
    bold_start = '\033[1m'
    table = table.replace('|', f'{bold_start}|{bold_end}')
    table = table.replace('-', f'{bold_start}-{bold_end}')
    return f'{bold_start}{table}{bold_end}'
```

```
# Apply for the above-mentioned bond

face_value=1000
mty=10 # Maturity of the Bond, in years
```

```
coupons=2.00 # Bond coupon, as a percentage of par value
SWsprd=50 # Bond spread over the interbank zero-coupon
curve, in basis points

bond_characteristics= bond_characteristics_
calculation(face_value, mty, coupons, SWsprd)
bond_characteristics.index+=1

print(printing_in_bold_type(bond_characteristics))
```

Output:

```
      Metric                      Value
 1    Face Value (€)              1000
 2    Bond Price (€)              900.43
 3    Bond Maturity (years)       10
 4    Coupon (€)                  20.0
 5    Coupon rate (%)             2.0
 6    Bond IRR (%)                3.18
 7    Duration (years)            9.1
 8    Modified Duration           8.82
 9    Discrete Convexity          91.15
10    Bond Cash-Flows             [-900.43, 20.0, 20.0, 20.0, 20.0,
20.0, 20.0, 20.0, 20.0, 20.0, 1020.0]
```

4.4 BUILDING A BOND PORTFOLIO

Building a bond portfolio is a strategic process that involves selecting bonds based on specific financial goals, risk tolerance, and market conditions. Here's a step-by-step guide to constructing a bond portfolio.

Step 1: Define Investment Objectives

- Income Generation: Focus on bonds that offer high coupon rates and consistent income.
- Capital Preservation: Prioritize high-quality bonds with low default risk, such as government bonds.
- Total Return: Aim for a combination of income and capital appreciation by selecting bonds with potential price increases.
- Duration Matching: Match the portfolio's duration with the time horizon of a specific financial goal (e.g., matching bond maturities with retirement dates).

Step 2: Assess Risk Tolerance

- Credit Risk: Determine the acceptable level of credit risk (likelihood of default). Investment-grade bonds (e.g., AAA to BBB ratings) have lower risk than high-yield bonds (junk bonds).

- Interest Rate Risk: Longer-duration bonds are more sensitive to interest rate changes. Assess your comfort with potential price volatility.

- Inflation Risk: Consider inflation-protected securities (e.g., TIPS) if you are concerned about purchasing power erosion.

Step 3: Set a Target Asset Allocation

- Diversification Across Sectors: Allocate investments across different bond sectors such as government, municipal, corporate, and international bonds.

- Duration and Maturity Mix: Diversify across short-term, intermediate-term, and long-term bonds to balance income with interest rate risk.

- Credit Quality Diversification: Mix high-quality bonds with some exposure to lower-rated bonds to optimize risk and return.

Step 4: Select Bonds

- Government Bonds: Choose from treasury securities, savings bonds, or sovereign bonds depending on risk tolerance.

- Corporate Bonds: Select bonds from companies with strong credit ratings for higher yields, balancing them with safer government bonds.

- International Bonds: Include bonds from foreign issuers to diversify geographically and potentially benefit from currency movements.

Step 5: Determine the Investment Strategy

- Laddering: Invest in bonds with staggered maturities to reduce interest rate risk and provide liquidity over time.

- Barbell Strategy: Invest in a mix of short-term and long-term bonds to benefit from both yield (from long-term bonds) and liquidity (from short-term bonds).

- Bullet Strategy: Focus on bonds that mature around the same time to meet a specific financial goal.

Step 6: Consider Tax Implications

- Taxable vs. Tax-Exempt Bonds: Some bonds (municipal bonds in the USA) offer tax-free interest income, which may be beneficial for investors in high tax brackets.
- Tax-Advantaged Accounts: Hold taxable bonds in tax-advantaged accounts to defer taxes on interest income.

Step 7: Conduct Due Diligence

- Credit Analysis: Review the issuer's credit rating, financial health, and likelihood of default.
- Interest Rate Outlook: Consider current and expected interest rate trends, as rising rates can negatively impact bond prices.
- Inflation Expectations: Assess inflation projections, which can erode the real return of fixed-income investments.

Step 8: Monitor and Rebalance

- Performance Review: Regularly review the portfolio's performance against benchmarks and objectives.
- Rebalancing: Adjust the portfolio periodically to maintain the desired asset allocation, especially if market conditions or personal financial goals change.
- Risk Management: Monitor credit and interest rate risk, making adjustments as necessary to protect the portfolio's value.

Step 9: Consider External Factors

- Market Conditions: Stay informed about economic indicators, central bank policies, and global events that can affect bond markets.
- Regulatory Changes: Be aware of any changes in tax laws or regulations that could impact bond investments.

Step 10: Implement and Execute

- Execution: Purchase the selected bonds, ensuring that transaction costs and fees are minimized.
- Record Keeping: Maintain accurate records of purchases, interest payments, and maturity dates to manage the portfolio effectively.

Step 11: Review and Adjust Strategy

- Periodic Review: Assess the portfolio periodically to ensure it continues to meet your objectives, especially if your financial situation or market conditions change.
- Adjustments: Make necessary changes to the bond selection, asset allocation, or strategy based on performance, changes in interest rates, or life events.

Conclusion: Building a bond portfolio requires careful planning and ongoing management to align with your financial goals. By defining your objectives, assessing risk, diversifying, and regularly monitoring the portfolio, you can create a bond portfolio that meets your income, preservation, or growth needs while managing risks effectively.

PRACTICAL EXERCISE #4.02 BOND OPTIMAL PORTFOLIO

Request: Consider the following list of bonds:

TABLE 4.3 Bond Characteristics

Bond	Face Value	Cupón (%)	Maturity (years)	YTM (%)	Price	Duration	Modified Duration	Convexity
Bond A	100	4,25%	2	2,12%	104,12	1,96	1,92	5,60
Bond B	100	7,70%	5	7,82%	99,54	4,33	4,02	21,25
Bond C	100	6,39%	8	6,99%	96,40	6,47	6,05	47,16
Bond D	100	5,59%	11	3,27%	121,12	8,76	8,48	90,57
Bond E	100	2,94%	14	3,09%	98,26	11,65	11,30	154,10
Bond F	100	2,94%	17	3,10%	97,85	13,58	13,17	212,06
Bond G	100	2,35%	20	3,83%	79,61	15,63	15,05	279,10
Bond H	100	7,20%	23	5,15%	127,25	13,10	12,46	224,26
Bond I	100	5,61%	26	4,59%	115,23	15,07	14,41	296,97
Bond J	100	6,25%	30	3,75%	144,61	16,74	16,14	375,13

Build a portfolio with a specific modified duration, maximizing the YTM of the portfolio.

Summary of the script. –

This code optimizes a bond portfolio by selecting bonds from a dataset, aiming to maximize the portfolio's yield-to-maturity while meeting a target modified duration constraint. It provides insights into optimal bond allocation, investment distribution, and portfolio characteristics. Key features of the code:

a) Automated Portfolio Optimization: The code optimizes bond allocations to maximize yield-to-maturity while ensuring the portfolio meets a target modified duration, balancing return and interest rate risk.

b) User-Friendly Inputs:
   - Users can easily select bonds, input investment amounts, and set duration targets.
   - Input validation ensures only valid bonds are included, preventing errors.

c) Flexible Portfolio Construction: The code adjusts bond allocations dynamically to match user preferences, ensuring full investment allocation and rounding bond quantities to whole units for practical implementation.

d) Risk and Return Metrics: Provides key financial insights such as YTM, modified duration, and convexity, helping investors assess the trade-offs between risk and return in the bond portfolio.

e) Professional Reporting Format: The final output is presented in a clear, well-structured table, showing bond allocations, investment amounts, and key metrics in a readable format for informed decision-making.

These features make the code an efficient tool for constructing and analysing fixed-income portfolios.

TABLE 4.4 Summary of Key Functions and Their Purposes

Function/Calculation	Purpose
pd.read_excel(file_path)	Reads the bond data from an Excel file into a DataFrame.
[bond.strip( ) for bond in portfolio_bonds_input.split(',')]	Processes and cleans the user input to create a list of selected bonds.
selected_bonds = df_bonds[df_bonds['Bond'].isin(portfolio_bonds)]	Filters the DataFrame to include only selected bonds.
np.dot(weights, modified_durations)	Computes the portfolio's modified duration using bond weights.
np.dot(weights, ytms)	Calculates the portfolio's weighted average yield to maturity.
minimize(objective, initial_weights, bounds=bounds, constraints=constraints)	Solves the optimization problem to find the best bond allocation.
optimal_weights = results.x	Extracts the optimized bond allocation weights.
securities_portfolio = np.ceil(investment_portfolio / selected_bonds['Price'].values)	Calculates the number of bonds to purchase based on the budget.
pd.concat([table_results_portfolio, row_portfolio], ignore_index=True)	Combines individual bond details with the overall portfolio summary.

Script execution and outputs. –

```
import pandas as pd
import numpy as np
from scipy.optimize import minimize

# Load the bond data from the Excel file

file_path = 'Set of bonds.xlsx'
df_bonds = pd.read_excel(file_path)

# Asking for bonds for the portfolio

portfolio_bonds_input = input("Enter the bond names for
the portfolio, separated by commas (e.g., 'Bond A, Bond
C'): ")


# Convert user input into a bond list

portfolio_bonds = [bond.strip() for bond in portfolio_
bonds_input.split(',')]


# Make sure that the bonds entered exist in the data

for bond in portfolio_bonds:
    if bond not in df_bonds['Bond'].values:
        raise ValueError(f"Bond {bond} not found in the
        bond table.")

# Request total investment

total_investment = float(input("Enter the total investment
amount (e.g., 1000000): "))

# Target modified duration

target_modified_duration = float(input("Enter the target
modified duration: "))


# Selected bonds for the portfolio

selected_bonds = df_bonds[df_bonds['Bond'].isin(portfolio_
bonds)]

# Modified durations and YTMs of selected bonds

modified_durations = selected_bonds['Modified
Duration'].values
```

```
ytms = selected_bonds['YTM (%)'].values

# Objective function: to maximize the portfolio's YTM
while targeting a specific modified duration

def objective(weights):
    portfolio_modified_duration = np.dot(weights, modified_
    durations)
    # Penalty for deviating from target duration
    penalty = (portfolio_modified_duration - target_
    modified_duration) ** 2
    portfolio_ytm = np.dot(weights, ytms)
    return -portfolio_ytm + penalty  # Negative because we
    are maximizing

# Constraint: the sum of the weights must be 100%

constraints = ({'type': 'eq', 'fun': lambda x: np.sum(x)
- 1})

# Additional constraints: weights must be non-negative
(between 0% and 100%)

bounds = [(0, 1) for _ in range(len(modified_durations))]

# Initial weights (equal to start)

initial_weights = np.full(len(modified_durations), 1 /
len(modified_durations))


# Solving the optimization

results = minimize(objective, initial_weights,
bounds=bounds, constraints=constraints)


# Extracting optimal weights

optimal_weights = results.x

# Calculate the investment in euros and number of
securities for the portfolio

investment_portfolio = optimal_weights * total_investment

# Always round up

securities_portfolio = np.ceil(investment_portfolio /
selected_bonds['Price'].values)
```

```
# Calculate final investment

final_investment_portfolio = securities_portfolio *
selected_bonds['Price'].values

# Calculate YTM (IRR), convexity, cost, and modified
duration of the portfolio using the optimal weights

ytm_optimal_portfolio = np.dot(optimal_weights, selected_
bonds['YTM (%)'].values)
convexity_optimal_portfolio = np.dot(optimal_weights,
selected_bonds['Convexity'].values)
cost_optimal_portfolio = np.dot(optimal_weights, selected_
bonds['Price'].values)
modified_duration_optimal_portfolio = np.dot(optimal_
weights, selected_bonds['Modified Duration'].values)

# Create a consolidated table with all portfolio
information

table_results_portfolio = pd.DataFrame({
    'Bond': selected_bonds['Bond'].values,
    'Weight (%)': optimal_weights * 100,  # Convert
    weights to %
    'Investment €': investment_portfolio,
    'Price €': selected_bonds['Price'].values,
    'Securities': securities_portfolio,
    'Final Investment €': final_investment_portfolio,
    'YTM (%)': selected_bonds['YTM (%)'].values * 100,  #
    Convert YTM to %
    'Modified Duration': selected_bonds['Modified
    Duration'].values,
    'Convexity': selected_bonds['Convexity'].values
})

# Create a row for the portfolio

row_portfolio = pd.DataFrame({
    'Bond': ['Optimal Portfolio'],
    'Weight (%)': [100.0],  # The complete portfolio
    weighs 100%
    'Investment €': [investment_portfolio.sum()],
    'Price €': [np.nan],  # Leave empty to not apply
    formatting
    'Securities': [np.nan],  # Leave empty to not apply
    formatting
```

```
    'Final Investment €': [final_investment_
    portfolio.sum()],
    'YTM (%)': [ytm_optimal_portfolio * 100],  # Convert
    YTM to %
    'Modified Duration': [modified_duration_optimal_
    portfolio],
    'Convexity': [convexity_optimal_portfolio]
})

# Concatenate all rows of the portfolio to the result
table

table_results = pd.concat([table_results_portfolio, row_
portfolio], ignore_index=True)

# Format all columns to display values to two decimal
places,
# excluding NaN cells

table_results['Weight (%)'] = table_results['Weight
(%)'].map('{:.2f}%'.format)
table_results['Investment €'] = table_results['Investment
€'].map('{:,.2f}'.format)
table_results['Price €'] = table_results['Price
€'].map(lambda x: '{:,.2f}'.format(x) if pd.notnull(x)
else '')
table_results['Securities'] = table_results['Securities']
.map(lambda x: '{:,.0f}'.format(x) if pd.notnull(x) else
'')
table_results['Final Investment €'] = table_results['Final
Investment €'].map('{:,.2f}'.format)
table_results['YTM (%)'] = table_results['YTM (%)'].map('{
:.2f}%'.format)
table_results['Modified Duration'] = table_results['Modified
Duration'].map('{:.2f}'.format)
table_results['Convexity'] = table_results['Convexity'].ma
p('{:.2f}'.format)

# Show the complete table

table_results
```

Output:

```
Enter the bond names for the portfolio, separated by commas
(e.g., 'Bond A, Bond C'): Bond B, Bond C, Bond G
```

```
Enter the total investment amount (e.g., 1000000): 1000000
Enter the target modified duration: 10
```

	Bond	Weight (%)	Investment €	Price €	Securities	Final Investment €	YTM (%)	Modified Duration	Convexity
0	Bond B	25.23%	252,262.23	99.54	2,535	252,328.70	7.82%	4.02	21.25
1	Bond C	25.23%	252,262.23	96.40	2,617	252,279.85	6.99%	6.05	47.16
2	Bond G	49.55%	495,475.53	79.61	6,224	495,516.94	3.83%	15.05	279.10
3	Optimal Portfolio	100.00%	1,000,000.00			1,000,125.49	5.63%	10.00	155.55

4.5 BULLET, BARBELL, AND LADDER PORTFOLIOS

4.5.1 Introduction to Bond Investment Strategies: Bullet, Barbell, and Ladder Portfolios

Investing in bonds offers a range of strategies that can be tailored to meet different financial goals and risk tolerances. Among the most commonly used strategies are the bullet, barbell, and ladder portfolios. Each of these approaches involves constructing a bond portfolio in a way that manages interest rate risk, optimizes returns, and meets specific investment needs.

4.5.2 Bullet Portfolio

A bullet portfolio is a bond investment strategy in which all the bonds in the portfolio have the same or similar maturity dates. The bullet portfolio has all of the bonds concentrated in a single maturity date (e.g. mid-term maturity). This strategy is typically used when an investor has a specific future financial goal, such as funding a child's college education or buying a house. By aligning the bond maturities with the investment horizon, the investor

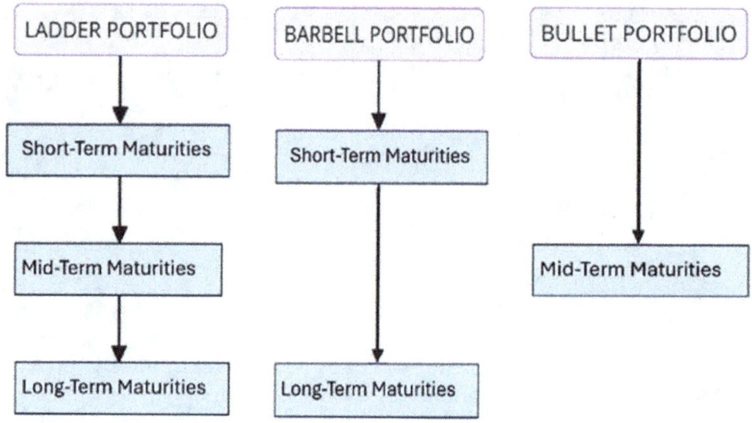

FIGURE 4.7 Ladder, Barbell, and Bullet Portfolios

can maximize returns while minimizing the reinvestment risk (the risk that maturing bonds will have to be reinvested at lower interest rates).

Advantages

- Targeted Objective: The bullet portfolio is ideal for investors with a specific future goal, ensuring that all funds mature at the same time.
- Interest Rate Risk Management: Since all bonds mature around the same time, the portfolio is less exposed to fluctuations in interest rates over the investment period.

Disadvantages

- Lack of Flexibility: The investor is locked into a specific maturity, which may limit opportunities to capitalize on changes in interest rates.
- Reinvestment Risk: If the interest rates drop by the time the bonds mature, the investor may have to reinvest at lower rates.

4.5.3 Barbell Portfolio

A barbell portfolio is a strategy where the investor holds bonds at two extremes of the maturity spectrum – short-term and long-term bonds, with little or no intermediate-term bonds. The short-term bonds provide liquidity and protect against rising interest rates, while the long-term bonds offer higher yields.

Advantages

- Flexibility and Liquidity: The short-term bonds can be reinvested frequently, allowing the investor to take advantage of rising interest rates.
- Higher Yield Potential: The long-term bonds typically offer higher yields, which can enhance the overall return of the portfolio.

Disadvantages

- Interest Rate Risk: While short-term bonds are less sensitive to interest rate changes, long-term bonds are more vulnerable to fluctuations in interest rates.
- Complexity: Managing a barbell portfolio can be more complex due to the need to balance the risks and rewards of different maturities.

4.5.4 Ladder Portfolio

A ladder portfolio involves purchasing bonds with staggered maturities, such as every year or every few years. As each bond matures, the proceeds are reinvested into a new bond at the longest maturity in the ladder. This strategy provides a balance between flexibility, yield, and risk management.

Advantages

- Interest Rate Risk Mitigation: By spreading bond maturities across time, a ladder portfolio reduces the impact of interest rate fluctuations.
- Steady Cash Flow: The regular maturity of bonds ensures a consistent cash flow, which can be reinvested or used as income.
- Diversification: The staggered maturities offer a diversified approach to bond investing, reducing the risk associated with any single bond.

Disadvantages

- Lower Yield Potential: Compared to a barbell portfolio, the ladder strategy might offer lower yields because it includes intermediate-term bonds, which usually yield less than long-term bonds.
- Reinvestment Risk: Although laddering mitigates some reinvestment risk, there's still a chance that maturing bonds will be reinvested at lower rates if interest rates decline.

4.5.4.1 Conclusion

Each of these strategies – bullet, barbell, and ladder portfolios – offers unique advantages and challenges. The choice of strategy depends on the investor's financial goals, risk tolerance, and market outlook. For investors seeking to meet a specific financial target, a bullet portfolio might be ideal. Those looking for flexibility and potential high yields may prefer a barbell approach, while a ladder portfolio offers a balanced strategy that manages interest rate risk and provides steady cash flow.

Understanding these strategies allows investors to make informed decisions and optimize their bond investments to achieve their financial objectives.

PRACTICAL EXERCISE #4.03 BULLET, BARBELL, LADDER PORTFOLIOS

Request: Consider the listed bonds of Table 4.4:

Build a barbell and a ladder portfolio with the same modified duration as a bullet portfolio with equally weighted bonds. Compare their metrics. To do this, you must choose bonds for the bullet portfolio, bonds for the barbell portfolio, and bonds for the ladder portfolio. You should also indicate the amount to invest.

Summary of the script. –

This code constructs and analyses three fixed-income investment strategies: bullet, barbell, and ladder portfolios, based on user-selected bonds from an Excel dataset. Key features of the code:

a) Automated Bond Selection & Allocation: Users input bond choices, and the system efficiently allocates investment using equal or optimized weighting.
b) Portfolio Diversification Strategies: Supports different portfolio structures (bullet, barbell, ladder) to align with varying investment goals.
c) Optimization for Risk Management: Ensures portfolio duration is controlled across different strategies.
d) Practical Considerations: Investment values are rounded to whole bond units to ensure realistic implementation.
e) Professional Reporting: Output is formatted with currency values and percentage figures for easy interpretation.

This code serves as an effective tool for investors and analysts to construct diversified bond portfolios and compare different investment strategies.

TABLE 4.5 Summary of Key Functions and Their Purposes

Function/Calculation	Purpose
[bond.strip( ) for bond in user_input.split(',')]	Converts user input into a cleaned list of selected bonds.
df_bonds[df_bonds['Bond'].isin(bullet_bonds)]	Filters the DataFrame for selected bonds in the bullet portfolio.
np.full(num_bonds, 1 / num_bonds) * total_investment	Calculates equal investment allocation for the bullet portfolio.
np.ceil(investment / bond_prices)	Determines the number of bonds to buy by rounding up.
np.dot(weights, selected_bonds['Modified Duration'])	Computes the portfolio's weighted modified duration.
minimize(target, initial_weights, bounds=bounds, constraints=constraints)	Optimizes bond allocation to match the bullet portfolio's duration.
pd.concat([. . .], ignore_index=True)	Combines the results from different portfolios into one table.

Script execution and outputs. –

```
import pandas as pd
import numpy as np
from scipy.optimize import minimize

# Upload the Excel file provided by the user

file_path = 'Set of bonds.xlsx'
df_bonds = pd.read_excel(file_path)

# Asking for bonds for the bullet portfolio

bullet_bonds_input = input("Enter the bond names for the bullet
portfolio, separated by commas. (e.g. 'Bond D, Bond E'): ")

# Convert user input into a bond list

bullet_bonds = [bond.strip() for bond in bullet_bonds_
input.split(',')]

# Make sure that the bonds entered exist in the data.

for bond in bullet_bonds:
    if bond not in df_bonds['Bond'].values:
        raise ValueError(f"Bond {bond} not found in the
        bond table.")

# Asking for bonds for the barbell portfolio

barbell_bonds_input = input("Enter the bond names for the
barbell portfolio, separated by commas. (e.g. 'Bond A,
Bond B, Bond C'): ")

# Convert user input into a bond list

barbell_bonds = [bond.strip() for bond in barbell_bonds_
input.split(',')]

# Make sure that the bonds entered exist in the data.

for bond in barbell_bonds:
    if bond not in df_bonds['Bond'].values:
        raise ValueError(f"Bond {bond} not found in the
        bond table.")

# Asking for bonds for the ladder portfolio

ladder_bonds_input = input("Enter the bond names for the
ladder portfolio, separated by commas. (e.g. 'Bond A, Bond
C, Bond G'): ")
```

```
# Convert user input into a bond list

ladder_bonds = [bond.strip() for bond in ladder_bonds_
input.split(',')]

# Make sure that the bonds entered exist in the data.

for bond in ladder_bonds:
    if bond not in df_bonds['Bond'].values:
        raise ValueError(f"Bond {bond} not found in the
        bond table.")



# Request total investment in euros

total_investment = float(input("Enter the total investment
in euros (e.g. 1000000): "))

# --------- Bullet Portfolio Calculation ---------

bullet_selected_bonds = df_bonds[df_
bonds['Bond'].isin(bullet_bonds)]
num_bonds_bullet = len(bullet_selected_bonds)

# Calculate equal weight for each bond in the bullet
portfolio

equal_weight = 1 / num_bonds_bullet

# Calculate the investment in euros for each bond in the
bullet portfolio

investment_bullet = np.full(num_bonds_bullet, equal_
weight) * total_investment

# Always round up

securities_bullet = np.ceil(investment_bullet / bullet_
selected_bonds['Price'].values)

# Calculate Final Investment

final_investment_bullet = securities_bullet * bullet_
selected_bonds['Price'].values

table_results_bullet = pd.DataFrame({
    'Bond': bullet_selected_bonds['Bond'].values,
    'Weight (%)': [equal_weight * 100] * num_bonds_bullet,
    # Equal weighting for all bonds
    'Investment €': investment_bullet,
```

```
    'Price €': bullet_selected_bonds['Price'].values,
    'Securities': securities_bullet,
    'Final Investment €': final_investment_bullet,
    'YTM (%)': bullet_selected_bonds['YTM (%)'].values *
    100,
    'Modified Duration': bullet_selected_bonds['Modified
    Duration'].values,
    'Convexity': bullet_selected_bonds['Convexity'].values
})

# Calculate the aggregate characteristics of the bullet
portfolio

bullet_portfolio_ytm = np.average(bullet_selected_
bonds['YTM (%)'], weights=investment_bullet)
bullet_portfolio_convexity = np.average(bullet_selected_
bonds['Convexity'], weights=investment_bullet)
bullet_portfolio_modified_duration = np.average(bullet_
selected_bonds['Modified Duration'], weights=investment_
bullet)

row_bullet_portfolio = pd.DataFrame({
    'Bond': ['Bullet Portfolio'],  # Summary row
    'Weight (%)': [100.0],
    'Investment €': [investment_bullet.sum()],
    'Price €': [np.nan],  # Leave empty to not apply
    formatting
    'Securities': [np.nan],  # Leave empty to not apply
    formatting
    'Final Investment €': [final_investment_bullet.sum()],
    'YTM (%)': [bullet_portfolio_ytm * 100],
    'Modified Duration': [bullet_portfolio_modified_
    duration],
    'Convexity': [bullet_portfolio_convexity]
})
```

```
# --------- Barbell Portfolio Calculation -------

selected_bonds = df_bonds[df_bonds['Bond'].isin(barbell_
bonds)]
modified_durations = selected_bonds['Modified Duration'].values

def target(weights):
    portfolio_modified_duration = np.dot(weights, modified_
    durations)
    return (portfolio_modified_duration - bullet_portfolio_
    modified_duration) ** 2

constraints = ({'type': 'eq', 'fun': lambda x: np.sum(x)
- 1})
```

```
bounds = [(0, 1) for _ in range(len(modified_durations))]
initial_weights = np.full(len(modified_durations), 1 /
len(modified_durations))

results = minimize(target, initial_weights, bounds=bounds,
constraints=constraints)
optimal_weights = results.x

investment_barbell = optimal_weights * total_investment

# Always round up

securities_barbell = np.ceil(investment_barbell /
selected_bonds['Price'].values)
# Calculate Final Investment
final_investment_barbell = securities_barbell * selected_
bonds['Price'].values

ytm_optimal_portfolio = np.dot(optimal_weights, selected_
bonds['YTM (%)'].values)
convexity_optimal_portfolio = np.dot(optimal_weights,
selected_bonds['Convexity'].values)
modified_duration_optimal_portfolio = np.dot(optimal_
weights, selected_bonds['Modified Duration'].values)

table_results_barbell = pd.DataFrame({
    'Bond': selected_bonds['Bond'].values,
    'Weight (%)': optimal_weights * 100,  # Convert
    weights to %
    'Investment €': investment_barbell,
    'Price €': selected_bonds['Price'].values,
    'Securities': securities_barbell,
    'Final Investment €': final_investment_barbell,
    'YTM (%)': selected_bonds['YTM (%)'].values * 100,  #
    Convert YTM to %
    'Modified Duration': selected_bonds['Modified
    Duration'].values,
    'Convexity': selected_bonds['Convexity'].values
})

row_barbell_portfolio = pd.DataFrame({
    'Bond': ['Barbell Portfolio'],
    'Weight (%)': [100.0],
    'Investment €': [investment_barbell.sum()],
    'Price €': [np.nan],  # Leave empty to not apply
    formatting
    'Securities': [np.nan],  # Leave empty to not apply
    formatting
    'Final Investment €': [final_investment_barbell.sum()],
    'YTM (%)': [ytm_optimal_portfolio * 100],  # Convert
    YTM to %
```

```
    'Modified Duration': [modified_duration_optimal_
    portfolio],
    'Convexity': [convexity_optimal_portfolio]
})
```

```
# --------- Ladder Portfolio Calculation ---------

ladder_selected_bonds = df_bonds[df_
bonds['Bond'].isin(ladder_bonds)]
modified_durations_ladder = ladder_selected_bonds['Modified
Duration'].values

# Optimization to match ladder portfolio's modified
duration with bullet portfolio's

def ladder_target(weights):
    portfolio_modified_duration = np.dot(weights, modified_
    durations_ladder)
    return (portfolio_modified_duration - bullet_portfolio_
    modified_duration) ** 2

constraints_ladder = ({'type': 'eq', 'fun': lambda x:
np.sum(x) - 1})
bounds_ladder = [(0, 1) for _ in range(len(modified_
durations_ladder))]
initial_weights_ladder = np.full(len(modified_durations_
ladder), 1 / len(modified_durations_ladder))

results_ladder = minimize(ladder_target, initial_weights_
ladder, bounds=bounds_ladder, constraints=constraints_
ladder)
optimal_weights_ladder = results_ladder.x

investment_ladder = optimal_weights_ladder * total_
investment

# Always round up

securities_ladder = np.ceil(investment_ladder / ladder_
selected_bonds['Price'].values)

# Calculate Final Investment

final_investment_ladder = securities_ladder * ladder_
selected_bonds['Price'].values

ytm_ladder_portfolio = np.dot(optimal_weights_ladder,
ladder_selected_bonds['YTM (%)'].values)
convexity_ladder_portfolio = np.dot(optimal_weights_
```

```
ladder, ladder_selected_bonds['Convexity'].values)
modified_duration_ladder_portfolio = np.dot(optimal_
weights_ladder, ladder_selected_bonds['Modified
Duration'].values)

table_results_ladder = pd.DataFrame({
    'Bond': ladder_selected_bonds['Bond'].values,
    'Weight (%)': optimal_weights_ladder * 100,  # Convert
    to %
    'Investment €': investment_ladder,
    'Price €': ladder_selected_bonds['Price'].values,
    'Securities': securities_ladder,
    'Final Investment €': final_investment_ladder,
    'YTM (%)': ladder_selected_bonds['YTM (%)'].values *
    100,  # Convert YTM to %
    'Modified Duration': ladder_selected_bonds['Modified
    Duration'].values,
    'Convexity': ladder_selected_bonds['Convexity'].values
})

row_ladder_portfolio = pd.DataFrame({
    'Bond': ['Ladder Portfolio'],
    'Weight (%)': [100.0],
    'Investment €': [investment_ladder.sum()],
    'Price €': [np.nan],  # Leave empty to not apply
    formatting
    'Securities': [np.nan],  # Leave empty to not apply
    formatting
    'Final Investment €': [final_investment_ladder.sum()],
    'YTM (%)': [ytm_ladder_portfolio * 100],
    'Modified Duration': [modified_duration_ladder_
    portfolio],
    'Convexity': [convexity_ladder_portfolio]
})

# --------- Concatenate All Results ---------

table_results = pd.concat([
    table_results_bullet, row_bullet_portfolio,
    table_results_barbell, row_barbell_portfolio,
    table_results_ladder, row_ladder_portfolio
], ignore_index=True)

# Format all columns to display values to two decimal
places, excluding NaN cells

table_results['Weight (%)'] = table_results['Weight
(%)'].map('{:.2f}%'.format)
table_results['Investment €'] = table_results['Investment
€'].map('{:,.2f}'.format)
table_results['Price €'] = table_results['Price
```

```
€'].map(lambda x: '{:,.2f}'.format(x) if pd.notnull(x)
else '')
table_results['Securities'] = table_results['Securities']
.map(lambda x: '{:,.0f}'.format(x) if pd.notnull(x) else
'')
table_results['Final Investment €'] = table_results['Final
Investment €'].map('{:,.2f}'.format)
table_results['YTM (%)'] = table_results['YTM (%)'].map('{
:.2f}%'.format)
table_results['Modified Duration'] = table_results['Modified
Duration'].map('{:.2f}'.format)
table_results['Convexity'] = table_results['Convexity'].ma
p('{:.2f}'.format)

# Show complete table

table_results
```

Input:

```
Enter the bond names for the bullet portfolio, separated by
commas. (e.g. 'Bond D, Bond E'): Bond C, Bond D
Enter the bond names for the barbell portfolio, separated by
commas. (e.g. 'Bond A, Bond B, Bond C'): Bond A, Bond B, Bond
E, Bond F
Enter the bond names for the ladder portfolio, separated by
commas. (e.g. 'Bond A, Bond C, Bond G'): Bond A, Bond B, Bond
C, Bond D, Bond E, Bond F
Enter the total investment in euros (e.g. 1000000): 1000000
```

Output:

	Bond	Weight (%)	Investment €	Price €	Securities	Final Investment €	YTM (%)	Modified Duration	Convexity
0	Bond C	50.00%	500,000.00	96.40	5,187	500,028.87	6.99%	6.05	47.16
1	Bond D	50.00%	500,000.00	121.12	4,128	500,003.63	3.27%	8.48	90.57
2	Bullet Portfolio	100.00%	1,000,000.00			1,000,032.50	5.13%	7.27	68.87
3	Bond A	29.44%	294,365.08	104.12	2,828	294,439.78	2.12%	1.92	5.60
4	Bond B	23.52%	235,211.86	99.54	2,364	235,307.71	7.82%	4.02	21.25
5	Bond E	23.52%	235,211.67	98.26	2,394	235,238.59	3.09%	11.30	154.10
6	Bond F	23.52%	235,211.39	97.85	2,404	235,236.47	3.10%	13.17	212.06
7	Barbell Portfolio	100.00%	1,000,000.00			1,000,222.55	3.92%	7.27	92.77
8	Bond A	19.94%	199,366.34	104.12	1,915	199,381.96	2.12%	1.92	5.60
9	Bond B	16.11%	161,088.19	99.54	1,619	161,151.94	7.82%	4.02	21.25
10	Bond C	15.99%	159,886.37	96.40	1,659	159,928.26	6.99%	6.05	47.16
11	Bond D	15.99%	159,886.37	121.12	1,321	160,006.01	3.27%	8.48	90.57
12	Bond E	15.99%	159,886.37	98.26	1,628	159,970.10	3.09%	11.30	154.10
13	Bond F	15.99%	159,886.37	97.85	1,634	159,890.34	3.10%	13.17	212.06
14	Ladder Portfolio	100.00%	1,000,000.00			1,000,328.62	4.31%	7.27	85.11

4.6 IMMUNIZATION

Bond immunization is a portfolio management strategy designed to protect a bond portfolio against interest rate risk. It involves structuring a portfolio in such a way that the portfolio's value is unaffected by changes in interest rates, ensuring the investor achieves a specified target return or liability at a future date.

This strategy is particularly useful for investors with defined future liabilities, such as pension funds, insurance companies, or individuals planning for retirement. By balancing the duration of assets (bonds) with the timing of liabilities, immunization provides a safeguard against the adverse effects of interest rate fluctuations.

Here are the key points about immunization:

- Matching Durations: Immunization involves matching the duration of assets with the duration of liabilities. Duration is a measure of the sensitivity of the price of a bond to changes in interest rates. By matching durations, the portfolio manager ensures that the values of assets and liabilities respond similarly to interest rate changes, thus offsetting each other.
- Interest Rate Risk: Interest rate changes can affect the present value of future cash flows. If the duration of the assets and liabilities are matched, a rise in interest rates, which typically decreases the present value of future cash flows, will have a similar impact on both sides of the balance sheet. This minimizes the net impact on the portfolio's value.
- Reinvestment Risk: Immunization also addresses reinvestment risk, which is the risk that future cash flows from an investment might have to be reinvested at a lower interest rate. By matching durations, the strategy ensures that cash flows from assets are timed to meet the liabilities as they come due, reducing the need for reinvestment.

Types of Immunization:

- Classical Immunization: This typically involves constructing a bond portfolio such that the duration of the assets equals the duration of the liabilities. It is most effective for single-period immunization where the liabilities are due at a single point in the future.

- Contingent Immunization: This allows for active management of the portfolio as long as certain conditions are met. If these conditions are not met, the strategy switches to a passive immunization approach to protect the portfolio's value.
- Dynamic Immunization: This involves continuously adjusting the portfolio to maintain the duration match as interest rates change over time. It requires more active management compared to static immunization.

Limitations:

Immunization relies on the assumption that the relationship between asset and liability durations remains constant over time, ensuring that changes in interest rates have a neutral effect on the portfolio's ability to meet future liabilities. However, in highly volatile markets, this relationship can be disrupted due to sudden and unpredictable movements in interest rates or other market dynamics. For instance, changes in the shape of the yield curve or unexpected economic events can lead to a mismatch between the portfolio's duration and the liability horizon, undermining the effectiveness of the immunization strategy.

Additionally, immunization assumes that changes in interest rates occur as parallel shifts in the yield curve, meaning that all maturities experience the same rate of change simultaneously. In reality, yield curve movements are often non-parallel, with short-term, medium-term, and long-term rates moving by different magnitudes or even in opposite directions. These non-parallel shifts, such as twists or humps in the curve, can cause the portfolio's performance to deviate from expectations, potentially exposing the investor to interest rate risk despite the immunization effort.

These limitations highlight the importance of regular monitoring and rebalancing of the portfolio to maintain alignment with liability durations, especially in the face of changing market conditions or unexpected yield curve behaviour.

PRACTICAL EXERCISE #4.04 IMMUNIZATION

Request: An investor must make a payment of 5,000,000 euros within 3 years. The following bonds are available to meet this amount in due course:

TABLE 4.6 Bond Cash Flows and Characteristics

year	0	1	2	3	4	5	Yield	Duration
Bond A	−1000	30	1030				3.00%	1.97
Bond B	−1000	35	35	35	1035		3.50%	3.80
Bond C	−1000	40	40	40	40	1040	4.00%	4.63

You are asked to: Construct a portfolio with these three bonds that secures as far as possible the obligated disbursement by year 3, indicating:

No. of securities of Bond A
No. of securities of Bond B
No. of securities of Bond C

After building the portfolio, check the quality of the immunization by simulating changes in interest rates. Good immunization guarantees that the amount invested in bonds will be sufficient to meet liabilities over the investment horizon, regardless of changes in interest rates.

Summary of the script. –

This code constructs an immunized bond portfolio to meet a future liability of €5,000,000 due in 3 years. The portfolio is designed to match the liability's duration and ensure the present value covers the future obligation by allocating funds among three available bonds.

Key features of the code:

a) Automated Portfolio Optimization: The code automatically allocates bond weights to match the target duration while ensuring the total investment is fully allocated and constraints are met.
b) Investment Calculation: It accurately determines the present value required to meet the future liability by using the portfolio's internal rate of return (IRR), ensuring precise funding.
c) Practical Implementation: Calculates the exact number of bond units to purchase, rounding up to whole units for real-world feasibility and efficient fund allocation.
d) Professional Reporting: Provides a well-structured table with formatted values for easy interpretation, presenting key metrics like investment amounts, yields, durations, and security counts.
e) Parallel shift stress test: Evaluates the immunization of a bond portfolio against interest rate changes. It defines three bonds (A, B, and C) with their respective cash-flows and a single liability of €5 million due in 3 years. Using several functions, it calculates the present value of cash flows, the prices of individual bonds, the total portfolio value, and the liability's value under different yield shifts. It then tests

how both the present value (t = 0) and the horizon value (t = 3) of the portfolio respond when all yields move up or down in 25-basis-point steps from –200 bps to +200 bps. Finally, it computes the worst-case deficit at the horizon and derives the minimum initial cash cushion needed today to ensure that no shortfall occurs under any interest-rate scenario.

These features make the code an effective tool for financial planning, allowing investors to construct liability-matching bond portfolios with precision and ease.

TABLE 4.7 Summary of Key Functions and Their Purposes

Function/Calculation	Purpose
duration_matching_minimize(weights)	Defines the objective function for duration matching optimization.
minimize(duration_matching_minimize, initial_weights, constraints=constraints)	Optimizes bond weights to achieve the target portfolio duration.
present_value(rate, future_value, years)	Calculates the present value of future liabilities using the portfolio IRR.
weights_solution = result.x	Extracts the optimized bond weights from the optimization results.
amount_invested_A = w_A * present_value_liability	Computes the amount to invest in each bond based on optimized weights.
no_securities_A = amount_invested_A / price_A	Calculates the number of bond units to purchase.
pd.concat([results, portfolio_details], ignore_index=True)	Combines bond details with portfolio summary in a single table.
pv(fv, r, t)	Present value of a single future amount.
price_from_cf(cf_dict, y)	Price of a cash-flow stream.
price_portfolio(y_shift)	Portfolio market value under a shift of yields.
pv_liability(y_shift)	Present value of the liability under a shift.
horizon_value_one_bond(cf_dict, y, shift, units, horizon=3)	Value of one bond at the horizon (t = 3).
horizon_value_assets(shift)	Total asset horizon value.

Script execution and outputs. –

```
import numpy as np
import pandas as pd
from scipy.optimize import minimize
```

```
# Initial data

required_payment = 5000000  # Future value in year 3
target_duration = 3

# Bond durations

duration_A = 1.97
duration_B = 3.80
duration_C = 4.63

# Current bond prices

price_A = 1000
price_B = 1000
price_C = 1000

# Bond Yields (discount rates)

y_A = 0.03
y_B = 0.035
y_C = 0.04

# Define the equations to be solved

def duration_matching_minimize(weights):
    w_A, w_B, w_C = weights


    # The duration of the portfolio should be 3 years.
    duration_constraint = (w_A * duration_A + w_B *
    duration_B + w_C * duration_C - 3)**2

    # Weights must add up to 100%.

    weights_sum_constraint = (w_A + w_B + w_C - 1)**2
    return duration_constraint + weights_sum_constraint

# Restrictions to ensure that weights are >= 0

constraints = (
    {'type': 'ineq', 'fun': lambda x: x[0]},  # w_A >= 0
    {'type': 'ineq', 'fun': lambda x: x[1]},  # w_B >= 0
    {'type': 'ineq', 'fun': lambda x: x[2]}   # w_C >= 0
)

# Initial assumptions for bond weights A, B and C

initial_weights = [0.33, 0.33, 0.34]
```

```
# Solve the equations to find the correct bond weights.

result = minimize(duration_matching_minimize, initial_
weights, constraints=constraints)
weights_solution = result.x

# Bond weights

w_A, w_B, w_C = weights_solution


# Calculate the IRR of the portfolio as the weighted
average of the bond IRRs.

portfolio_yield = w_A * y_A + w_B * y_B + w_C * y_C

# Calculate the present value of the liability using the
IRR of the portfolio.

def present_value(rate, future_value, years):
    return future_value / (1 + rate)**years

present_value_liability = present_value(portfolio_yield,
required_payment, 3)

# Calculate the amount to invest in each bond

amount_invested_A = w_A * present_value_liability
amount_invested_B = w_B * present_value_liability
amount_invested_C = w_C * present_value_liability

# Calculate the number of units of each bond

no_securities_A = amount_invested_A / price_A
no_securities_B = amount_invested_B / price_B
no_securities_C = amount_invested_C / price_C

# Create the results DataFrame

results = pd.DataFrame({
    'Bond': ['A', 'B', 'C'],
    'Weight': [w_A, w_B, w_C],
    'Amount Invested': [amount_invested_A, amount_
    invested_B, amount_invested_C],
    'Current Price': [price_A, price_B, price_C],
    'Number of Securities': [round(no_securities_A,0),
    round(no_securities_B,0), round(no_securities_C,0)],
    'Bond Yield(%)': [y_A*100, y_B*100, y_C*100],
    'Duration': [duration_A, duration_B, duration_C]
})
```

```
# Round IRR Bond to four decimal places

results['Bond Yield(%)'] = results['Bond
Yield(%)'].apply(lambda x: '{:.2f}'.format(x))

# Add additional portfolio details

portfolio_yield_rounded = '{:.2f}'.format(portfolio_
yield*100)
present_value_liability_rounded = round(present_value_
liability, 2)

# Create an additional row for portfolio details

portfolio_details = pd.DataFrame({
    'Bond': ['Inmunized Portfolio'],
    'Weight': [1.0],
    'Amount Invested': [present_value_liability_rounded],
    'Current Price': ['-'],
    'Number of Securities': ['-'],
    'Bond Yield(%)': [portfolio_yield_rounded],
    'Duration': [target_duration]
})

# Concatenate the results table with the portfolio details
row

final_results= pd.concat([results, portfolio_details],
ignore_index=True)

# Display results without scientific notation and with
thousands separator

pd.set_option('display.float_format', lambda x:
'{:,.2f}'.format(x))
final_results
```

Output:

	Bond	Weight	Amount Invested	Current Price	Number of Securities	Bond Yield(%)	Duration
0	A	0.52	2,371,080.87	1000	2,371.00	3.00	1.97
1	B	0.29	1,300,479.59	1000	1,300.00	3.50	3.80
2	C	0.19	860,017.53	1000	860.00	4.00	4.63
3	Inmunized Portfolio	1.00	4,531,577.71	-	-	3.33	3.00

Now let's check that immunization is effective by simulating changes in interest rates.

```
# Parallel shift test (stress-test immunization).
# We are going to bump all discount rates up and down by
the same amount and reprice the asset portfolio and the
liability (5M due at year 3)

# Inputs from before
nA = int(round(no_securities_A))
nB = int(round(no_securities_B))
nC = int(round(no_securities_C))

# liability
FV_liab = float(required_payment)
T_liab = 3

# cash-flow schedules (year -> CF)
cf_A = {1: 30, 2: 1030}
cf_B = {1: 35, 2: 35, 3: 35, 4: 1035}
cf_C = {1: 40, 2: 40, 3: 40, 4: 40, 5: 1040}


def pv(fv, r, t): # annual compounding
    return fv / (1 + r) ** t

def price_from_cf(cf_dict, y):
    return sum(cf / (1 + y) ** t for t, cf in cf_
    dict.items())

def price_portfolio(y_shift):
    pA = price_from_cf(cf_A, y_A + y_shift)
    pB = price_from_cf(cf_B, y_B + y_shift)
    pC = price_from_cf(cf_C, y_C + y_shift)
    return nA * pA + nB * pB + nC * pC

def pv_liability(y_shift):
    return pv(FV_liab, portfolio_yield + y_shift, T_liab)

def horizon_value_one_bond(cf_dict, y, shift, units,
horizon=3):
    y_s = y + shift
    # cashflows up to horizon are reinvested to horizon
    before = sum(cf * (1 + y_s) ** (horizon - t) for t, cf
in cf_dict.items() if t <= horizon)
    # remaining cashflows are priced at horizon
    after_price = sum(cf / (1 + y_s) ** (t - horizon) for
    t, cf in cf_dict.items() if t > horizon)
    return units * (before + after_price)

def horizon_value_assets(shift):
    return (
```

```
        horizon_value_one_bond(cf_A, y_A, shift, nA) +
        horizon_value_one_bond(cf_B, y_B, shift, nB) +
        horizon_value_one_bond(cf_C, y_C, shift, nC)
    )

# run parallel shifts (±200 bps in 25-bp steps)
bps_grid = np.arange(-200, 201, 25)
shifts = bps_grid / 10_000

# PV at t0 test
pv_rows = []
for s in shifts:
    pv_rows.append({
        "Shift (bps)": int(s * 10_000),
        "PV Assets": price_portfolio(s),
        "PV Liability": pv_liability(s)
    })
pv_df = pd.DataFrame(pv_rows)
pv_df["PV Surplus"] = pv_df["PV Assets"] - pv_df["PV
Liability"]

# Horizon-value (t=3) test
hv_rows = []
for s in shifts:
    hv_rows.append({
        "Shift (bps)": int(s * 10_000),
        "Horizon Asset Value": horizon_value_assets(s),
        "Liability at t=3": float(FV_liab)
    })
hv_df = pd.DataFrame(hv_rows)
hv_df["Horizon Surplus"] = hv_df["Horizon Asset Value"] -
hv_df["Liability at t=3"]

# Worst-case deficits and minimum cash cushion today (for
the horizon test)
worst_hv_deficit_t3 = max(0.0, -hv_df["Horizon
Surplus"].min())     # need at t=3
min_cushion_today = worst_hv_deficit_t3 / (1 + port_yield)
** T_liab # deposit today

# prints
print("PV stress (t=0):")
print(pv_df.to_string(index=False))
print("\nHorizon stress (t=3):")
print(hv_df.to_string(index=False))
print(f"\nMinimum cash cushion today to avoid any horizon
shortfall: €{min_cushion_today:,.2f}")
```

Output:

```
PV stress (t=0):
 Shift (bps)      PV Assets   PV Liability  PV Surplus
        -200 4,805,721.64  4,805,225.55       496.09
        -175 4,770,034.27  4,769,835.30       198.97
        -150 4,734,742.89  4,734,791.73       -48.84
        -125 4,699,841.84  4,700,090.61      -248.77
        -100 4,665,325.56  4,665,727.76      -402.20
         -75 4,631,188.56  4,631,699.06      -510.50
         -50 4,597,425.48  4,598,000.48      -575.00
         -25 4,564,031.02  4,564,628.00      -596.98
           0 4,531,000.00  4,531,577.71      -577.71
          25 4,498,327.30  4,498,845.72      -518.42
          50 4,466,007.91  4,466,428.20      -420.29
          75 4,434,036.88  4,434,321.39      -284.52
         100 4,402,409.36  4,402,521.58      -112.22
         125 4,371,120.59  4,371,025.11        95.48
         150 4,340,165.87  4,339,828.36       337.51
         175 4,309,540.58  4,308,927.78       612.80
         200 4,279,240.20  4,278,319.87       920.33

Horizon stress (t=3):
Shift (bps)  Horizon Asset      Liability          Horizon
             Value              at t=3             Surplus
    -200     5,001,957.12       5,000,000.00       1,957.12
    -175     5,001,490.58       5,000,000.00       1,490.58
    -150     5,001,072.97       5,000,000.00       1,072.97
    -125     5,000,703.89       5,000,000.00         703.89
    -100     5,000,382.92       5,000,000.00         382.92
     -75     5,000,109.64       5,000,000.00         109.64
     -50     4,999,883.66       5,000,000.00        -116.34
     -25     4,999,704.58       5,000,000.00        -295.42
       0     4,999,571.99       5,000,000.00        -428.01
      25     4,999,485.52       5,000,000.00        -514.48
      50     4,999,444.77       5,000,000.00        -555.23
      75     4,999,449.37       5,000,000.00        -550.63
     100     4,999,498.92       5,000,000.00        -501.08
     125     4,999,593.07       5,000,000.00        -406.93
     150     4,999,731.45       5,000,000.00        -268.55
     175     4,999,913.67       5,000,000.00         -86.33
     200     5,000,139.40       5,000,000.00         139.40

Minimum cash cushion today to avoid any horizon
shortfall: €503.21
```

4.7 CASH FLOW MATCHING

Cash flow matching is a passive bond investing strategy. Cash flow matching involves putting together a portfolio of bonds with cash flow receipts that match the timing and scale of expected cash flow payments. The idea is to construct a portfolio of low-cost bonds so that their cash flows (generated by coupons and principal) can satisfy a stream of payments due. The aim is to establish a time structure of cash inflows that matches the structure of cash outflows.

To the extent that the asset and liability cash flows match, the portfolio is risk free in the sense that it will always be able to meet its payments.

Also called dedicating a portfolio, this is an alternative to multiperiod immunization that calls for the manager to match the maturity of each element in the liability stream, working backward from the last liability to assure all required cash flows, as illustrated in the following exhibit (Figure 4.9). Let us assume 5 bonds with the following maturities: Bond A with a 5-year maturity, Bond B with a 4-year maturity, Bond C with a 3-year maturity, Bond D with a 2-year maturity, and Bond E with a 1-year maturity. Let us also assume five cash flows corresponding to liabilities (L_i). The matching process begins with the bond with the longest maturity funding the liability with the longest maturity. In this case:

- Liability of year 5 (L5) is funded by Bond A with its face value and coupon.
- Liability of year 4 (L_4) is funded by the face value and coupon of Bond B, plus the coupon from Bond A.

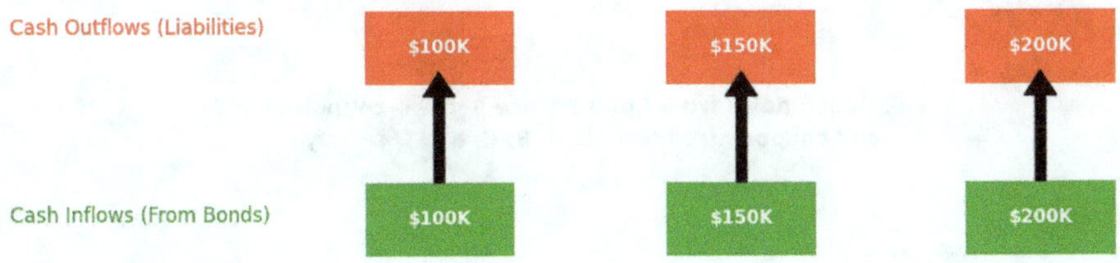

FIGURE 4.8 Cash-Flow Matching

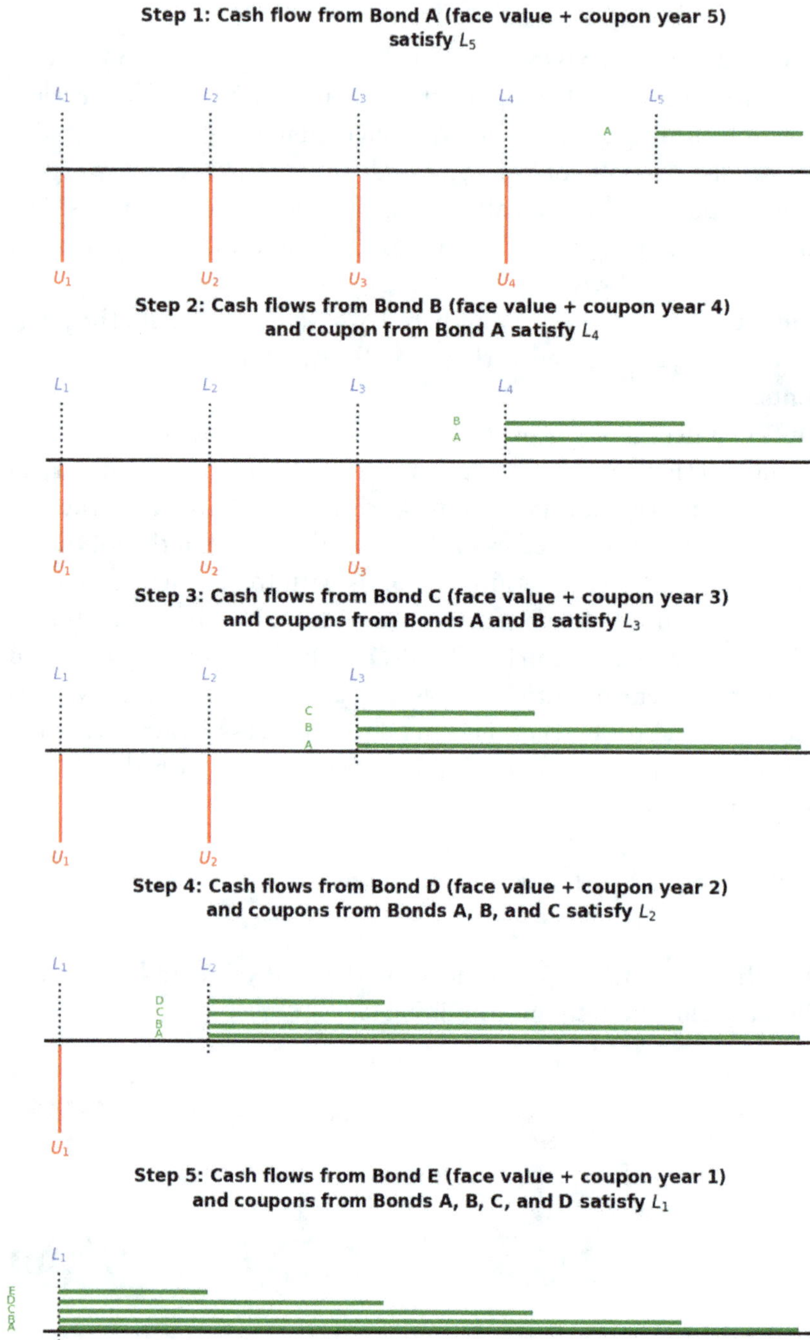

FIGURE 4.9 Cash Flow Matching Steps

- Liability of year 3 (L_3) is funded by the face value and coupon of Bond C, plus the coupons from Bonds A and B.
- Liability of year 2 (L_2) is funded by the face value and coupon of Bond D, plus the coupons from Bonds A, B, and C.
- Finally, the liability of year 1 (L_1) is funded by the face value and coupon of Bond E, plus the coupons from Bonds A, B, C, and D.

To determine the number of bonds needed to fund the liabilities, we divide the unfunded liability for a year *i* (U_i) by the face value plus the coupon of the bond maturing in year *i*. We did this every year. It is important that the cost of the bond portfolio (bonds multiplied by their market prices) does not exceed the present value of the liabilities.

PRACTICAL EXERCISE #4.05 CASH FLOW MATCHING

Request: Consider the following asset (portfolio of bonds) and liability (loan):

TABLE 4.8 Asset and Liability Characteristics

Liability	Loan amount	Maturity (years)	Interest rate
	15.000.000,00 €	5	3%

Asset	Bond	Face value (€)	Coupon rate	Maturity (years)	YTM
	A	100	1.50%	1	1.55%
	B	500	1.75%	2	2,00%
	C	1000	2,00%	3	2.25%
	D	1000	2.50%	4	2.75%
	E	500	2.75%	5	3.15%

The purpose is to build a portfolio of bonds whose cash flows match the cash flows of the loan.

Summary of the script. –

This code implements a cash flow matching strategy for managing liabilities using a bond portfolio. The process involves selecting a set of bonds with different maturities and yields to ensure that future liability cash flows are fully covered by the bond cash flows. Key steps in the code:

a) Cash Flow Matching Process:
   - Defines bond cash flows and liability cash flows.
   - Iterates through bonds (starting from longest maturity) to match liabilities.
   - Rounds up the number of bonds needed and calculates the total cash flows generated.

b) Bond Pricing Calculation:
   - Calculates bond prices using discounted cash flows based on respective yields.
   - Computes total cost by multiplying bond quantity by price.

c) Result Presentation:
   - Generates a summary DataFrame with bond quantities, prices, and total costs.
   - Adds a row to display the total investment required.
   - Calculates and displays the surplus or shortfall relative to the loan amount.

This code effectively implements a cash flow matching (immunization) strategy, ensuring that the bond portfolio meets liability requirements over time.

TABLE 4.9 Summary of Key Functions and Their Purposes

Function/Calculation	Purpose
cover_flows(bond, year, bonds_needed, loan_flows)	Determines the number of bonds required to cover liability cash flows for each year.
sum(num * bond_flows[bond][year] for bond, num in bonds_needed.items( ))	Computes total cash flows generated by the selected bonds.
calculate_bond_price(flows, yield_to_maturity)	Calculates the price of a bond based on its cash flows and yield to maturity.
df_bond_details.loc[len(df_bond_details)] = [. . .]	Adds a total row to summarize overall bond cost.

Script execution and outputs. –

```
import numpy as np
import pandas as pd

# Bond cash flows

bond_flows = {
    'A': [101.5, 0, 0, 0, 0],
    'B': [8.75, 508.75, 0, 0, 0],
    'C': [20, 20, 1020, 0, 0],
    'D': [25, 25, 25, 1025, 0],
    'E': [13.75, 13.75, 13.75, 13.75, 513.75]
}

# Cash flows from liabilities

loan_flows = [450000, 450000, 450000, 450000, 15450000]

# Initialize the number of b required

bonds_needed = {bond: 0 for bond in bond_flows.keys()}

# Function to match liability cash flows with bond cash flows

def cover_flows(bond, year, bonds_needed, loan_flows):
    num_bonds = loan_flows[year] / bond_flows[bond][year]
    bonds_needed[bond] += num_bonds
    for y in range(5):
        loan_flows[y] -= num_bonds * bond_flows[bond][y]
    return bonds_needed, loan_flows

# Cover liability cash flows starting with the longest maturity

for bond, year in zip(['E', 'D', 'C', 'B', 'A'], range(4,
-1, -1)):
    bonds_needed, loan_flows = cover_flows(bond, year,
    bonds_needed, loan_flows)

# Round up the amounts of bonds needed

bonds_needed = {bond: round(num,0) for bond, num in bonds_
needed.items()}

# Calculate the cash flows generated

generated_flows = [
    round(sum(num * bond_flows[bond][0] for bond, num in
```

```
bonds_needed.items())),
    round(sum(num * bond_flows[bond][1] for bond, num in
bonds_needed.items())),
    round(sum(num * bond_flows[bond][2] for bond, num in
bonds_needed.items())),
    round(sum(num * bond_flows[bond][3] for bond, num in
bonds_needed.items())),
    round(sum(num * bond_flows[bond][4] for bond, num in
    bonds_needed.items()))
]

# Show results

print("Bonds required:", bonds_needed)
print("Cash flows generated:", generated_flows)
print("Outstanding balances:", loan_flows)
```

Output:

```
Bonds required: {'A': 338.0, 'B': 69.0, 'C': 35.0, 'D': 36.0,
'E': 30073.0}
Cash flows generated: [450014, 450208, 450104, 450404, 15450004]
Outstanding balances: [0.0, 0.0, 0.0, 0.0, 0.0]
```

Portfolio cost and surplus

```
import pandas as pd

# Bond data
bond_yields = {
    'A': 0.0155,
    'B': 0.02,
    'C': 0.0225,
    'D': 0.0275,
    'E': 0.0315
}

bond_flows = {
    'A': [101.5, 0, 0, 0, 0],
    'B': [8.75, 508.75, 0, 0, 0],
    'C': [20, 20, 1020, 0, 0],
    'D': [25, 25, 25, 1025, 0],
    'E': [13.75, 13.75, 13.75, 13.75, 513.75]
}
```

```
bonds_needed = {'A': 338.0, 'B': 69.0, 'C': 35.0, 'D':
36.0, 'E': 30073.0}
loan_amount = 15000000  # Amount of the loan


# Function to calculate the price of a bond
def calculate_bond_price(flows, yield_to_maturity):
    return sum(flow / (1 + yield_to_maturity) ** (t + 1)
for t, flow in enumerate(flows))

# Calculating bond prices
bond_prices = {bond: calculate_bond_price(flows, bond_
yields[bond]) for bond, flows in bond_flows.items()}

# Create the DataFrame
df_bond_details = pd.DataFrame({
    'Bond': bonds_needed.keys(),
    'Quantity': bonds_needed.values(),
    'Price': [bond_prices[bond] for bond in bonds_
    needed],
    'Total Cost': [bonds_needed[bond] * bond_prices[bond]
for bond in bonds_needed]
})

# Add total sum row without values in Quantity and Price
df_bond_details.loc[len(df_bond_details)] = ['Total', '',
'', df_bond_details['Total Cost'].sum()]

# Format the columns
df_bond_details['Quantity'] = df_bond_details['Quantity'].
apply(lambda x: f"{x:,.2f}" if x != '' else '')
df_bond_details['Price'] = df_bond_
details['Price'].apply(lambda x: f"{x:,.2f}" if x != ''
else '')
df_bond_details['Total Cost'] = df_bond_details['Total
Cost'].apply(lambda x: f"{x:,.2f}")

# Calculate the difference with the loan amount
total_cost_sum = df_bond_details.loc[df_bond_
details['Bond'] == 'Total', 'Total Cost'].replace({',':
''}, regex=True).astype(float).values[0]
difference = loan_amount-total_cost_sum

# Add the difference to the DataFrame
df_bond_details['Loan surplus'] = ''
df_bond_details.loc[df_bond_details['Bond'] == 'Total',
'Loan surplus'] = f"{difference:,.2f}"
```

```
# Reset index and hide index column
df_bond_details.reset_index(drop=True, inplace=True)
df_bond_details.style.hide(axis='index')
```

Output:

Bond	Quantity	Price	Total Cost	Loan Surplus
A	338.00	99.95	33,783.36	
B	69.00	497.57	34,332.54	
C	35.00	992.83	34,748.88	
D	36.00	990.65	35,663.45	
E	30,073.00	490.88	14,762,224.70	
Total			14,900,752.93	99,247.07

Limitations of Cash Flow Matching

Cash flow matching, while effective for mitigating certain financial risks, has several limitations:

a) Lack of Flexibility:

- Bonds or other fixed-income securities chosen for matching specific liabilities may not allow for adjustments if liabilities change over time.
- Unplanned cash flows, such as early liability settlements, can disrupt the matching strategy.

b) Market Constraints:

- Suitable bonds may not always be available in the market, particularly for liabilities with specific timing or irregular cash flows.
- Limited liquidity in the bond market can make it challenging to acquire or sell bonds at desired prices.

c) Cost Considerations:

- Cash flow matching often requires purchasing long-term bonds, which may have higher prices and lower yields compared to shorter-term alternatives.

- The overall cost of the portfolio may exceed alternative risk management strategies, such as immunization.

d) Interest Rate Risk: Although cash flow matching reduces interest rate risk for planned liabilities, it does not protect against reinvestment risk for intermediate cash flows (e.g., coupons) if they need to be reinvested at lower rates.

e) Incompleteness for Complex Liabilities:

- Complex liabilities with uncertain amounts or timings (e.g., insurance claims) cannot always be matched precisely with available bonds.
- Inflation-indexed liabilities require inflation-protected bonds, which may not be readily available or may carry higher costs.

f) High Initial Investment:

- Implementing a cash flow matching strategy often requires a significant upfront capital outlay to acquire the necessary bonds.
- This can make the strategy less feasible for entities with constrained budgets.

g) Opportunity Cost:

- By focusing exclusively on matching liabilities, investors may forgo potentially higher returns from alternative investment strategies.
- It limits portfolio diversification as assets are concentrated in fixed-income instruments with specific maturities.

h) Operational Complexity:

- Designing and maintaining a cash flow matching strategy requires precise planning and monitoring.
- Changes in liabilities or bond availability may necessitate frequent adjustments, increasing operational effort.

i) Assumption of Certainty: Cash flow matching assumes that bond payments (coupons and face value) will occur exactly as scheduled, which may not hold in cases of issuer default or early bond redemption.

By understanding these limitations, investors and financial managers can weigh the trade-offs and decide if cash flow matching is the appropriate strategy for their specific financial objectives.

CHAPTER 5

Python Applied to Return Attribution

5.1 CHAPTER OVERVIEW

This chapter explores how performance attribution techniques can be implemented in Python to evaluate and decompose portfolio returns. It begins with a conceptual overview of return attribution, emphasizing its role in distinguishing between market movements and managerial skill. The chapter presents the Brinson–Fachler model (Brinson & Fachler, 1985) for equity portfolios, which breaks down excess returns into allocation, selection, and interaction effects, and provides a Python script to perform the calculations using sector data. It then transitions to fixed income attribution, addressing the added complexity of bond portfolios by analysing components like duration, yield curve shifts, credit spreads, carry, convexity, and selection effects. The chapter includes a detailed Python script to compute these effects and normalize them against the portfolio's excess return, offering practical tools for analysing performance in both equity and fixed income contexts. Throughout, the focus is on turning theory into actionable code, enhancing transparency and decision-making in asset management.

5.2 INTRODUCTION

Return attribution is a performance analysis technique used in asset management to break down and understand the sources of a portfolio's returns. It helps investors and portfolio managers assess how different

DOI: 10.1201/9781003781394-5

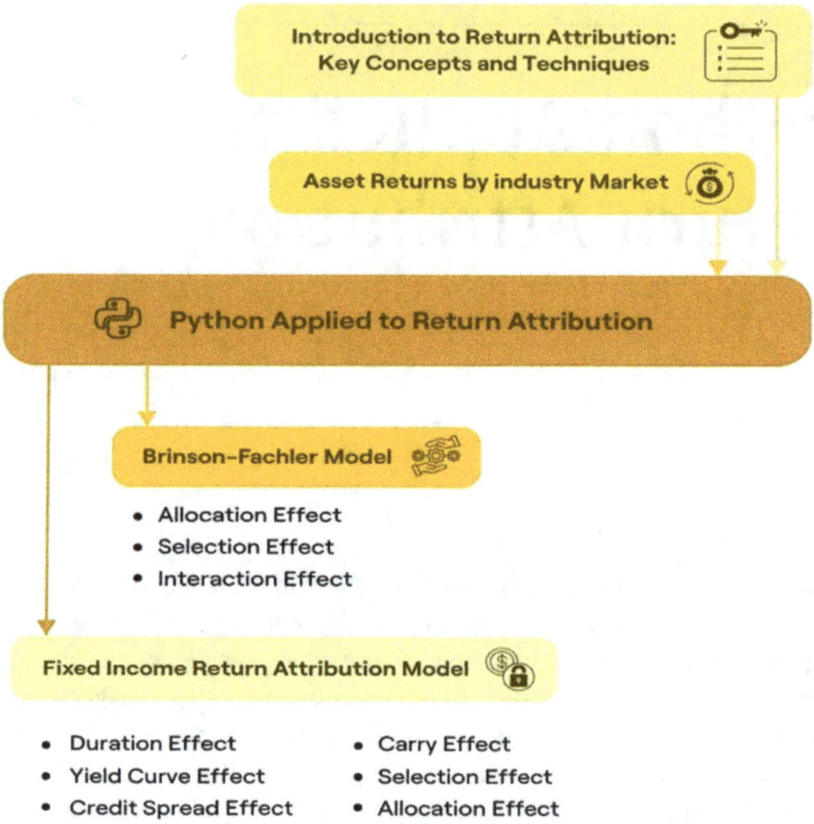

FIGURE 5.1 Python in Return Attribution: Models and Techniques

factors have contributed to overall performance, distinguishing between market-driven effects and active management decisions.

This process involves comparing the actual returns of a portfolio against a benchmark or expected performance, identifying the impact of asset allocation, security selection, and other investment decisions. By analysing return attribution, managers can determine whether returns were generated by strategic positioning, skilful selection of assets, or broader market movements.

Return attribution is crucial for evaluating the effectiveness of investment strategies, improving decision-making, and providing transparency to clients and stakeholders. It enables investment professionals to refine their approaches, optimize asset allocation, and justify their investment choices based on measurable contributions to portfolio performance.

Various attribution methods exist, each suited to different asset classes and investment strategies. While equity portfolios typically focus on allocation and selection effects, fixed income portfolios incorporate interest rate movements and credit risk factors. Factor-based attribution, on the other hand, examines how broader economic and financial variables influence returns.

By applying return attribution, investment managers can refine their decision-making, optimize portfolio strategies, and better communicate the rationale behind performance results. This enhances investor confidence and contributes to more informed portfolio adjustments over time.

5.3 BRINSON–FACHLER RETURN ATTRIBUTION MODEL (EQUITY PORTFOLIOS)

Brinson attribution is one of the most widely used methods for analysing the performance of equity portfolios. It provides a structured framework to assess how different investment decisions contribute to overall returns by comparing a portfolio's performance against a benchmark. This method helps portfolio managers determine whether their returns stem from asset allocation choices, security selection, or a combination of both.

At its core, Brinson attribution evaluates how a portfolio's weighting across various sectors, industries, or regions influences its returns relative to a benchmark. It distinguishes between the impact of allocating capital to different segments of the market and the selection of individual securities within those segments. By quantifying these effects, investors can identify whether outperformance or underperformance is driven by macro-level strategic positioning or specific investment decisions.

This method is particularly useful for active portfolio managers, as it helps assess whether their strategy is adding value compared to passive investing. It also enhances transparency by providing a clear breakdown of performance drivers, which is essential for client reporting and investment oversight.

Brinson attribution serves as a powerful diagnostic tool, guiding portfolio managers in refining their investment approach and making more informed decisions about asset allocation and stock selection. By continuously analysing past performance through this framework, investors can improve their strategies and align them with their long-term objectives.

Brinson–Fachler attribution is an extension of the classic Brinson attribution model, designed to provide a more precise and consistent evaluation of portfolio performance. Developed by Brinson and Fachler in 1985, this method refines the way returns are decomposed, particularly in how it treats the allocation and selection effects. While it retains the core principles of Brinson–Hood–Beebower (BHB) attribution, it adjusts the formulas to ensure a more intuitive interpretation of results.

The main goal of Brinson–Fachler attribution is to break down a portfolio's excess return (also known as active return) into three primary components:

a) Allocation Effect: Analyses the impact of the manager's decision to overweight or underweight different asset classes, sectors, or regions compared to the benchmark.

b) Selection Effect: Evaluates the impact of choosing specific securities within those sectors or asset classes relative to the benchmark.

c) Interaction Effect: Considers the combined impact of both allocation and selection decisions.

By quantifying these effects, Brinson–Fachler attribution provides insight into whether a portfolio's performance is driven by strategic asset allocation or skilful security selection.

5.3.1 Allocation Effect

This effect measures the impact of the portfolio manager's decision to overweight or underweight certain sectors, industries, or asset classes relative to the benchmark. If a manager assigns a higher weight to a sector that outperforms the market, it will contribute positively to performance. Conversely, if they overweight a sector that underperforms, it will have a negative impact.

The formula for the allocation effect is:

$$\text{Allocation Effect} = \sum \left(w_p - w_b\right) \times \left(r_p - r_T\right)$$

where:

- w_p = weight of the sector in the portfolio
- w_b = weight of the sector in the benchmark
- r_b = return of the sector in the benchmark
- r_T = total benchmark return

A positive allocation effect means that the manager successfully allocated more capital to sectors that performed better than the overall market.

5.3.2 Selection Effect

This effect measures the performance impact of selecting specific stocks within a given sector, rather than the overall allocation to that sector. Even if the portfolio's allocation to a sector is identical to the benchmark's, superior or inferior stock-picking within that sector can lead to outperformance or underperformance.

The formula for the selection effect is:

$$\text{Selection Effect} = \sum w_b \times \left(r_p - r_b\right)$$

where:

- w_b = weight of the sector in the benchmark
- r_p = return of the sector in the portfolio
- r_b = return of the sector in the benchmark

A positive selection effect indicates that the portfolio manager successfully picked better-performing stocks within a sector compared to the benchmark.

5.3.3 Interaction Effect

Brinson–Fachler attribution includes an interaction term that accounts for the combined effect of allocation and selection decisions. This occurs when the portfolio manager overweights or underweights a sector and selects stocks within that sector that perform differently than the benchmark.

The formula for the interaction effect is:

$$\text{Interaction Effect} = \sum \left(w_p - w_b\right) \times \left(r_p - r_b\right)$$

where:

- w_p = weight of the sector in the portfolio
- w_b = weight of the sector in the benchmark
- r_p = return of the sector in the portfolio
- r_b = return of the sector in the benchmark

If a portfolio manager overweighted a sector and also picked strong-performing stocks within it, the interaction effect will be positive. Conversely, if they overweighted a sector but chose poor-performing stocks, the interaction effect will be negative.

5.3.4 Conclusion

By analysing these components, portfolio managers can refine their investment approach and focus on areas where they have demonstrated expertise. For example:

- If the allocation effect is consistently negative but the selection effect is positive, it may suggest that the manager is good at picking stocks but poor at choosing sectors.
- If the selection effect is weak but the allocation effect is strong, the manager may be better suited for macro-level asset allocation strategies rather than stock picking.

Additionally, Brinson–Fachler attribution helps investment firms provide clear and detailed reports to clients, demonstrating the value added by active management.

Brinson–Fachler attribution is a fundamental framework for understanding the drivers of portfolio performance in equity markets. By decomposing returns into allocation, selection, and sometimes interaction effects, it helps investment managers assess the effectiveness of their decisions and adjust their strategies accordingly. While it has limitations, it remains a crucial tool for performance evaluation, risk management, and investor communication.

PRACTICAL EXERCISE #5.01 EQUITY PORTFOLIO RETURN ATTRIBUTION

Request: You are a portfolio manager analysing the performance of your equity portfolio relative to a benchmark. Your objective is to break down the excess return into three key components using Brinson–Fachler attribution.

The portfolio is invested in five sectors with the following weights and returns:

TABLE 5.1 Portfolio Sectors

Sector	Portfolio Weight	Benchmark Weight	Portfolio Return (%)	Benchmark Return (%)
Tech	30%	25%	12.0	10.0
Healthcare	25%	20%	8.5	7.0
Finance	20%	25%	6.0	6.5
Energy	15%	20%	4.0	5.0
Consumer	10%	10%	7.5	7.0

Using Python, you will calculate each of the attribution effects and determine whether the portfolio outperformed or underperformed due to sector allocation, stock selection, or their interaction.

Summary of the script. –

The script calculates the Brinson–Fachler attribution using sector weights and returns:

a) Compute Attribution Effects:
   - Allocation Effect: Impact of sector weight differences.
   - Selection Effect: Impact of stock selection within sectors.
   - Interaction Effect: Combined effect of allocation and selection.

b) Calculate Portfolio and Benchmark Total Returns:
   - Compute weighted returns for portfolio and benchmark.
   - Determine the excess return.

c) Normalize and Display Results:
   - Ensure attribution effects sum to excess return.
   - Print sector-wise and total attribution effects.

TABLE 5.2 Summary of Key Functions and Their Purposes

Function	Purpose
df["Allocation_Effect"]	Calculates the impact of sector weighting differences.
df["Selection_Effect"]	Computes the impact of selecting better/worse stocks.
df["Interaction_Effect"]	Measures the combined effect of allocation and selection.
portfolio_total_return	Computes the total return of the portfolio.
benchmark_total_return	Computes the total return of the benchmark.
expected_excess_return	Difference between portfolio and benchmark returns.
scaling_factor	Ensures attribution effects sum to expected excess return.
total_effects	Stores the final attribution effect values.

Script execution and outputs. –

```
import pandas as pd
import numpy as np

# Sample input data
sectors = ["Tech", "Healthcare", "Finance", "Energy",
     "Consumer"]
data = {
    "Sector": sectors,
    "Weight_Portfolio": [0.30, 0.25, 0.20, 0.15, 0.10],
       # Portfolio Weights
```

```
    "Weight_Benchmark": [0.25, 0.20, 0.25, 0.20, 0.10],
       # Benchmark Weights
    "Return_Portfolio": [12.0, 8.5, 6.0, 4.0, 7.5],
       # Portfolio Sector Returns (%)
    "Return_Benchmark": [10.0, 7.0, 6.5, 5.0, 7.0]
       # Benchmark Sector Returns (%)
}

df = pd.DataFrame(data)
# Compute Benchmark Total Return
benchmark_total_return = sum(df["Weight_Benchmark"] *
df["Return_Benchmark"])

# Compute Attribution Effects using the correct formula
df["Allocation_Effect"] = (df["Weight_Portfolio"] -
df["Weight_Benchmark"]) * (df["Return_Benchmark"] -
benchmark_total_return)
df["Selection_Effect"] = df["Weight_Benchmark"] *
(df["Return_Portfolio"] - df["Return_Benchmark"])
df["Interaction_Effect"] = (df["Weight_Portfolio"] -
df["Weight_Benchmark"]) * (df["Return_Portfolio"] -
df["Return_Benchmark"])

# Summarizing total effects
total_effects = {
    "Allocation Effect": df["Allocation_Effect"].sum(),
    "Selection Effect": df["Selection_Effect"].sum(),
    "Interaction Effect": df["Interaction_Effect"].sum()
}

# Compute Portfolio and Benchmark Total Returns
portfolio_total_return = sum(df["Weight_Portfolio"] *
df["Return_Portfolio"])
expected_excess_return = portfolio_total_return -
benchmark_total_return

# Normalize total attribution effect to match expected
excess return
scaling_factor = expected_excess_return / sum(total_effects.
values()) if sum(total_effects.values()) != 0 else 1
total_effects = {key: value * scaling_factor for key,
value in total_effects.items()}

# Compute total attribution effect
total_attribution_effect = sum(total_effects.values())

# Display results
print(f"\nPortfolio Total Return: {portfolio_total_
return:.4f}%")
print(f"Benchmark Total Return: {benchmark_total_
return:.4f}%")
```

```
print(f"Expected Excess Return: {expected_excess_
return:.4f}%")

print(f"\nEffects:")
print(df[["Sector", "Allocation_Effect", "Selection_
Effect", "Interaction_Effect"]])
print("\nTotal Attribution Effects:")
for key, value in total_effects.items():
    print(f"{key}: {value:.4f}%")

print(f"\nDiscrepancy (Attribution - Expected Excess
Return): {total_attribution_effect - expected_excess_
return:.4f}%")
```

Output:

```
Portfolio Total Return: 8.2750%
Benchmark Total Return: 7.2250%
Expected Excess Return: 1.0500%

Effects:
   Sector       Allocation_   Selection_   Interaction_
                Effect        Effect       Effect
0  Tech             0.13875        0.500          0.100
1  Healthcare      -0.01125        0.300          0.075
2  Finance          0.03625       -0.125          0.025
3  Energy           0.11125       -0.200          0.050
4  Consumer        -0.00000        0.050          0.000

Total Attribution Effects:
Allocation Effect: 0.2750%
Selection Effect: 0.5250%
Interaction Effect: 0.2500%

Discrepancy (Attribution - Expected Excess Return): 0.0000%
```

Interpretation

The portfolio outperformed the benchmark by 1.05%, primarily driven by:

- Strong stock selection (+0.5250%) in Tech and Healthcare.
- Effective sector allocation (+0.2750%), particularly in Tech and Energy.
- A positive interaction effect (+0.2500%), reinforcing that the combination of allocation and selection worked well.

Areas of Concern:

- Negative selection effect in Finance (−0.125%) and Energy (−0.200%) suggests that stock choices in these sectors underperformed their benchmark counterparts.
- The Healthcare allocation effect (0.01125%) was slightly negative, meaning the weighting in this sector could have been better optimized.

5.4 FIXED INCOME RETURN ATTRIBUTION MODEL

Fixed income attribution is a method used to analyse the sources of a bond portfolio's performance relative to a benchmark. Unlike equity attribution, where returns are primarily driven by asset allocation and stock selection, fixed income attribution is more complex due to multiple return drivers such as interest rates, credit spreads, yield curve shifts, and carry effects.

This framework helps portfolio managers assess whether their excess returns (active return) come from strategic positioning, security selection, or macroeconomic factors. It also provides insights into risk exposure, portfolio adjustments, and overall investment effectiveness.

Fixed income returns can be broken down into several key components, depending on the chosen attribution model. The most common return drivers include:

a) Yield Curve Effect: Impact of changes in the interest rate curve.

b) Duration Effect: Impact of interest rate movements based on bond maturity.

c) Credit Spread Effect: Changes in credit risk premiums.

d) Carry Effect: Return generated from the yield of held securities.

e) Convexity Effect: Impact of nonlinear price changes due to interest rate fluctuations.

f) Selection Effect: Returns from individual bond selection within sectors or rating categories.

g) Currency Effect (for international portfolios): Impact of foreign exchange rate fluctuations.

Each of these components captures a distinct source of return, allowing a deeper understanding of portfolio performance.

5.4.1 Yield Curve Effect

Measures the impact of shifts in the yield curve (e.g., parallel shifts, steepening, or flattening). A manager can benefit from positioning the portfolio correctly in response to expected interest rate changes. For example, if long-term interest rates decline, bonds with longer durations gain more value, benefiting portfolios with high duration exposure.

The yield curve effect is calculated using the formula:

$$\textit{Yield Curve Effect} = (\textit{Duration}_{Portfolio} - \textit{Duration}_{Benchmark}) \times (\Delta \textit{Interest Rate}) \times \textit{Weight}_{Portfolio}$$

5.4.2 Duration Effect

It measures how sensitive the portfolio is to changes in interest rates. Bonds with longer durations are more affected by rate movements. A portfolio with higher duration than the benchmark will outperform when rates decline and underperform when rates rise.

Formula:

$$\textit{Duration Effect} = \left(D_p - D_b\right) \times \Delta Y$$

where:

- D_p = Portfolio duration
- D_b = Benchmark duration
- ΔY = Change in yield

5.4.3 Credit Spread Effect

It measures the impact of changes in credit spreads, which reflect perceived credit risk. If a portfolio holds more corporate bonds than the benchmark and credit spreads tighten, it benefits. Conversely, widening spreads hurt corporate bond-heavy portfolios. Formula:

$$\textit{Credit Spread Effect} = \left(CS_p - CS_b\right) \times \Delta CS$$

where:

- CS_p = Portfolio credit spread
- CS_b = Benchmark credit spread
- ΔCS = Change in credit spread

5.4.4 Carry Effect

It represents the income earned from holding bonds over time. Includes interest income and roll-down return (when bonds move down the yield curve as they approach maturity). Carry is positive when the bond's yield is higher than the benchmark's yield and remains stable over time. Formula:

$$Carry\ Effect = Y_p - Y_b$$

where:

- Y_p = Portfolio yield
- Y_b = Benchmark yield

5.4.5 Convexity Effect

It captures nonlinear price movements due to large interest rate changes. Bonds with higher convexity experience greater price gains when interest rates decline and smaller losses when rates rise. Formula:

$$Convexity\ Effect = \frac{1}{2} C\ x (\Delta Y)^2$$

where: C = Portfolio convexity

5.4.6 Selection Effect

Measures the manager's ability to pick individual bonds that perform better than similar securities in the benchmark. If a portfolio manager selects bonds that provide higher returns than their benchmark counterparts, the selection effect is positive. It isolates the return difference due to choosing specific bonds rather than just sector weighting.

Formula:

$$Selection\ Effect = \sum_i Weight_{Benchmark,i}\ x \left(Return_{Portfolio,i} - Return_{Benchmark,i} \right)$$

where:

$Weight_{Benchmark,i}$: Weight of bond *i* in the benchmark

$Return_{Portfolio,i}$: Return of bond *i* in the portfolio

$Return_{Benchmark,i}$: Return of bond *i* in the benchmark

5.4.7 Currency Effect (for Global Bond Portfolios)

Arises when investing in bonds denominated in foreign currencies. If a currency appreciates relative to the investor's base currency, the portfolio benefits.

5.4.8 Models

Several models are used to apply fixed income attribution, each offering different levels of complexity:

- Campisi Model – Breaks down returns into interest rate, spread, and selection effects.
- Lehmann & Modest Model – Expands on Campisi by including convexity effects.
- Fisher–Weil Model – Uses duration and convexity to explain bond price movements.
- JPMorgan & Barclays Models – Proprietary frameworks widely used in asset management.

5.4.9 Conclusion

Fixed income attribution is a critical tool for bond portfolio analysis, breaking down returns into components that reflect active management decisions and market movements. By examining factors like duration, credit spreads, yield curve positioning, and carry effects, investors can gain valuable insights into performance drivers and risks. This analytical approach helps fixed income managers refine their strategies, enhance risk-adjusted returns, and communicate more effectively with stakeholders.

PRACTICAL EXERCISE #5.02 FIXED INCOME PORTFOLIO RETURN ATTRIBUTION

Request: You are a fixed income portfolio manager overseeing a bond portfolio that consists of various bonds with different maturities, credit spreads, and yields. The portfolio is benchmarked against a market index, and you need to evaluate the performance of your strategy over a given period.

In the following table, you are given data on portfolio and benchmark bond weights, bond yields (for both the portfolio and benchmark), duration, credit spreads (for both the portfolio and benchmark), total returns of each bond in the portfolio and benchmark. Additionally, external market factors such as interest rate changes and yield curve shifts are provided. Analyse the attribution results and compare them to the portfolio's excess return over the benchmark.

TABLE 5.3 Return Attribution: Bond Portfolio

Bond	Weight Portfolio (%)	Weight Benchmark (%)	Yield Portfolio (%)	Yield Benchmark (%)	Duration Portfolio (Years)	Duration Benchmark (Years)	Credit Spread Portfolio (bp)	Credit Spread Benchmark (bp)	Return Portfolio (%)	Return Benchmark (%)
Bond A	0.20	0.15	2.5	2.3	5.0	4.5	1.5	1.3	1.2	1.0
Bond B	0.30	0.25	3.0	2.8	7.0	6.5	2.0	1.8	2.5	2.2
Bond C	0.15	0.20	3.5	3.2	4.0	4.2	2.5	2.2	2.0	1.8
Bond D	0.25	0.30	4.0	3.8	6.0	5.8	3.0	2.8	3.0	2.7
Bond E	0.10	0.10	2.8	2.6	3.0	2.9	1.8	1.6	1.5	1.3
									2.19	**2.00**

Summary of the script. –

The script decomposes a fixed income portfolio's excess return over a benchmark into six attribution effects:

a) Carry Effect: Measures the impact of holding higher-yielding bonds.
b) Duration Effect: Captures the impact of interest rate changes.
c) Yield Curve Effect: Evaluates shifts in the yield curve.
d) Credit Spread Effect: Assesses the impact of credit spread movements.
e) Selection Effect: Measures the performance of selected bonds vs. benchmark bonds.
f) Allocation Effect: Evaluates the impact of asset weight differences.

It converts Macaulay duration to modified duration for accurate sensitivity calculations and applies market changes (interest rate shifts, yield curve movements, and credit spread changes) to assess portfolio performance.

Finally, the script normalizes attribution effects to match the portfolio's excess return (0.19%), ensuring accuracy. It outputs a table of attribution results and highlights key performance drivers.

TABLE 5.4 Summary of Key Functions and Their Purposes

Function	Purpose
df["Duration_Modified_Portfolio"]	Converts Macaulay duration to modified duration to adjust for interest rate sensitivity.
df["Carry_Effect"]	Computes the impact of yield differences between the portfolio and benchmark.

TABLE 5.4 (*Continued*) Summary of Key Functions and Their Purposes

Function	Purpose
df["Duration_Effect"]	Measures the effect of interest rate changes on portfolio performance.
df["Yield_Curve_Effect"]	Assesses the impact of shifts in the yield curve on the portfolio.
df["Credit_Spread_Effect"]	Evaluates how changes in credit spreads influenced portfolio returns.
df["Selection_Effect"]	Measures the contribution of bond selection within the portfolio.
df["Allocation_Effect"]	Analyses how differences in asset allocation affected performance.

Script execution and output. –

```
import pandas as pd
import numpy as np

# Sample input data
data = {
    "Bond": ["Bond A", "Bond B", "Bond C", "Bond D",
    "Bond E"],
    "Weight_Portfolio": [0.2, 0.3, 0.15, 0.25, 0.1],   #
    Portfolio Weights
    "Weight_Benchmark": [0.15, 0.25, 0.2, 0.3, 0.1],   #
    Benchmark Weights
    "Yield_Portfolio": [2.5, 3.0, 3.5, 4.0, 2.8],   # Yield
    of Bonds in Portfolio (%)
    "Yield_Benchmark": [2.3, 2.8, 3.2, 3.8, 2.6],   # Yield
    of Bonds in Benchmark (%)
    "Macaulay_Duration_Portfolio": [5, 7, 4, 6, 3],   #
    Macaulay Duration of Bonds in Portfolio
    "Macaulay_Duration_Benchmark": [4.5, 6.5, 4.2, 5.8,
    2.9],  # Macaulay Duration in Benchmark
    "Credit_Spread_Portfolio": [1.5, 2.0, 2.5, 3.0, 1.8],
    # Credit Spread in bps
    "Credit_Spread_Benchmark": [1.3, 1.8, 2.2, 2.8, 1.6],
    # Credit Spread in bps
    "Return_Portfolio": [1.2, 2.5, 2.0, 3.0, 1.5],   #
    Portfolio Bond Returns (%)
    "Return_Benchmark": [1.0, 2.2, 1.8, 2.7, 1.3],   #
    Benchmark Bond Returns (%)
}

df = pd.DataFrame(data)
```

```
# Convert Macaulay Duration to Modified Duration
df["Duration_Modified_Portfolio"] = df["Macaulay_Duration_
Portfolio"] / (1 + df["Yield_Portfolio"] / 100)
df["Duration_Modified_Benchmark"] = df["Macaulay_Duration_
Benchmark"] / (1 + df["Yield_Benchmark"] / 100)

# Market Changes
interest_rate_change = -0.0025  # Converted from bps to %
yield_curve_shift = -0.0015  # Parallel shift in yield
curve
credit_spread_change = -0.0010  # Converted from bps to %

# Compute Attribution Effects
df["Carry_Effect"] = (df["Yield_Portfolio"] - df["Yield_
Benchmark"]) * df["Weight_Portfolio"]
df["Duration_Effect"] = (df["Duration_Modified_Portfolio"] -
df["Duration_Modified_Benchmark"]) * interest_rate_change *
df["Weight_Portfolio"]
df["Yield_Curve_Effect"] = (df["Duration_Modified_
Portfolio"] - df["Duration_Modified_Benchmark"]) * yield_
curve_shift * df["Weight_Portfolio"]
df["Credit_Spread_Effect"] = (df["Credit_Spread_Portfolio"] -
df["Credit_Spread_Benchmark"]) * credit_spread_change *
df["Weight_Portfolio"]
df["Selection_Effect"] = (df["Return_Portfolio"] -
df["Return_Benchmark"]) * df["Weight_Benchmark"]
df["Allocation_Effect"] = (df["Weight_Portfolio"] -
df["Weight_Benchmark"]) * df["Return_Benchmark"]

# Summarizing total effects
total_effects = {
    "Duration Effect": df["Duration_Effect"].sum(),
    "Yield Curve Effect": df["Yield_Curve_Effect"].sum(),
    "Credit Spread Effect": df["Credit_Spread_Effect"].sum(),
    "Carry Effect": df["Carry_Effect"].sum(),
    "Selection Effect": df["Selection_Effect"].sum(),
    "Allocation Effect": df["Allocation_Effect"].sum(),
}

# Compute Portfolio and Benchmark Total Returns
portfolio_total_return = sum(df["Weight_Portfolio"] *
df["Return_Portfolio"])
benchmark_total_return = sum(df["Weight_Benchmark"] *
df["Return_Benchmark"])
expected_excess_return = portfolio_total_return -
benchmark_total_return
```

```
# Normalize total attribution effect to match expected
excess return
scaling_factor = expected_excess_return / sum(total_
effects.values()) if sum(total_effects.values()) != 0
else 1
total_effects = {key: value * scaling_factor for key,
value in total_effects.items()}

# Calculate total attribution effect
total_attribution_effect = sum(total_effects.values())
total_effects["Total Attribution Effect"] = total_
attribution_effect

# Display results
print(df[["Bond", "Duration_Effect", "Yield_Curve_Effect",
"Credit_Spread_Effect", "Carry_Effect", "Selection_
Effect", "Allocation_Effect"]])
print("\nTotal Attribution Effects:")
for key, value in total_effects.items():
    print(f"{key}: {value:.4f}%")
print(f"\nExpected Excess Return: {expected_excess_
return:.4f}%")
print(f"Discrepancy (Attribution - Expected Excess
Return): {total_attribution_effect - expected_excess_
return:.4f}%")
```

Output:

```
    Bond    Duration_   Yield_Curve_   Credit_Spread_
            Effect      Effect         Effect
0   Bond A  -0.000240      -0.000144        -0.000040
1   Bond B  -0.000355      -0.000213        -0.000060
2   Bond C   0.000077       0.000046        -0.000045
3   Bond D  -0.000113      -0.000068        -0.000050
4   Bond E  -0.000023      -0.000014        -0.000020

   Carry_Effect  Selection_Effect  Allocation_Effect
0         0.040             0.030              0.050
1         0.060             0.075              0.110
2         0.045             0.040             -0.090
3         0.050             0.090             -0.135
4         0.020             0.020              0.000

Total Attribution Effects:
Duration Effect: -0.0003%
```

```
Yield Curve Effect: -0.0002%
Credit Spread Effect: -0.0001%
Carry Effect: 0.1012%
Selection Effect: 0.1200%
Allocation Effect: -0.0306%
Total Attribution Effect: 0.1900%

Expected Excess Return: 0.1900%
Discrepancy (Attribution - Expected Excess Return): -0.0000%
```

Interpretation. –

The carry effect (+0.1012%) and selection effect (+0.1200%) were the primary drivers of outperformance. Interest rate (yield curve effect, −0.0002%; duration effect, −0.0003%) and credit spread positioning (−0.0001%) had a minimal effect, meaning that the portfolio's exposure to macroeconomic factors was relatively neutral. Asset allocation differences (0.0306%) were slightly negative, but they did not significantly drag down performance.

CHAPTER 6

Python Applied to Investment Funds

6.1 CHAPTER OVERVIEW

This chapter introduces how Python can be leveraged to analyse and evaluate investment funds through practical, data-driven approaches. It begins by explaining the structure, types, and management styles of various funds, including mutual funds, ETFs, hedge funds, and REITs, while contrasting active and passive strategies, as well as growth vs. value and income vs. growth approaches. The chapter then shifts to performance evaluation, detailing key financial metrics like annualized return, volatility, Sharpe and Sortino ratios, alpha, beta, tracking error, information ratio, and Calmar ratio. These concepts are implemented in Python through three practical exercises: one using simulated data, one comparing results using the *empyrical* library, and another using real data from Yahoo Finance to compare an index mutual fund and an ETF against the S&P 500 benchmark. With step-by-step coding examples, readers learn how to calculate risk-adjusted performance, interpret fund behaviour relative to benchmarks, and visually assess fund performance over time – bridging theory with hands-on application for fund analysis.

6.2 INTRODUCTION TO INVESTMENT FUNDS

Investment funds are pooled investment vehicles where multiple investors combine their capital to invest collectively in securities such as stocks,

DOI: 10.1201/9781003781394-6

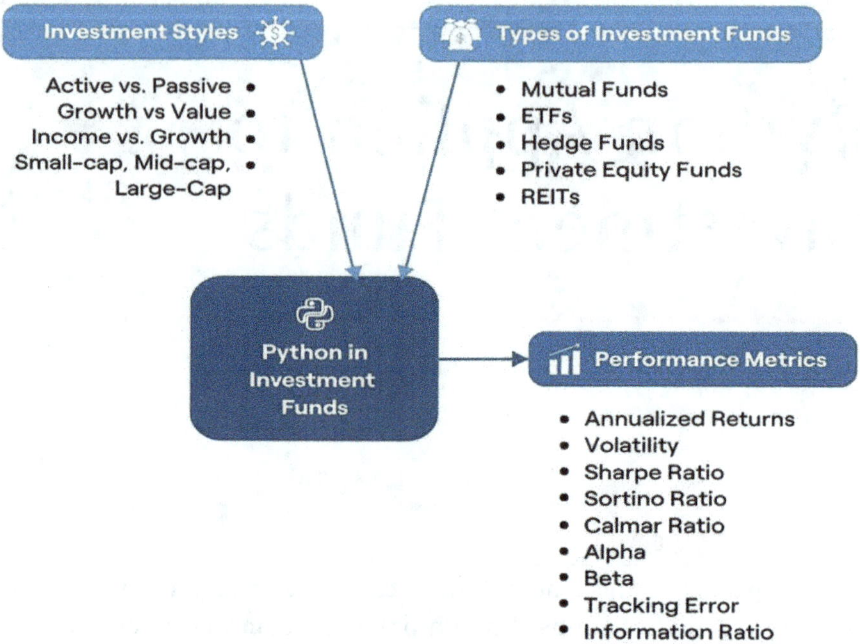

FIGURE 6.1 Python in Investment Funds: Types, Styles & Metrics

bonds, or other assets. Managed by professional fund managers, these funds offer diversification, professional management, and economies of scale, making investing accessible to both individual and institutional investors.

Python has become a key tool in asset management due to its flexibility, efficiency, and extensive ecosystem of libraries for data analysis, portfolio management, and automation. When applied to investment funds, Python provides significant advantages over traditional tools like Excel or Bloomberg Terminal scripting:

- Python simplifies the retrieval, cleaning, and analysis of fund data from Yahoo Finance, Morningstar, Bloomberg, and other sources.
- Libraries like *pandas* and *numpy* make working with large datasets more efficient than spreadsheets.
- Time-series analysis for NAV tracking, performance attribution, and factor analysis is seamless with *statsmodels* and *scipy*.

- Fund managers can automate portfolio monitoring, rebalancing, and reporting, saving time and reducing human error.
- Web scraping and APIs allow for real-time tracking of fund inflows/outflows and market conditions.
- Python can execute automated strategies that rebalance portfolios based on predefined rules.

The following is an introduction to the characteristics and types of the investment funds, their styles, and the main metrics of their performance.

6.2.1 Types of Investment Funds

6.2.1.1 Mutual Funds

Mutual funds pool money from numerous investors to buy a diversified portfolio of stocks, bonds, or other securities. They are typically open-ended, meaning they can issue and redeem shares daily at their net asset value (NAV). There are several subtypes:

a) Equity Funds: Invest primarily in stocks.

b) Bond Funds: Focus on fixed-income securities.

c) Balanced (Hybrid) Funds: Combine stocks and bonds.

d) Money Market Funds: Invest in short-term, low-risk debt securities.

6.2.1.2 Exchange-Traded Funds (ETFs)

ETFs are similar to mutual funds but trade like stocks on an exchange. They often track indexes (passive management) but may also be actively managed.

6.2.1.3 Hedge Funds

Hedge funds are alternative investments employing various strategies like leveraging, short selling, and derivatives. They aim for high returns, often with higher risks, and are typically accessible only to accredited investors.

6.2.1.4 Private Equity Funds

These funds invest in private companies or buy out public companies to delist them. They aim for long-term capital appreciation and typically have a long investment horizon (5–10 years).

6.2.1.5 Real Estate Investment Trusts (REITs)

REITs invest directly in real estate properties or mortgages. They trade on exchanges like stocks and provide investors with exposure to real estate markets, usually offering regular dividend income.

6.2.2 Investment Styles

Investment styles refer to the approaches fund managers or investors take to select securities and manage portfolios, focusing on different objectives like growth, value, income, or size of companies.

6.2.2.1 Active vs. Passive Management

The key focus here is the performance relative to market or benchmark indexes. *Active management* fund managers actively select securities, aiming to outperform market benchmarks through research and analysis. *Passive management* funds aim to replicate the performance of a benchmark index, typically involving lower fees and less frequent trading.

6.2.2.2 Growth vs. Value

The key focus here is expected growth vs. undervaluation. *Growth investing* involves investing in companies expected to grow faster than the market average, often characterized by high earnings growth. *Value investing* focuses on companies trading at a price below their intrinsic value, based on fundamental analysis, aiming for eventual price appreciation

6.2.2.3 Income vs. Growth

The key focus of these styles is the immediate income generation vs. long-term capital appreciation. *Income investing* seeks regular and reliable income through dividends or interest payments, suitable for investors prioritizing cash flow. *Growth investing* prioritizes capital appreciation, aiming for an increase in investment value over time rather than immediate income.

6.2.2.4 Small-Cap, Mid-Cap, and Large-Cap

The key focus of these styles is the size of the companies in which the fund invests. *Small-cap funds* invest in smaller companies with high growth potential but higher risk and volatility. *Mid-cap funds* focus on mid-sized companies, balancing growth opportunities with relatively moderate risk. *Large-cap funds* invest in large, well-established companies, generally providing more stability and lower risk.

Investment funds provide investors with an efficient way to diversify and access professional management. Understanding the various types and styles can help investors select funds aligned with their investment goals, risk tolerance, and financial objectives.

6.3 METRICS TO EVALUATE FUND PERFORMANCE

Evaluating fund performance requires understanding specific metrics that shed light on returns, risks, and efficiency. This section provides a look at the most important metrics, including their explanations, formulas, and practical relevance.

6.3.1 Annualized Returns

Annualized returns standardize returns on an annual basis, allowing investors to compare the performance of investments over different periods effectively:

$$Annualized\,Return = \left(\frac{Ending\,Value}{Beginning\,Value} \right)^{1/n} - 1$$

where "n" is number of years

Annualized returns enable comparison across various funds, irrespective of their holding periods.

6.3.2 Volatility (Annualized Standard Deviation)

Volatility measures the degree of variation in a fund's returns over a specified period. Annualizing volatility helps standardize this risk metric:

$$Annualized\,Volatility = \sigma_p x \sqrt{Number\,of\ periods}$$

where "σ_p" is standard deviation of periodic returns.

Higher volatility implies higher risk, reflecting larger swings in fund performance. This metrics is Important for assessing risk levels, especially for investors with low-risk tolerance or when comparing funds with similar returns but different risk levels.

6.3.3 Sharpe Ratio

The Sharpe ratio is one of the most widely used metrics for evaluating fund performance on a risk-adjusted basis. It measures how much excess return a fund generates per unit of volatility compared to a risk-free asset:

$$Sharpe\ Ratio = \frac{R_p - R_f}{\sigma_p}$$

where

- R_p: Fund return
- R_f: Risk-free rate (e.g., yield on treasury bills)
- σ_p: Standard deviation of the fund's returns

A higher Sharpe ratio indicates better risk-adjusted performance. It is especially useful for comparing funds with similar objectives. Ideal for comparing funds with similar objectives, especially when assessing whether higher returns justify increased risk.

6.3.4 Sortino Ratio

The Sortino ratio is similar to the Sharpe ratio but differentiates harmful volatility from total volatility by considering only downside risk:

$$Sortino\ Ratio = \frac{R_p - R_f}{\sigma_{downside}}$$

where "$\sigma_{downside}$" is the standard deviation of negative (downside) returns.

A higher Sortino ratio suggests a better risk-adjusted performance, especially in volatile markets, by penalizing downside volatility more heavily.

6.3.5 Calmar Ratio

The Calmar ratio assesses the risk-adjusted return of a fund by comparing its annualized return to its maximum drawdown:

$$Calmar\ Ratio = \frac{Annualized\ Return}{Maximum\ Drawdown}$$

A higher Calmar ratio suggests that a fund delivers strong returns relative to its worst historical losses, making it particularly useful for evaluating hedge funds and mutual funds with significant volatility.

6.3.6 Alpha

Alpha measures the value added by a fund manager through active management, reflecting the excess returns compared to a benchmark adjusted for risk.

$$\alpha = R_p' - \left(R_f + \beta_p\left(R_b - R_f\right)\right)$$

where

- R_p' is the return obtained by the fund
- B_p is the beta of the fund relative to the benchmark
- R_b is the benchmark or market return
- R_f is the risk-free rate

Positive alpha indicates the manager's skill in generating returns above the expected level based on the fund's risk profile. Negative alpha suggests underperformance. Alpha is best used for evaluating actively managed funds, assessing whether the manager provides value beyond market movements.

6.3.7 Beta

Beta measures a fund's sensitivity to movements in its benchmark or the overall market. It is a measure of systematic risk:

$$\beta_p = \frac{\text{cov}_{p,b}}{\sigma_b^2}$$

where

- $\text{cov}_{p,M}$ is the covariance of fund returns and benchmark returns
- $\sigma^2{}_M$ is the variance of the benchmark

A beta greater than 1 implies that the fund is expected to move more than the market, both up and down. A beta less than 1 indicates lower sensitivity to market movements. Beta is ideal for determining a fund's relative risk exposure and how it might behave in different market conditions.

6.3.8 Tracking Error

Tracking error measures the consistency of a fund's returns relative to its benchmark by calculating the standard deviation of excess returns over the benchmark:

$$Tracking\ Error = \sqrt{\frac{\sum\left(R_p - R_b\right)^2}{n-1}}$$

where

- R_p is the return obtained by the fund
- R_b is the benchmark or market return
- n is the number of return periods

A lower tracking error indicates that the fund closely follows its benchmark, while a higher tracking error suggests greater deviation, which may be expected in actively managed funds.

6.3.9 Information Ratio

The information ratio measures a fund manager's ability to generate excess returns relative to a benchmark, adjusted for tracking error:

$$Information\,Ratio = \frac{R_p - R_b}{Tracking\ Error}$$

A higher information ratio suggests that the fund consistently generates excess returns relative to its benchmark, making it a valuable metric for assessing active management performance.

PRACTICAL EXERCISE #6.01 COMPARING FUND WITH BENCHMARK PERFORMANCES

Request: Using Python, simulate daily returns for both the fund and its benchmark, then compute essential financial metrics such as annualized return, volatility, Sharpe ratio, Sortino ratio, tracking error, information ratio, alpha, beta, and Calmar ratio. Additionally, the exercise should include a visual comparison of cumulative fund returns against benchmark returns, helping to illustrate performance trends over time.

Summary of the script. –

This Python script simulates and analyses the performance of an investment fund compared to a benchmark over a one-year period (252 trading days). It calculates key risk and return metrics, displaying both numerical results and a cumulative return plot. Steps:

a) Data Simulation: generates daily returns, ensures reproducibility, stores the simulated returns.
b) Return Metrics: annualized return, benchmark annualized return.
c) Risk Metrics: annualized volatility, Sharpe ratio, Sortino ratio, maximum drawdown.
d) Performance vs. Benchmark: tracking error, information ratio, beta, alpha, Calmar ratio.
e) Results Display and Visualization.

TABLE 6.1 Summary of Key Functions and Their Purposes

Function/Calculation	Purpose
np.random.normal( )	Generates simulated daily returns for the fund and benchmark.
pd.DataFrame( )	Stores and organizes fund and benchmark returns.
set_index('Date')	Sets the date as the index for time-series analysis.
calculate_metrics (df, risk_free_rate)	Computes key performance metrics of the fund.
cumulative_return	Computes the total return over the period.
annualized_return	Converts cumulative return into an annualized rate.
annualized_volatility	Measures fund return fluctuations, annualized.
sharpe_ratio	Evaluates risk-adjusted performance using total volatility.
sortino_ratio	Evaluates risk-adjusted performance using downside risk only.
max_drawdown	Captures the worst peak-to-trough decline.
tracking_error	Measures deviation from the benchmark.
information_ratio	Evaluates fund manager's skill in outperforming the benchmark.
beta	Measures the fund's sensitivity to the benchmark's movements.
alpha	Determines excess return after adjusting for risk (outperformance).
calmar_ratio	Assesses risk-adjusted return based on maximum drawdown.

Script execution and output. –

```
import numpy as np
import pandas as pd
import matplotlib.pyplot as plt
```

```
# Sample data: Simulated daily returns of a fund and benchmark
np.random.seed(42)
dates = pd.date_range(start='2025-01-01', periods=252,
freq='B')
fund_returns = np.random.normal(0.0005, 0.01, len(dates))
# Simulating daily fund returns
benchmark_returns = np.random.normal(0.0004, 0.009,
len(dates))  # Simulating benchmark returns

# Convert to pandas DataFrame
data = pd.DataFrame({'Date': dates, 'Fund_Returns': fund_
returns, 'Benchmark_Returns': benchmark_returns})
data.set_index('Date', inplace=True)

# Risk-free rate (annualized)
risk_free_rate = 0.02
trading_days = 252  # Annual trading days

# Function to calculate key metrics
def calculate_metrics(df, risk_free_rate):
    excess_returns = df['Fund_Returns'] - df['Benchmark_
    Returns']
    cumulative_return = (1 + df['Fund_Returns']).prod() - 1
    annualized_return = (1 + cumulative_return) **
    (trading_days / len(df)) - 1
    benchmark_cumulative_return = (1 + df['Benchmark_
    Returns']).prod() - 1
    benchmark_annualized_return = (1 + benchmark_
    cumulative_return) ** (trading_days / len(df)) - 1
    annualized_volatility = df['Fund_Returns'].std() *
    np.sqrt(trading_days)
    sharpe_ratio = (annualized_return - risk_free_rate) /
    annualized_volatility
    sortino_ratio = (annualized_return - risk_free_rate) /
    (df[df['Fund_Returns'] < 0]['Fund_Returns'].std() *
    np.sqrt(trading_days))
    max_drawdown = (df['Fund_Returns'].cumsum().expanding().
    max() - df['Fund_Returns'].cumsum()).max()
    tracking_error = np.std(excess_returns) *
    np.sqrt(trading_days)
    information_ratio = (annualized_return -
    df['Benchmark_Returns'].mean() * trading_days) /
    tracking_error
    beta = np.cov(df['Fund_Returns'], df['Benchmark_
    Returns'])[0,1] / np.var(df['Benchmark_Returns'])
    alpha = annualized_return - (risk_free_rate + beta *
    (df['Benchmark_Returns'].mean() * trading_days - risk_
    free_rate))
    calmar_ratio = annualized_return / abs(max_drawdown)
```

```
    return {
        'Annualized Return': annualized_return,
        'Benchmark Annualized Return': benchmark_
        annualized_return,
        'Annualized Volatility': annualized_volatility,
        'Sharpe Ratio': sharpe_ratio,
        'Sortino Ratio': sortino_ratio,
        'Maximum Drawdown': max_drawdown,
        'Tracking Error': tracking_error,
        'Information Ratio': information_ratio,
        'Beta': beta,
        'Alpha': alpha,
        'Calmar Ratio': calmar_ratio
    }

# Calculate metrics
metrics = calculate_metrics(data, risk_free_rate)

# Display results
for metric, value in metrics.items():
    print(f"{metric}: {value:.4f}")

# Plot Fund vs. Benchmark Returns Over Time
plt.figure(figsize=(10, 5))
plt.plot(data.index, data['Fund_Returns'].cumsum(),
label='Fund', color='blue')
plt.plot(data.index, data['Benchmark_Returns'].cumsum(),
label='Benchmark', color='orange')
plt.xlabel("Date")
plt.ylabel("Cumulative Returns")
plt.title("Comparison of Fund and Benchmark Cumulative
Returns")
plt.legend()
plt.show()
```

Output:

```
Annualized Return: 0.1105
Benchmark Annualized Return: 0.1593
Annualized Volatility: 0.1535
Sharpe Ratio: 0.5892
Sortino Ratio: 1.0758
Maximum Drawdown: 0.1434
Tracking Error: 0.2072
Information Ratio: -0.2299
Beta: 0.0238
Alpha: 0.0872
Calmar Ratio: 0.7702
```

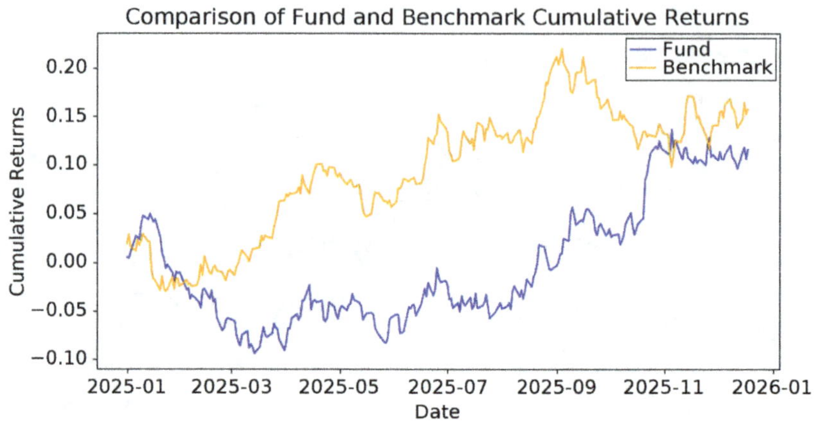

PRACTICAL EXERCISE #6.02 COMPARING FUND WITH BENCHMARK PERFORMANCES

Request: Repeat the former exercise but using the *empyrical* module.

Script execution and output. –

```
import numpy as np
import pandas as pd
import matplotlib.pyplot as plt
import empyrical as ep  # Importing empyrical for financial
metrics

# Sample data: Simulated daily returns of a fund and benchmark
np.random.seed(42)
dates = pd.date_range(start='2025-01-01', periods=252,
freq='B')
fund_returns = np.random.normal(0.0005, 0.01, len(dates))
# Simulating daily fund returns
benchmark_returns = np.random.normal(0.0004, 0.009,
len(dates))  # Simulating benchmark returns

# Convert to pandas DataFrame
data = pd.DataFrame({'Date': dates, 'Fund_Returns': fund_
returns, 'Benchmark_Returns': benchmark_returns})
data.set_index('Date', inplace=True)

# Risk-free rate (daily rate)
risk_free_rate = 0.02 / 252  # Convert annual rate to daily

# Function to calculate key metrics using empyrical
def calculate_metrics(df, risk_free_rate):
    fund = df['Fund_Returns']
```

```
    benchmark = df['Benchmark_Returns']
    excess_returns = fund - benchmark  # Required for
    tracking error and information ratio

    annualized_return = ep.annual_return(fund)
    benchmark_annualized_return = ep.annual_
    return(benchmark)
    annualized_volatility = ep.annual_volatility(fund)
    sharpe_ratio = ep.sharpe_ratio(fund, risk_free=risk_
    free_rate)
    sortino_ratio = ep.sortino_ratio(fund, required_
    return=risk_free_rate)
    max_drawdown = ep.max_drawdown(fund)

    # FIX: Manually calculate Tracking Error
    tracking_error = excess_returns.std() * np.sqrt(252)

    # FIX: Manually calculate Information Ratio
    excess_annualized_return = annualized_return -
    benchmark_annualized_return
    information_ratio = excess_annualized_return /
    tracking_error if tracking_error != 0 else np.nan

    beta = ep.beta(fund, benchmark)
    alpha = ep.alpha(fund, benchmark, risk_free=risk_free_rate)
    calmar_ratio = ep.calmar_ratio(fund)

    return {
        'Annualized Return': annualized_return,
        'Benchmark Annualized Return': benchmark_
        annualized_return,
        'Annualized Volatility': annualized_volatility,
        'Sharpe Ratio': sharpe_ratio,
        'Sortino Ratio': sortino_ratio,
        'Maximum Drawdown': max_drawdown,
        'Tracking Error': tracking_error,
        'Information Ratio': information_ratio,
        'Beta': beta,
        'Alpha': alpha,
        'Calmar Ratio': calmar_ratio
    }

# Calculate metrics
metrics = calculate_metrics(data, risk_free_rate)

# Display results
for metric, value in metrics.items():
    print(f"{metric}: {value:.4f}")

# Plot Fund vs. Benchmark Returns Over Time
plt.figure(figsize=(10, 5))
```

```
plt.plot(data.index, data['Fund_Returns'].cumsum(),
label='Fund', color='blue')
plt.plot(data.index, data['Benchmark_Returns'].cumsum(),
label='Benchmark', color='orange')
plt.xlabel("Date")
plt.ylabel("Cumulative Returns")
plt.title("Comparison of Fund and Benchmark Cumulative
Returns")
plt.legend()
plt.show()
```

Output:

```
Annualized Return: 0.1105
Benchmark Annualized Return: 0.1593
Annualized Volatility: 0.1535
Sharpe Ratio: 0.6286
Sortino Ratio: 0.9458
Maximum Drawdown: -0.1353
Tracking Error: 0.2076
Information Ratio: -0.2354
Beta: 0.0238
Alpha: 0.0977
Calmar Ratio: 0.8167
```

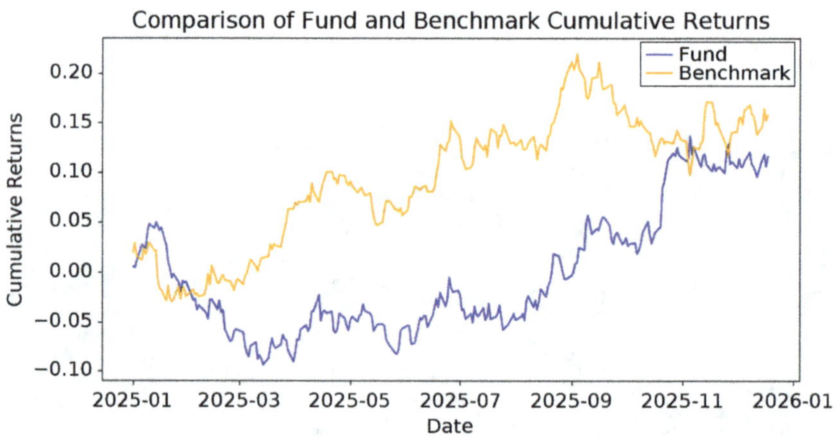

The discrepancies between the original results (#6.01) and the results using the module *empyrical* (#6.02) are small, but let's analyse where they come from:

- Sharpe Ratio (0.5892 → 0.6286): *empyrical.sharpe_ratio()* uses a rolling method for excess returns, possibly leading to a small difference in calculation. Moreover, the manual calculation likely used simple effects, while *empyrical* accounts for compounding effects.

- Sortino Ratio (1.0758 → 0.9458): *empyrical.sortino_ratio()* may calculate downside deviation differently. The manual calculation might not be annualizing downside deviation the same way.
- Alpha (0.0872 → 0.0977): This is calculated using *empyrical.alpha()*, which might use a more refined regression-based approach than the manual method.
- Maximum Drawdown (0.1434 → 0.1353): The manual calculation uses daily drawdowns directly, while *Empyrical* ensures logarithmic compounding and may apply a rolling window to smooth data.
- Calmar Ratio (0.7702 → 0.8167): This depends on the annualized return and drawdown calculation. Since *empyrical.max_drawdown()* gives a slightly different result, it affects Calmar ratio.

PRACTICAL EXERCISE #6.03 COMPARING FUND WITH BENCHMARK PERFORMANCES

Request: In this exercise, you will compare the performance of an index mutual fund with the performance of an ETF relative to their market benchmark using real-world financial data from Yahoo Finance. You will compute key risk-adjusted metrics such as Sharpe ratio, alpha, beta, tracking Error, Sortino ratio, maximum drawdown, and Calmar ratio with the *Empyrical* module. Additionally, you will plot the rebased performance of the fund vs. the benchmark.

Summary of the script. –

This Python script analyses the performance of a mutual fund relative to a market benchmark using real financial data from Yahoo Finance. It computes key risk-adjusted metrics and visualizes performance over time. Steps:

a) Data Collection
   - Yahoo Finance (yfinance) is used to download daily adjusted closing prices for:
   - Fund: "VFINX" (Vanguard 500 Index Fund)
   - ETF: "IVV" (iShares Core S&P 500 ETF)
   - Benchmark: "^GSPC" (S&P 500 Index)

b) Performance Metrics Calculation

c) Visualization: Rebased Performance Plot

TABLE 6.2 Summary of Key Functions and Their Purposes

Function Name	Purpose
yf.download( )	Fetches historical price data for funds and benchmark from Yahoo Finance.
.align( )	Ensures all datasets have the same date index to avoid mismatches.
.pct_change( ) .dropna( ).squeeze( )	Computes daily returns and ensures they are 1D pandas series.
compute_metrics_ empyrical( )	Computes key performance metrics using the empyrical library.
ep.annual_return( )	Calculates the annualized return of a fund.
ep.annual_volatility( )	Computes the annualized standard deviation of returns (volatility).
ep.sharpe_ratio( )	Measures risk-adjusted return relative to the risk-free rate.
ep.sortino_ratio( )	Similar to Sharpe but penalizes only downside risk.
ep.max_drawdown( )	Finds the largest peak-to-trough loss during the period.
ep.beta( )	Measures the fund's sensitivity to the benchmark.
ep.alpha( )	Calculates the fund's excess return over the benchmark, adjusted for risk.
ep.calmar_ratio( )	Compares annualized return to maximum drawdown (risk-adjusted performance).

Script execution and output. –

```
import yfinance as yf
import pandas as pd
import numpy as np
import matplotlib.pyplot as plt
import empyrical as ep

# Define tickers for funds and benchmark
fund1_ticker = "IVV"    # iShares Core S&P 500 ETF
fund2_ticker = "VFINX" # Vanguard 500 Index Fund
benchmark_ticker = "^GSPC"  # S&P 500 Index

# Fetch historical price data
start_date = "2020-01-01"
end_date = "2025-01-01"

fund1_data = yf.download(fund1_ticker, start=start_date,
end=end_date, auto_adjust=True, progress=False)['Close']
fund2_data = yf.download(fund2_ticker, start=start_date,
end=end_date, auto_adjust=True, progress=False)['Close']
benchmark_data = yf.download(benchmark_ticker,
start=start_date, auto_adjust=True, end=end_date,
progress=False)['Close']
```

```
# Align data to avoid mismatches
fund1_data, benchmark_data = fund1_data.align(benchmark_
data, join='inner', axis=0)
fund2_data, benchmark_data = fund2_data.align(benchmark_
data, join='inner', axis=0)


# Compute daily returns (Ensure 1D pandas Series)
fund1_returns = fund1_data.pct_change().dropna().squeeze()
fund2_returns = fund2_data.pct_change().dropna().squeeze()
benchmark_returns = benchmark_data.pct_change().dropna().s
queeze()

# --- EMPYRICAL CALCULATIONS FUNCTION ---
def compute_metrics_empyrical(fund_returns, benchmark_
returns, risk_free_rate=0.02 / 252):
    # Ensure inputs are 1D pandas Series
    fund_returns = fund_returns.squeeze()
    benchmark_returns = benchmark_returns.squeeze()

    annualized_return = ep.annual_return(fund_returns)
    annualized_volatility = ep.annual_volatility(fund_returns)
    sharpe_ratio = ep.sharpe_ratio(fund_returns, risk_
    free=risk_free_rate)
    sortino_ratio = ep.sortino_ratio(fund_returns,
    required_return=risk_free_rate)
    max_drawdown = ep.max_drawdown(fund_returns)
    beta = ep.beta(fund_returns, benchmark_returns)
    alpha = ep.alpha(fund_returns, benchmark_returns,
    risk_free=risk_free_rate)
    calmar_ratio = ep.calmar_ratio(fund_returns)

    # Manually compute missing metrics
    tracking_error = (fund_returns - benchmark_
    returns).std() * np.sqrt(252)
    excess_return = ep.annual_return(fund_returns) -
    ep.annual_return(benchmark_returns)
    information_ratio = excess_return / tracking_error if
    tracking_error != 0 else np.nan

    return [annualized_return, annualized_volatility,
    sharpe_ratio, alpha, beta,
            tracking_error, information_ratio, sortino_
            ratio, max_drawdown, calmar_ratio]

# Compute metrics for both funds AND the S&P 500 index
metrics_labels = ["Annualized Return", "Annualized
Volatility", "Sharpe Ratio", "Alpha (Annualized)", "Beta",
                  "Tracking Error", "Information Ratio",
                  "Sortino Ratio", "Maximum Drawdown",
                  "Calmar Ratio"]
```

```
fund1_metrics = compute_metrics_empyrical(fund1_returns,
benchmark_returns)
fund2_metrics = compute_metrics_empyrical(fund2_returns,
benchmark_returns)
sp500_metrics = compute_metrics_empyrical(benchmark_
returns, benchmark_returns)  # S&P 500 self-comparison

# Create DataFrame for display
performance_metrics_df = pd.DataFrame({
    "Metric": metrics_labels,
    fund1_ticker: fund1_metrics,
    fund2_ticker: fund2_metrics,
    "S&P 500": sp500_metrics
})

# Display comparison table
print(performance_metrics_df)

# ========== PLOTTING REBASED PERFORMANCE ==========
plt.figure(figsize=(12, 6))

# Rebase all three series to 100
fund1_rebased = (fund1_data / fund1_data.iloc[0]) * 100
fund2_rebased = (fund2_data / fund2_data.iloc[0]) * 100
benchmark_rebased = (benchmark_data / benchmark_
data.iloc[0]) * 100

# Plot Funds vs. Benchmark
plt.plot(fund1_rebased, label=fund1_ticker, color='blue',
linewidth=2, alpha=0.7)
plt.plot(fund2_rebased, label=fund2_ticker, color='green',
linewidth=2, alpha=0.7)
plt.plot(benchmark_rebased, label=benchmark_ticker,
color='red', linestyle="dashed", linewidth=2, alpha=0.7)

# Formatting
plt.title("Rebased Performance (100 at Start)")
plt.xlabel("Date")
plt.ylabel("Index Value (Rebased to 100)")
plt.legend()
plt.grid()

# Show plot
plt.show()
```

Output:

```
                Metric       IVV     VFINX   S&P 500
0    Annualized Return  0.143275  0.141970  0.125734
1 Annualized Volatility 0.213286  0.213420  0.213399
2         Sharpe Ratio  0.641304  0.635688  0.568602
3   Alpha (Annualized)  0.015730  0.014427  0.000000
4                 Beta  0.998633  1.000045  1.000000
5       Tracking Error  0.008726  0.002204  0.000000
6    Information Ratio  2.010198  7.366336       NaN
7        Sortino Ratio  0.895058  0.887638  0.791845
8     Maximum Drawdown -0.339031 -0.338297 -0.339250
9         Calmar Ratio  0.422600  0.419660  0.370624
```

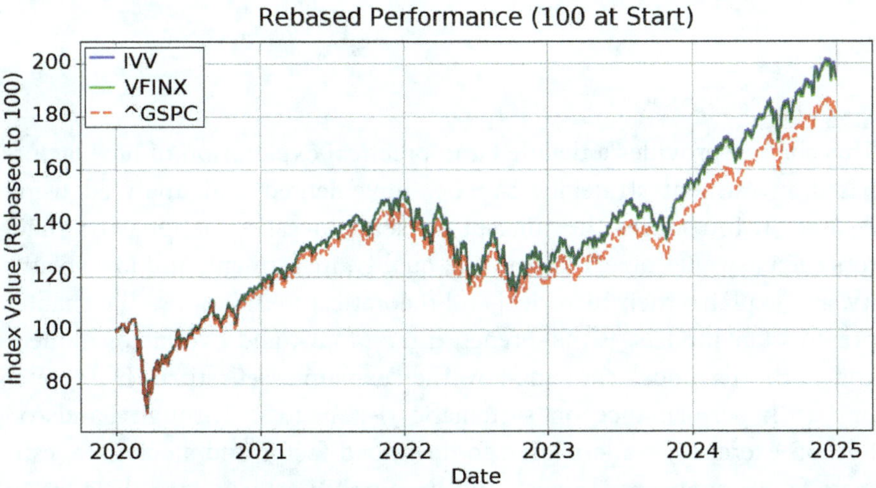

CHAPTER 7

Python Applied to Factor Investing

7.1 CHAPTER OVERVIEW

This chapter provides a detailed and practical exploration of how factor-based investment strategies can be implemented and analysed using Python. It introduces the concept of factor investing, emphasizing factors such as value, size, momentum, quality, investment, and low volatility, and explains their historical and theoretical foundations. The chapter presents key models, Fama–French three-, four-, and five-factor models, and Carhart's model, showing how they explain asset returns by regressing stock performance on systematic risk factors. Through hands-on Python exercises, readers learn to download factor and stock data, estimate factor exposures (betas), and decompose returns into their factor contributions. The chapter also explores Smart Beta strategies, comparing equally weighted and momentum-based IBEX 35 portfolios against traditional benchmarks. It culminates in an in-depth analysis of Fama–French five-factor portfolios using regression, heatmaps, and performance metrics, offering students and professionals a powerful toolkit to understand, apply, and evaluate factor-based investing in real markets.

7.2 PYTHON APPLIED TO FACTOR INVESTING

Factor investing has emerged as a prominent strategy in the world of asset management, providing a systematic approach to capturing specific drivers of returns across asset classes. By focusing on various factors, such

DOI: 10.1201/9781003781394-7

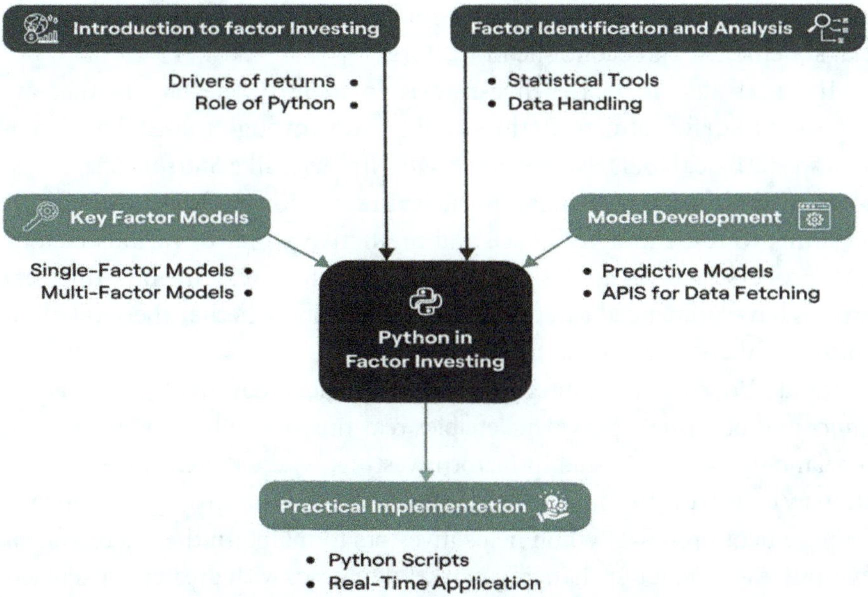

FIGURE 7.1 Python in Factor Investing: Structure and Applications

as value, momentum, size, and quality, investors can construct portfolios that are designed to outperform traditional benchmarks. In recent years, Python has become an indispensable tool in the implementation and analysis of factor investing strategies, offering a powerful and flexible platform for data analysis, model development, and portfolio optimization.

Factor investing involves identifying and harnessing the influence of specific factors that drive returns in the financial markets. These factors, such as value, momentum, size, and volatility, represent underlying characteristics that can explain the performance of stocks and other assets over time. The challenge for investors lies in accurately identifying these factors, constructing portfolios that are exposed to them, and continuously monitoring and adjusting those exposures to maintain optimal performance.

Python's extensive library ecosystem makes it particularly well suited for factor investing. It provides tools for data collection, processing, and analysis, which are essential for identifying factors and constructing factor-based portfolios. Libraries like *Pandas* and *NumPy* allow investors to efficiently manipulate large datasets, such as historical price data, financial statements, and economic indicators.

The first step in factor investing is to identify the factors that are expected to drive returns. Python enables this through robust data analysis and statistical tools. For instance, with libraries like *Statsmodels*, investors can apply statistical methods, such as regression analysis and machine learning, to test the significance and predictive power of various factors. This process involves analysing historical data to determine how different factors have influenced asset prices over time and whether these relationships are likely to persist in the future.

In addition, Python's integration with financial data APIs, such as *yfinance* and other data providers, enables real-time portfolio monitoring and rebalancing. This is crucial in factor investing, where the effectiveness of a strategy can change as market conditions evolve. By automating the portfolio management process, Python helps investors to maintain the desired factor exposures and adapt to changing market dynamics with greater efficiency.

Another advantage of using Python in factor investing is its ability to enhance transparency and customization. Unlike proprietary software, Python's open-source nature allows investors to fully understand and control the models and algorithms used in their strategies. This transparency is important for managing risk and ensuring that the strategy aligns with the investor's objectives and risk tolerance.

7.3 ANALYSING FACTOR EVOLUTION

Factor investing, also known as factor-based investing, is a strategic approach to portfolio management that focuses on specific factors that have demonstrated significant influence on the returns of financial assets (Blitz, 2015). These factors can include characteristics such as market value, company size, profitability, and other aspects that go beyond simple asset diversification.

Unlike traditional asset allocation strategies based on asset class diversification, factor investing seeks to exploit systemic anomalies in financial markets by leveraging specific characteristics that impact asset performance.

Factor-based portfolio management provides investors with additional tools to understand and manage the risk and performance of their portfolios. It enables investment managers to make more informed decisions by considering not only historical returns but also the specific characteristics of assets that may influence their future behaviour. Instead of focusing on a single factor, many investors are integrating multiple factors into their investment strategies to capture a broader range of potential sources of return and reduce the specific risk of each factor.

The extension of the CAPM model by Fama and French introduced the factors of size and value, providing a more comprehensive framework for explaining stock returns. As market conditions evolve and investor preferences change, new investment factors are likely to emerge while others may lose relevance (Blitz, 2015).

Typically, besides the market, the following six investment style factors are used to select individual stocks: value, size, volatility, momentum, quality, and investment.

- The value factor is referred to as HML (high minus low) and it is the return of companies with high book value relative to their market value minus the return of companies with low book value relative to their market value.
- The size factor is known as SMB (small minus big) and refers to the excess returns that small-cap companies generate over large-cap companies in the long term. Small-cap companies typically have a market capitalization between USD 300 million and USD 2 billion.
- The quality factor is known as RMW (robust minus weak) and aims to capture the differences in performance between companies with robust operating profitability and those with weaker operating profitability.
- The investment factor is known as CMA (conservative minus aggressive) and aims to capture the differences in performance between companies with small investments and companies with large investments.
- The momentum (MOM) factor is known as UMD (up minus down) or WML (winners minus losers) and is represented by the weighted average performance of the top 30% of stocks with the highest momentum, minus the weighted average performance of the bottom 30% of stocks with the lowest momentum, reset every month.
- The low volatility factor captures the excess risk-adjusted returns of low-volatility stocks (low beta or idiosyncratic risk) compared to high-volatility stocks (Blitz & van Vliet, 2007).

The premises on which these factors are based on are as follows:

- Value: Undervalued stocks outperform overvalued ones.
- Size: Smaller stocks outperform larger ones.

- Quality: High returns on capital are better than low ones.
- Investment: Lower investment beats higher investment.
- Volatility: Low-volatility stocks outperform high-volatility ones.
- Momentum: Stocks that are trending upward will continue to do so.

PRACTICAL EXERCISE #7.01 FACTOR EVOLUTION

Request: Analyse the evolution of the investing factors in the last ten years in the US market.

Summary of the script. –
This code downloads and processes financial factor data from Ken French's Data Library, specifically the Fama–French 5 factors and momentum factor, to analyse their cumulative performance over time. Key steps in the code:

a) Download Data:
   - The code downloads two ZIP files containing:
     i) Fama–French 5 Factors (Mkt-RF, SMB, HML, RMW, CMA)
     ii) Momentum Factor
   - The ZIP files are extracted, and the CSV files are saved locally.

b) Load and Preprocess Data:
   - The CSV files are read into Pandas DataFrames.
   - The first column is renamed to "Date".
   - Non-convertible date values are removed.
   - The date format is converted to datetime.

c) Merge and Clean Data:
   - The two datasets are merged on the "Date" column using an outer join to ensure complete coverage.
   - The data is sorted by date.
   - Missing values (NaNs) are dropped.
   - The risk-free rate column (RF) is removed, as it is not needed for analysis.

d) Column Renaming:
   - Factors are renamed for better readability:

e) Filter Data by Date Range:
   - Filters the data between July 1980 and May 2024 to focus on a specific period.
   - Handles potential date conversion errors.

f) Cumulative Index Calculation (Base 100):
   - Each factor starts at an index of 100.

- The cumulative sum of daily returns is added to this base to track performance over time.

g) Visualization:
   - A line plot is created to visualize the cumulative evolution of factors.
   - The graph includes titles, labels, and a legend for clarity.

This code is useful for financial researchers, analysts, and portfolio managers who want to analyse the long-term behaviour of various risk factors affecting stock returns.

TABLE 7.1 Summary of Key Functions and Their Purposes

Function/Calculation	Purpose
requests.get(url)	Downloads the ZIP file containing factor data from Ken French's website.
with open(zip_path, 'wb') as f: f.write(response.content)	Saves the downloaded ZIP file locally.
pd.read_csv(filepath, skiprows=N, low_memory=False)	Reads the extracted CSV file into a Pandas DataFrame, skipping metadata rows.
df_combined = pd.merge(df1, df2, on='Date', how='outer')	Merges the factor and momentum datasets on the Date column.
df_combined.sort_values(by='Date')	Sorts the combined data chronologically.
filtered_factors = df_combined[(df_combined['Date'] >= start_date) & (df_combined['Date'] <= end_date)]	Filters data within the specified date range.
accumulated_factors[column] = 100 + accumulated_factors[column].cumsum( )	Calculates the cumulative return of each factor starting from base 100.

Script execution and outputs. –

```
import pandas as pd
import numpy as np
import requests
import zipfile
from datetime import datetime
import matplotlib.pyplot as plt
```

```
#FF Data Library file download

url = 'https://mba.tuck.dartmouth.edu/pages/faculty/ken.
french/ftp/F-F_Research_Data_5_Factors_2x3_daily_csv.zip'

# Specify the path where you want the file to be saved
zip_path1 = 'F-F_Research_Data_5_Factors_2x3_daily_csv.
zip'

# Make HTTP request to download the file
response = requests.get(url)
with open(zip_path1, 'wb') as f:
            f.write(response.content)
            print(f"File downloaded and saved as: {zip_
            path1}")

with zipfile.ZipFile(zip_path1, 'r') as z:

    # List the names of files in the ZIP to identify the
    CSV
    csv_files = [f for f in z.namelist() if f.endswith('.
    csv')]
    csv_file_name = csv_files[0]
    z.extract(csv_file_name, '.')
    print(f"File '{csv_file_name}' extracted correctly.")
```

Output:

```
File downloaded and saved as: F-F_Research_Data_5_Factors_2x3_
daily_csv.zip
File 'F-F_Research_Data_5_Factors_2x3_daily.csv' extracted
correctly.
```

```
# Load the CSV file, assuming the first column should be
named 'Date'
# and skipping the header

filepath='F-F_Research_Data_5_Factors_2x3_
daily.csv'
factors = pd.read_csv(filepath, skiprows=3, low_
memory=False)
factors.rename(columns={factors.columns[0]: 'Date'},
inplace=True)
factors.tail()
```

Output:

	Date	Mkt-RF	SMB	HML	RMW	CMA	RF
15642	20250826	0.43	0.25	0.13	-0.47	-0.46	0.02
15643	20250827	0.24	0.48	0.27	0.09	0.12	0.02
15644	20250828	0.35	-0.35	-0.52	-0.62	-0.46	0.02
15645	20250829	-0.68	0.22	0.85	0.05	0.55	0.02

```
# Momentum factor
url = 'https://mba.tuck.dartmouth.edu/pages/faculty/ken.
french/ftp/F-F_Momentum_Factor_daily_csv.zip'

# Specify the path where you want the file to be saved
zip_path2 = 'F-F_Momentum_Factor_daily_csv.zip'

# Make HTTP request to download the file
response = requests.get(url)
with open(zip_path2, 'wb') as f:
            f.write(response.content)
            print(f"File downloaded and saved as: {zip_
            path2}")

with zipfile.ZipFile(zip_path2, 'r') as z:

    # List the names of files in the ZIP to identify the
    CSV
    csv_files2 = [f for f in z.namelist() if f.endswith('.
    csv')]
    csv_file_name2 = csv_files2[0]
    z.extract(csv_file_name2, '.')
    print(f"File '{csv_file_name2}' extracted correctly.")
```

Output:

```
File downloaded and saved as: F-F_Momentum_Factor_daily_csv.zip
File 'F-F_Momentum_Factor_daily.csv' extracted correctly.
```

```
# --- Load and clean the Momentum file ---
filepath2 = 'F-F_Momentum_Factor_daily.csv'

# Load the CSV file, skipping the non-data header rows
momentum = pd.read_csv(filepath2, skiprows=13, low_
memory=False)
```

```
momentum.rename(columns={momentum.columns[0]: 'Date'},
inplace=True)

# Extract only 8-digit date strings (YYYYMMDD)
momentum['Date'] = (
    momentum['Date']
    .astype(str)
    .str.extract(r'(\d{8})', expand=False)
)

# Convert 'Date' to datetime format and drop invalid rows
momentum['Date'] = pd.to_datetime(momentum['Date'],
format='%Y%m%d', errors='coerce')
momentum.dropna(subset=['Date'], inplace=True)


# --- Clean the Fama-French 5 Factors file ---
df1 = pd.DataFrame(factors).copy()
df1.columns = df1.columns.str.strip()  # remove extra
spaces in column names

# Rename the date column if it appears with a different
name (e.g., 'DATE')
if 'Date' not in df1.columns:
    date_col = [c for c in df1.columns if c.lower() ==
    'date']
    if date_col:
        df1.rename(columns={date_col[0]: 'Date'},
        inplace=True)

# Extract and convert date values to datetime
df1['Date'] = (
    df1['Date']
    .astype(str)
    .str.extract(r'(\d{8})', expand=False)
)
df1['Date'] = pd.to_datetime(df1['Date'], format='%Y%m%d',
errors='coerce')
df1.dropna(subset=['Date'], inplace=True)

# --- Merge both datasets on 'Date' ---
df_combined = pd.merge(df1, momentum, on='Date',
how='outer')

# --- Sort and clean the merged DataFrame ---
df_combined = df_combined.sort_values(by='Date').dropna()

# --- Display the result ---
print(df_combined.tail())
```

Output:

```
             Date  Mkt-RF   SMB   HML   RMW   CMA    RF   Mom
25960 2025-08-25   -0.48 -0.50  0.45  0.48 -0.02  0.02  0.73
25961 2025-08-26    0.43  0.25  0.13 -0.47 -0.46  0.02  1.15
25962 2025-08-27    0.24  0.48  0.27  0.09  0.12  0.02 -0.51
25963 2025-08-28    0.35 -0.35 -0.52 -0.62 -0.46  0.02  0.73
25964 2025-08-29   -0.68  0.22  0.85  0.05  0.55  0.02 -1.19
```

```
# Drop 'ColumnName'
df_combined.drop('RF', axis=1, inplace=True)
df_combined.head()

# Create a replacement dictionary
replacement = {
    'Mkt-RF': 'Market',
    'SMB': 'Size',
    'HML': 'Value',
    'RMW': 'Quality',
    'CMA': 'Investment',
    'Mom   ': 'Momentum',
    }
# Rename headings
df_combined.rename(columns=replacement, inplace=True)

# See the new headings
df_combined.tail()
```

Output:

```
           Date  Market  Size  Value  Quality  Investment  Momentum
25960 2025-08-25  -0.48 -0.50   0.45     0.48       -0.02      0.73
25961 2025-08-26   0.43  0.25   0.13    -0.47       -0.46      1.15
25962 2025-08-27   0.24  0.48   0.27     0.09        0.12     -0.51
25963 2025-08-28   0.35 -0.35  -0.52    -0.62       -0.46      0.73
25964 2025-08-29  -0.68  0.22   0.85     0.05        0.55     -1.19
```

```
#Filtering data by date
start_date = pd.to_datetime('19800701',format='%Y%m%d')
end_date = pd.to_datetime('20250829',format='%Y%m%d')
try:
    filtered_factors = df_combined[(df_combined['Date'] >=
start_date) & (df_combined['Date'] <= end_date)]
```

```
except TypeError as e:
    print("TypeError encountered:", e)
    print("Re-checking the data types...")
    print(data.dtypes)  # This will help identify if
there's still a data type issue.

# Initialize base 100 for each factor
accumulated_factors = filtered_factors.copy()

# Start each column (factor) at 100 and accumulate daily
changes
for column in accumulated_factors.columns[1:]:
    accumulated_factors[column] = 100 + accumulated_
factors[column].cumsum()


# Graph the cumulative evolution of each factor.
plt.figure(figsize=(10, 6))
for column in accumulated_factors.columns[1:]:
    plt.plot(accumulated_factors['Date'], accumulated_
factors[column], label=column)

# Add title and tags
plt.title('Cumulative Evolution of Factors with Base 100')
plt.xlabel('Date')
plt.ylabel('Index(Base 100)')
plt.legend()
plt.grid(True)
```

Output:

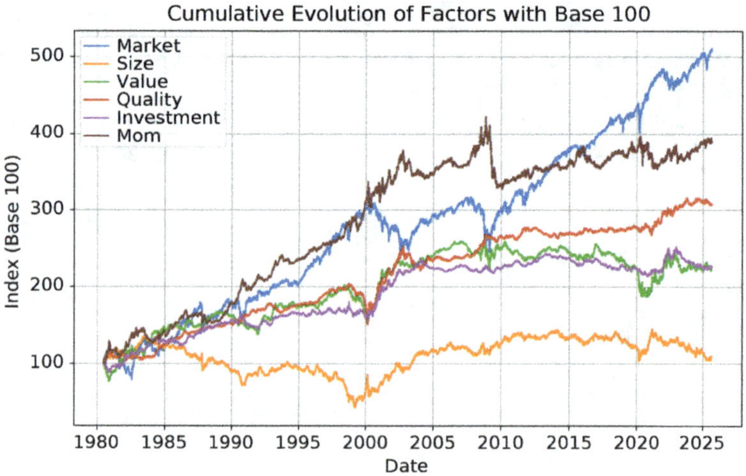

```
# ===========  CORRELATIONS BETWEEN FACTORS  =============

import seaborn as sns

def compute_correlations(df: pd.DataFrame, method: str =
"pearson") -> pd.DataFrame:
    """
    Calculate the correlation matrix between the factors.
    method: 'pearson' (lineal), 'spearman' (ranges) or
    'kendall'.
    """
    # Only numeric columns and no excessive NaNs
    df_num = df.select_dtypes(include=[np.number]).dropna(
    how="any")
    corr = df_num.corr(method=method)
    return corr

def plot_correlation_heatmap(corr: pd.DataFrame, title:
str = "Correlation between factors") -> None:
    """
    Plots a heat map of the correlation matrix.
    """
    plt.figure(figsize=(8,6))
    sns.heatmap(corr, annot=True, fmt=".2f",
    cmap="coolwarm", center=0)
    plt.title(title)
    plt.tight_layout()
    plt.show()

# ---------- Calculation ----------
corr_factors = compute_correlations(df_combined)
print("Correlation matrix (Pearson):")
print(corr_factors.round(3))

# ---------- Heat map ----------
plot_correlation_heatmap(corr_factors, title="Factor
Correlations in USA (daily)")
```

Output:

```
Correlation matrix (Pearson):
            Market   Size  Value  Quality  Investment  Momentum
Market       1.000 -0.054 -0.168   -0.211      -0.345    -0.122
Size        -0.054  1.000  0.148   -0.281       0.023    -0.069
Value       -0.168  0.148  1.000    0.065       0.542    -0.273
Quality     -0.211 -0.281  0.065    1.000       0.117     0.083
Investment  -0.345  0.023  0.542    0.117       1.000     0.034
Momentum    -0.122 -0.069 -0.273    0.083       0.034     1.000
```

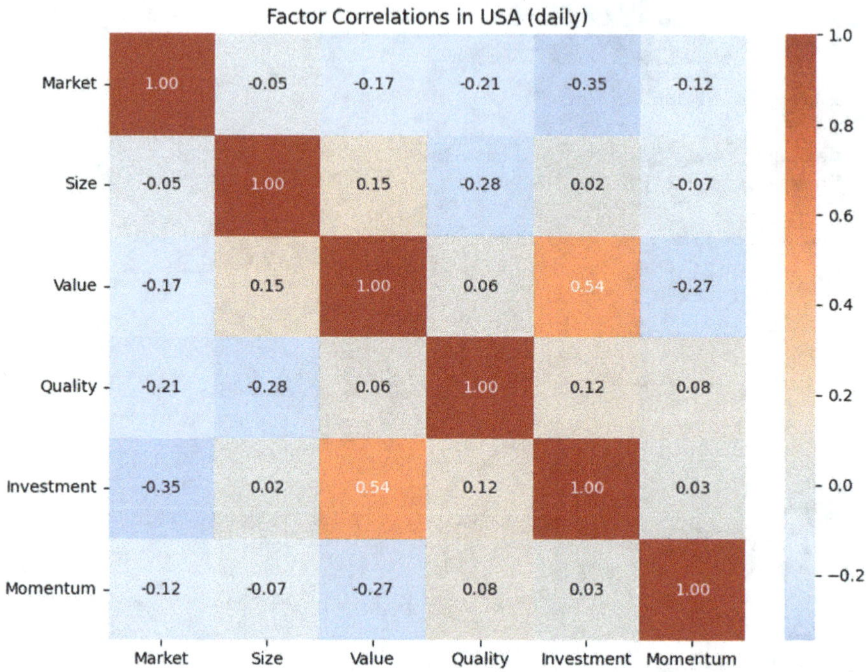

7.4 MODELS IN FACTOR INVESTING

Factor models are quantitative tools used to identify, measure, and incorporate factors into portfolio construction. The main types of factor models are:

a) Single-Factor Models: These models focus on one factor at a time. For instance, a value-based single-factor model evaluates assets based solely on their valuation metrics (e.g., price-to-earnings or price-to-book ratios).

b) Multi-Factor Models: These models combine multiple factors to explain returns more comprehensively. For example, a portfolio might use a combination of momentum, size, and quality factors to achieve better diversification and performance. The main multi-factor models in factor investing are the following:

    i) Three-Factor Model (Fama–French, 1993): This model proposes that the performance of a portfolio can be explained by three main risk factors: the overall market return (market factor), the size of the company (size factor), and the relative value of the company (value factor).

ii) Four-Factor Model (Carhart): The Carhart model is an extension of the Fama–French three-factor model that adds a fourth factor, the momentum factor, to capture the performance of stocks that have had strong recent returns.

iii) Five-Factor Model (Fama–French, 2015): The five-factor model, developed mainly by Eugene Fama and Kenneth French, extends the Fama–French three-factor model by adding two additional factors: firm profitability (RMW) and firm investment (CMA).

c) Risk-Based Factor Models: These models focus on the risk contributions of various factors to the overall portfolio, helping in risk management and portfolio optimization.

d) Smart Beta Approaches: These models apply systematic factor exposures to traditional passive investing. They aim to improve the risk-return profile over market-cap-weighted indexes by tilting toward specific factors.

Factor investing has evolved from its theoretical roots into a practical and applied approach in investment management. The evolution of factors in investing has been marked by changes in popularity, the expansion of the universe of factors, the integration of multiple factors, improvements in construction methodology, and increased attention to ESG considerations. These developments continue to shape the landscape of factor-based investing and offer opportunities for innovation and growth in the future.

7.4.1 The Fama–French's Three-Factor Model

Fama and French (1992) conducted an empirical investigation studying the beta of the initial CAPM model, concluding that this variable does not fully explain the profitability of financial assets. In a subsequent investigation (Fama & French, 1993), they search for factors that significantly explain expected stock returns, using a sample of stocks from the US market (NYSE, AMEX, and NASDAQ) in the period from July 1963 to December 1991. They conclude that variables related to company size and ratios such as P/E, debt/equity, or book-to-market (book value/market value) most significantly explained stock returns.

Based on this finding, Fama and French (1993) developed, from the classic CAPM model, the so-called three-factor model, incorporating two new variables to be studied:

- SMB (*Small Minus Big*): The difference between the return on the smallest asset size and the return on the largest asset size in a portfolio, also called the premium size, or size premium. It measures the additional expected return that investors have historically been acquiring by investing in different assets of companies with a relatively small capitalization. The assumption behind this variable is that smaller companies are more sensitive to risk factors than larger companies because they have less capacity to absorb negative factors in the economy.
- HML (*High Minus Low*): The difference between the return on assets of the company with the highest book-to-market ratio and the return on assets of the company with the lowest book-to-market ratio. This difference is also known as premium value or premium for value. It measures the additional expected return that investors have historically acquired by investing in different assets of companies with a high book-to-market ratio. The assumption behind this variable is that companies with higher book-to-market ratios are more vulnerable to financial shocks than companies with lower book-to-market ratios.

The methodology for calculating these premiums can be found on Professor French's website.[1] The mathematical expression of this model is as follows:

$$E(R_i) - R_f = \alpha_i + \beta_i\left(E(R_M) - R_f\right) + \beta_{SMB}E(R_{SMB}) + \beta_{HML}E(R_{HML}) + \epsilon_i$$

where

- $E(R_{SMB})$ is the expected return on the SMB factor.
- $E(R_{HML})$ is the expected return on the HML factor.
- B_{SMB} and β_{HML} are the sensitivities of the asset return to variations in the corresponding premiums.

PRACTICAL EXERCISE #7.02 FAMA–FRENCH THREE-FACTOR MODEL

Request: Calculate the required return of seven S&P500 stocks and decompose their returns into factors following the Fama–French's three-factor model.

Summary of the script. –

This code analyses the performance of selected stocks using the Fama–French three-factor model, which explains stock returns based on three key factors: market risk (Mkt-RF), size (SMB), and value (HML). The goal is to estimate the exposure of each stock to these factors, calculate expected annualized returns, and decompose returns into factor contributions. Key steps in the code:

a) Data Download and Preprocessing:
   - Downloads stock data from Yahoo Finance.
   - Retrieves and processes Fama–French factor data from the official source.
   - Merges both datasets and aligns them by date.

b) Factor Model Estimation:
   - Runs the Fama–French three-factor regression model for each stock.
   - Extracts alpha (abnormal return) and factor betas (market, size, value).
   - Stores regression results for later analysis.

c) Return Estimation:
   - Computes the expected annualized returns based on factor exposure.
   - Incorporates the risk-free rate and factor contributions.

d) Return Decomposition:
   - Breaks down annualized returns into contributions from each factor and the risk-free rate.
   - Provides insight into the drivers of stock performance.

e) Result Presentation:
   - Displays tables with factor betas, estimated returns, and their decomposition.

This code is useful for portfolio managers and analysts looking to evaluate stocks based on the Fama–French three-factor model, estimate expected returns, and decompose sources of returns.

TABLE 7.2 Summary of Key Functions and Their Purposes

Function/Calculation	Purpose
download_stock_data(symbols, start_date, end_date)	Downloads adjusted closing prices of selected stocks from Yahoo Finance.
stock_data.pct_change( ).dropna( ) * 100	Computes daily percentage returns for the stocks.
clean_fama_french_data(file_content)	Cleans and processes Fama–French data, extracting usable rows.
stock_returns.subtract(ff_factors['RF'], axis=0)	Computes excess returns by subtracting the risk-free rate (RF).
fama_french_3factor_regression(stock_returns, factors)	Runs OLS regression to estimate factor exposures (alphas and betas).
calculate_annualized_returns(betas_table, factors)	Computes the annualized expected returns based on factor betas and averages.
decompose_returns(betas_table, factors)	Decomposes annualized returns into contributions from market, size, value, and risk-free factors.
pd.merge(df1, df2, on='Date', how='outer')	Merges stock return and factor data based on the common date.
betas_table.loc[stock, betas_table.columns[1:]] * avg_factors_annualized	Calculates the contribution of each factor to stock returns.

Script execution and outputs. –

```
import pandas as pd
import numpy as np
import statsmodels.api as sm
import yfinance as yf
import zipfile
import requests
from io import BytesIO

# Define the stocks and the date range
symbols = ['AAPL', 'AMZN', 'META', 'GOOGL', 'MSFT',
'NVDA', 'TSLA']
start_date = '2014-01-03'
end_date = pd.Timestamp.today().strftime('%Y-%m-%d')

# Download stock price data from Yahoo Finance
def download_stock_data(symbols, start_date, end_date):
    data = yf.download(symbols, start=start_date, end=end_
    date, auto_adjust=False, actions=False)['Adj Close']
    return data
```

```
stock_data = download_stock_data(symbols, start_date, end_
date)

# Calculate daily returns
stock_returns = stock_data.pct_change().dropna() * 100

# Clean the Fama-French data
def clean_fama_french_data(file_content):
    lines = file_content.decode('utf-8').splitlines()
    start_line = next(i for i, line in enumerate(lines) if
    line.strip() and line[0].isdigit())
    data = "\n".join(lines[start_line:])
    df = pd.read_csv(BytesIO(data.encode('utf-8')), skip_
    blank_lines=True, index_col=0)
    return df

# Download Fama-French 3-factor data
url = 'https://mba.tuck.dartmouth.edu/pages/faculty/ken.
french/ftp/F-F_Research_Data_Factors_daily_CSV.zip'
response = requests.get(url)
with zipfile.ZipFile(BytesIO(response.content)) as z:
    file_name = z.namelist()[0]
    with z.open(file_name) as f:
        ff_factors = clean_fama_french_data
        (f.read())

# Rename columns and process dates
ff_factors.columns = ['Mkt-RF', 'SMB', 'HML', 'RF']
ff_factors.index = pd.to_datetime(ff_factors.index,
format='%Y%m%d', errors='coerce')
ff_factors = ff_factors.dropna()
ff_factors = ff_factors.loc[start_date:end_date]

# Ensure both indexes are tz-naive
stock_returns.index = stock_returns.index.tz_
localize(None)
ff_factors.index = ff_factors.index.tz_localize(None)

# Get the common set of dates between returns and factors
data
common_dates = stock_returns.index.intersection(ff_
factors.index)

# Filter both DataFrames by the common dates
stock_returns = stock_returns.loc[common_dates]
ff_factors = ff_factors.loc[common_dates]

# Subtract the risk-free rate (RF) to get excess returns
excess_returns = stock_returns.subtract(ff_factors['RF'],
axis=0)
```

```
# Function to fit the Fama-French 3-factor model
results = {}
def fama_french_3factor_regression(stock_returns, factors):
    betas = pd.DataFrame(index=stock_returns.columns,
    columns=['Alpha', 'Mkt-RF', 'SMB', 'HML'])
    for stock in stock_returns.columns:
        Y = stock_returns[stock]  # Stock returns
        X = factors[['Mkt-RF', 'SMB', 'HML']]  # Fama-
        French 3 factors
        X = sm.add_constant(X)  # Add constant term
        model = sm.OLS(Y, X).fit()
        results[stock] = model
        betas.loc[stock, 'Alpha'] = model.params['const']
        betas.loc[stock, ['Mkt-RF', 'SMB', 'HML']] =
        model.params[1:]  # Exclude constant
    return betas

factors = ff_factors[['Mkt-RF', 'SMB', 'HML']]
betas_table = fama_french_3factor_regression(excess_
returns, ff_factors)

# Display the betas table
print("Betas Table:")
print(betas_table)

# Calculate estimated returns based on the 3-factor model,
including RF
def calculate_annualized_returns(betas_table, factors):
    avg_factors = factors.mean()  # Average daily values
    of the factors
    trading_days = 252  # Approximate number of trading
    days in a year

    # Annualize the average daily factor values
    avg_factors_annualized = avg_factors * trading_
    days

    # Calculate annualized returns for each stock
    annualized_returns = pd.DataFrame(index=betas_
    table.index, columns=['Total Return'])
    for stock in betas_table.index:
        rf_annualized = avg_factors_annualized['RF']  #
        Annualized risk-free rate
        factor_contributions = (betas_table.loc[stock,
        betas_table.columns[1:]] * avg_factors_
        annualized[betas_table.columns[1:]]).sum()
        total_return = rf_annualized + factor_
        contributions
```

```
        annualized_returns.loc[stock, 'Total Return'] =
        total_return

    return annualized_returns


# Calculate annualized returns
annualized_returns = calculate_annualized_returns(betas_
table, ff_factors)

# Display annualized returns
print("\nAnnualized Returns:")
print(annualized_returns)

# Decompose annualized returns into factor contributions
def decompose_returns(betas_table, factors):
    avg_factors = factors.mean()  # Average daily values
    of the factors
    trading_days = 252  # Approximate number of trading
    days in a year

    # Annualize the average daily factor values
    avg_factors_annualized = avg_factors * trading_days

    # Create a DataFrame to store contributions
    decomposition = pd.DataFrame(index=betas_table.index,
    columns=factors.columns[:-1].tolist() + ['RF',
    'Total'])

    for stock in betas_table.index:
        rf_annualized = avg_factors_annualized['RF']  #
        Annualized risk-free rate
        factor_contributions = betas_table.loc[stock,
        betas_table.columns[1:]] * avg_factors_
        annualized[betas_table.columns[1:]]

        # Populate the DataFrame
        decomposition.loc[stock, factors.columns[:-1]] =
        factor_contributions
        decomposition.loc[stock, 'RF'] = rf_annualized
        decomposition.loc[stock, 'Total'] = rf_annualized
        + factor_contributions.sum()

    return decomposition

# Calculate the decomposition
returns_decomposition = decompose_returns(betas_table, ff_
factors)
```

```
# Display the decomposition
print("\nReturns Decomposition:")
print(returns_decomposition)
```

Output:

```
Betas Table:
           Alpha    Mkt-RF       SMB       HML
Ticker
AAPL    0.036369  1.168003 -0.302957 -0.377376
AMZN    0.036027  1.133559 -0.148882  -0.73362
GOOGL   0.019459  1.109596  -0.22264 -0.422596
META    0.042998  1.254247 -0.141646 -0.677521
MSFT    0.038648  1.164656 -0.434984 -0.457394
NVDA    0.160033  1.654036  0.008838 -0.957463
TSLA    0.105554  1.482322  0.619013 -0.754626

Annualized Returns:
       Total Return
Ticker
AAPL      17.480016
AMZN       17.37492
GOOGL     16.664083
META      18.733133
MSFT      17.893372
NVDA      23.819651
TSLA       19.92778

Returns Decomposition:
          Mkt-RF       SMB       HML        RF      Total
Ticker
AAPL   14.329206  0.696509  0.711537  1.742764  17.480016
AMZN    13.90664  0.342286   1.38323  1.742764   17.37492
GOOGL  13.612663  0.511857  0.796799  1.742764  16.664083
META   15.387264   0.32565  1.277456  1.742764  18.733133
MSFT   14.288152  1.000045  0.862411  1.742764  17.893372
NVDA   20.291923 -0.020319  1.805282  1.742764  23.819651
TSLA   18.185314 -1.423133  1.422836  1.742764   19.92778
```

7.4.2 Carhart's Four-Factor Model

The Carhart four-factor model is an extension of the Fama and French three-factor model and was introduced by Mark M. Carhart in 1997 in his influential article "On Persistence in Mutual Fund Performance" published in the *Journal of Finance*. This model emerged as a response to the need to better explain financial asset returns, particularly in the context of mutual fund performance persistence.

Mark M. Carhart introduced the fourth factor, momentum, to address one of the most persistent anomalies in financial markets. The momentum effect was documented by Narasimhan Jegadeesh and Sheridan Titman in 1993 (Jegadeesh & Titman, 1993), who showed that stocks that had performed well over the past 3 to 12 months tended to continue to outperform in the short term.

Carhart included this factor in his model to better explain persistence in mutual fund performance and stock returns. His model showed that a significant portion of the performance of mutual funds that outperformed the market could be explained by their exposure to these four factors rather than by the skill of the fund manager.

The momentum factor (WML, *winner minus loser*): Captures the momentum effect, which is the tendency of stocks that have performed well in the recent past (winners) to continue to perform well, and vice versa. WML is the difference between the return of a portfolio of stocks that have performed well over the past 12 months and a portfolio of stocks that have underperformed over the same period.

The mathematical expression of the model is as follows:

$$E(R_i) - R_f = \alpha_i + \beta_i\left(E(R_M) - R_f\right) + \beta_{SMB}E(R_{SMB}) + \beta_{HML}E(R_{HML})f + \beta_{WML}E(R_{WML}) + \epsilon_i$$

Carhart's model, along with Fama and French's three-factor model, laid the groundwork for more advanced multifactor models in finance. In 2015, Fama and French expanded their model to a five-factor model to include profitability and investment growth, reflecting the continuing evolution in the understanding of the factors that drive returns in financial markets.

PRACTICAL EXERCISE #7.03 CARHART FOUR-FACTOR MODEL

Request: Calculate the required return of seven S&P500 stocks and decompose their returns into factors following the Carhart's four-factor model.

Summary of the script. –

This code implements a Carhart four-factor model to analyse stock returns based on four key factors: market risk (Mkt-RF), size (SMB), value (HML), and momentum (MOM). It downloads historical stock prices and factor data, calculates stock exposures to these factors, and estimates their expected returns. Key steps in the code:

a) Download Factor Data:
   - Retrieves Fama–French three-factor data and momentum factor from the Ken French Data Library.
   - Cleans and processes the data by converting dates and merging the datasets.
b) Download Stock Data:
   - Uses Yahoo Finance to obtain adjusted closing prices for selected stocks.
   - Calculates daily percentage returns and aligns them with the factor data.
c) Calculate Factor Betas:
   - Runs an ordinary least squares (OLS) regression to estimate stock exposure to the market, size, value, and momentum factors.
   - Stores the results, including alpha (excess return unexplained by factors).
d) Annualized Return Calculation:
   - Computes expected annualized returns for each stock based on factor exposures.
   - Incorporates the risk-free rate and annualizes factor values based on 252 trading days.
e) Return Decomposition:
   - Breaks down annualized returns into contributions from market, size, value, and momentum factors.
   - Provides insight into the sources of stock performance.
f) Result Presentation:
   - Displays factor betas, annualized expected returns, and decomposition of returns into their respective components.

The code is useful for portfolio managers, analysts, and researchers to:

- Evaluate the factor exposures of stocks.
- Estimate future returns based on historical factor performance.
- Gain insights into the sources of returns and risk.

TABLE 7.3 Summary of Key Functions and Their Purposes

Function	Purpose
download_carhart_factors( )	Downloads and processes the Carhart four-factor data (Fama–French + Momentum).

(Continued)

TABLE 7.3 *(Continued)* Summary of Key Functions and Their Purposes

Function	Purpose
yf.download(symbols, start=start_date)	Downloads historical stock prices from Yahoo Finance.
stock_returns.pct_change( ).dropna( )	Calculates daily percentage returns for stocks.
calculate_betas(stock_returns, factors)	Estimates stock betas using the Carhart four-factor model via OLS regression.
sm.OLS(Y, X).fit( )	Runs ordinary least squares regression to estimate factor exposures.
calculate_annualized_returns(betas, factors)	Computes the annualized expected returns based on factor exposures.
decompose_returns(betas, factors)	Breaks down returns into factor contributions and the risk-free rate.
stock_returns.index.intersection(carhart_factors.index)	Aligns stock returns and factor data based on common dates.

Script execution and outputs. –

```
import pandas as pd
import requests
import zipfile
from io import BytesIO
import yfinance as yf
import statsmodels.api as sm

# Download Carhart factors (Fama-French 3 factors +
Momentum)
def download_carhart_factors():
    ff_url = 'https://mba.tuck.dartmouth.edu/pages/faculty/
    ken.french/ftp/F-F_Research_Data_Factors_daily_CSV.
    zip'
    response_ff = requests.get(ff_url)
    with zipfile.ZipFile(BytesIO(response_ff.content)) as z:
        file_name = z.namelist()[0]
        with z.open(file_name) as f:
            ff_raw_lines = f.read().decode('utf-
            8').splitlines()
            ff_data_start = next((i for i, line in
            enumerate(ff_raw_lines) if line.strip() and
            line[0].isdigit()), None)
            ff_cleaned_data = '\n'.join(ff_raw_lines[ff_data_
            start:])
            fama_french_factors = pd.read_csv(
                BytesIO(ff_cleaned_data.encode('utf-8')),
                index_col=0, header=None, names=['Mkt-RF',
                'SMB', 'HML', 'RF'], skip_blank_lines=True
            )
```

```
    mom_url = 'https://mba.tuck.dartmouth.edu/pages/
    faculty/ken.french/ftp/F-F_Momentum_Factor_daily_CSV.
    zip'
    response_mom = requests.get(mom_url)
    with zipfile.ZipFile(BytesIO(response_mom.content)) as
    z:
        file_name = z.namelist()[0]
        with z.open(file_name) as f:
            mom_raw_lines = f.read().decode('utf-
            8').splitlines()
            mom_data_start = next((i for i, line in
            enumerate(mom_raw_lines) if line.strip() and
            line[0].isdigit()), None)
            mom_cleaned_data = '\n'.join(mom_raw_
            lines[mom_data_start:])
            momentum_factor = pd.read_csv(
                BytesIO(mom_cleaned_data.encode('utf-8')),
                index_col=0, header=None, names=['MOM'],
                skip_blank_lines=True
            )

    fama_french_factors = fama_french_factors[fama_french_
    factors.index.astype(str).str.match(r'^\d{8}$')]
    fama_french_factors.index = pd.to_datetime(fama_
    french_factors.index, format='%Y%m%d',
    errors='coerce')
    fama_french_factors = fama_french_factors.dropna()


    momentum_factor = momentum_factor[momentum_factor.inde
    x.astype(str).str.match(r'^\d{8}$')]
    momentum_factor.index = pd.to_datetime(momentum_
    factor.index, format='%Y%m%d', errors='coerce')
    momentum_factor = momentum_factor.dropna()

    carhart_factors = pd.merge(fama_french_factors,
    momentum_factor, left_index=True, right_index=True,
    how='inner')

    return carhart_factors

def download_stock_data(symbols, start_date):
    data = yf.download(symbols, start=start_date, auto_
    adjust=False, actions=False)['Adj Close']
    return data.pct_change().dropna() * 100
def calculate_betas(stock_returns, factors):
    betas = pd.DataFrame(index=stock_returns.columns,
    columns=['Alpha'] + list(factors.columns.
    drop('RF')))
    for stock in stock_returns.columns:
        Y = stock_returns[stock].dropna()
```

```
        X = factors.drop(columns=['RF']).loc[Y.index].drop
        na()

        if X.empty or Y.empty:
            continue

        try:
            X = sm.add_constant(X)
            model = sm.OLS(Y, X).fit()
            betas.loc[stock, 'Alpha'] =
            model.params['const']
            for factor in factors.columns.drop('RF'):
                betas.loc[stock, factor] =
                model.params.get(factor, None)
        except Exception as e:
            print(f"Error processing {stock}: {e}")

    return betas.dropna()

def calculate_annualized_returns(betas, factors):
    avg_factors = factors.mean()
    trading_days = 252
    avg_factors_annualized = avg_factors * trading_days

    annualized_returns = pd.DataFrame(index=betas.index,
    columns=['Total Return'])
    for stock in betas.index:
        rf_annualized = factors['RF'].mean() * trading_
        days
        factor_contributions = (betas.loc[stock,
        betas.columns[1:]] * avg_factors_annualized[betas.
        columns[1:]]).sum()
        total_return = rf_annualized + factor_
        contributions

        annualized_returns.loc[stock, 'Total Return'] =
        total_return

    return annualized_returns

def decompose_returns(betas, factors):
    avg_factors = factors.mean()
    trading_days = 252
    avg_factors_annualized = avg_factors * trading_days

    decomposition = pd.DataFrame(index=betas.index, co
    lumns=factors.columns.drop('RF').tolist() + ['RF',
    'Total'])
    for stock in betas.index:
        rf_annualized = factors['RF'].mean() * trading_days
```

```
        factor_contributions = betas.loc[stock,
        betas.columns[1:]] * avg_factors_annualized[betas.
        columns[1:]]
        total_return = rf_annualized + factor_
        contributions.sum()

        decomposition.loc[stock, factors.columns.drop('
RF')] = factor_contributions
        decomposition.loc[stock, 'RF'] = rf_annualized
        decomposition.loc[stock, 'Total'] = total_
        return

    return decomposition

symbols = ['AAPL', 'AMZN', 'META', 'GOOGL', 'MSFT',
'NVDA', 'TSLA']
start_date = '2014-01-01'

carhart_factors = download_carhart_factors()
stock_returns = download_stock_data(symbols, start_date)

stock_returns.index = stock_returns.index.tz_
localize(None)
carhart_factors.index = carhart_factors.index.tz_
localize(None)
carhart_factors = carhart_factors.apply(pd.to_numeric,
errors='coerce')

common_dates = stock_returns.index.intersection(carhart_
factors.index)
stock_returns = stock_returns.loc[common_dates]
carhart_factors = carhart_factors.loc[common_dates]

stock_returns = stock_returns.dropna()
carhart_factors = carhart_factors.dropna()

betas = calculate_betas(stock_returns, carhart_
factors)
annualized_returns = calculate_annualized_returns(betas,
carhart_factors)
returns_decomposition = decompose_returns(betas, carhart_
factors)


# Print results
print("Betas (including Alpha):")
print(betas)

print("\nAnnualized Returns:")
print(annualized_returns)
```

```
print("\nReturns Decomposition:")
print(returns_decomposition)
```

Output:

```
Betas (including Alpha):

          Alpha    Mkt-RF       SMB       HML       MOM
Ticker
AAPL   0.042545  1.167986 -0.304151 -0.377972  -0.00083
AMZN   0.043215  1.129475 -0.161836 -0.750503 -0.040589
GOOGL  0.026395   1.10697 -0.231227 -0.433575 -0.026187
META   0.050362  1.248738 -0.158967 -0.700221 -0.054766
MSFT   0.044674  1.171504 -0.414209 -0.429579  0.068345
NVDA   0.164737  1.671319  0.061519 -0.887101  0.172049
TSLA   0.111735  1.487128  0.633403 -0.735196  0.047914

Annualized Returns:

       Total Return
Ticker
AAPL      17.467773
AMZN      17.263593
GOOGL     16.588269
META      18.585998
MSFT      18.049667
NVDA      24.251697
TSLA      20.065408

Returns Decomposition:

          Mkt-RF       SMB       HML       MOM        RF      Total
Ticker
AAPL   14.327122  0.689345  0.711443 -0.002306  1.742169  17.467773
AMZN   13.854732  0.366795  1.412646 -0.112749  1.742169  17.263593
GOOGL  13.578676  0.524064  0.816103 -0.072744  1.742169  16.588269
META   15.317668  0.360291     1.318 -0.152131  1.742169  18.585998
MSFT    14.37028  0.938785  0.808582  0.189851  1.742169  18.049667
NVDA   20.501273 -0.139431  1.669759  0.477926  1.742169  24.251697
TSLA   18.241885 -1.435577  1.383833  0.133098  1.742169  20.065408
```

7.4.3 The Fama–French Five-Factor Model

In 2015 and as a continuation of the three-factor model, Fama and French developed a new asset valuation model. The new model includes size, capitalization ratio, operating profitability of the business and corporate investment patterns in assets, in addition to market risk.

Fama and French (2015) incorporate two new variables:

- RMW (*Robust Minus Weak*): the difference in stock market returns between companies with strong business operating returns and those with weak returns. The assumption behind this variable is that companies that are more robust in operating margins are more sensitive to risk factors than weaker companies.
- CMA (*Conservative Minus Aggressive*): the difference in stock market returns between companies with low and high corporate investments in assets. The assumption behind this variable is that companies with lower investments are more vulnerable to financial shocks than companies with higher investments.

The methodology of its calculation can be viewed on Professor French's website.[2] The mathematical formulation of the model is as follows:

$$E(R_i)-R_f=\alpha_i+\beta_i\left(E(R_M)-R_f\right)+\beta_{SMB}E(R_{SMB})+\beta_{HML}E(R_{HML})$$
$$+\beta_{RMW}E(R_{RMW})+\beta_{CMA}E(R_{CMA})+\epsilon_i$$

where

- $E(R_{RMW})$ is the expected return on the RMW factor.
- $E(R_{CMA})$ is the expected return on the CMA factor.
- β_{RMW} and β_{CMA} are the sensitivities of the asset return to changes in the corresponding premiums.

Fama and French conducted an empirical analysis with company returns between July 1963 and December 2013, concluding that the model is able to explain asset returns 71–94% of the time. But in performing the model, some empirical problems also emerged: The main problem is that it fails to reflect the low average returns of small-cap stocks whose returns behave like those of firms that invest despite their low profitability. The model's performance is not sensitive to the way its factors are defined. With the introduction of business operating profitability and business investment in assets, the value factor of the three-factor model becomes redundant for the description of the average returns of the sample used.

PRACTICAL EXERCISE #7.04 FAMA–FRENCH FIVE-FACTOR MODEL

Request: Calculate the required return of seven S&P500 stocks and decompose their returns into factors following the Fama–French five-factor model.

Summary of the script. –

This code analyses the performance of selected technology stocks using the Fama–French five-factor model, which explains stock returns based on five key factors: market risk (Mkt-RF), size (SMB), value (HML), profitability (RMW), and investment (CMA). The goal is to estimate factor loadings (betas), calculate expected annualized returns, and decompose those returns into factor contributions.

Key Steps in the Code:

a) Data Acquisition:
   - Downloads daily adjusted closing prices of selected stocks (AAPL, AMZN, etc.) from Yahoo Finance.
   - Retrieves the daily Fama–French five-factor dataset from the Ken French Data Library.
   - Cleans and merges stock returns with factor data by aligning dates.

b) Excess Return Calculation:
   - Computes stock excess returns by subtracting the risk-free rate (RF) from daily stock returns.

c) Factor Model Estimation (Regression Analysis):
   - Runs ordinary least squares (OLS) regression to estimate stock exposures to the five factors.
   - Extracts the intercept (alpha) and factor loadings (betas) for each stock.

d) Annualized Return Calculation:
   - Computes the expected annualized returns for each stock using the factor betas and average factor values.
   - Includes the contribution of the risk-free rate.

e) Return Decomposition:
   - Breaks down annualized returns into contributions from market, size, value, profitability, investment, and risk-free factors.

f) Result Presentation:
   - Displays tables showing factor betas, estimated annualized returns, and decomposition of returns.

The code is useful for portfolio managers, analysts, and researchers to:

- Evaluate the risk-return characteristics of stocks based on the Fama–French five-factor model.
- Estimate future returns based on historical factor performance.
- Gain insights into the sources of returns and risk.

TABLE 7.4 Summary of Key Functions and Their Purposes

Function	Purpose
clean_fama_french_data(file_content)	Cleans and processes raw Fama–French factor data for analysis.
pd.to_datetime(ff_factors.index, format='%Y%m%d', errors='coerce')	Converts date strings to datetime format.
stock_returns.subtract(ff_factors['RF'], axis=0)	Computes excess stock returns by removing the risk-free rate.
fama_french_5factor_regression(stock_returns, factors)	Performs OLS regression to estimate factor loadings (betas) and alpha.
sm.OLS(Y, X).fit( )	Runs the OLS regression to fit the Fama–French five-factor model.
calculate_annualized_returns(betas_table, factors)	Computes expected annualized returns using factor betas and averages.
factors.mean( )	Computes the average value of each factor over the selected period.
decompose_returns(betas_table, factors)	Breaks down returns into contributions from market, size, value, and profitability factors.
betas_table.loc[stock, betas_table.columns[1:]] * avg_factors_annualized[betas_table.columns[1:]]	Calculates factor contributions for each stock.

Script execution and outputs. –

```
import pandas as pd
import numpy as np
import statsmodels.api as sm
import yfinance as yf
import zipfile
import requests
from io import BytesIO

# Define the stocks and the date range
symbols = ['AAPL', 'AMZN', 'META', 'GOOGL', 'MSFT',
'NVDA', 'TSLA']
start_date = '2014-01-03'
end_date = pd.Timestamp.today().strftime('%Y-%m-%d')

# Download stock price data from Yahoo Finance
def download_stock_data(symbols, start_date, end_date):
    data = yf.download(symbols, start=start_date, end=end_
    date, auto_adjust=False, actions=False)['Adj Close']
    return data

stock_data = download_stock_data(symbols, start_date,
end_date)
```

```
# Calculate daily returns
stock_returns = stock_data.pct_change().dropna() * 100

# Clean the Fama-French data
def clean_fama_french_data(file_content):
    lines = file_content.decode('utf-8').splitlines()
    start_line = next(i for i, line in enumerate(lines) if
    line.strip() and line[0].isdigit())
    data = "\n".join(lines[start_line:])
    df = pd.read_csv(BytesIO(data.encode('utf-8')), skip_
    blank_lines=True, index_col=0)
    return df

# Download Fama-French 5-factor data
url = 'https://mba.tuck.dartmouth.edu/pages/faculty/ken.
french/ftp/F-F_Research_Data_5_Factors_2x3_daily_CSV.zip'
response = requests.get(url)
with zipfile.ZipFile(BytesIO(response.content)) as z:
    file_name = z.namelist()[0]
    with z.open(file_name) as f:
        ff_factors = clean_fama_french_data(f.read())

# Rename columns and process dates
ff_factors.columns = ['Mkt-RF', 'SMB', 'HML', 'RMW',
'CMA', 'RF']
ff_factors.index = pd.to_datetime(ff_factors.index,
format='%Y%m%d', errors='coerce')
ff_factors = ff_factors.dropna()
ff_factors = ff_factors.loc[start_date:end_date]

# Ensure both indexes are tz-naive
stock_returns.index = stock_returns.index.tz_
localize(None)
ff_factors.index = ff_factors.index.tz_localize(None)

# Get the common set of dates between returns and factors
data
common_dates = stock_returns.index.intersection(ff_
factors.index)

# Filter both DataFrames by the common dates
stock_returns = stock_returns.loc[common_dates]
ff_factors = ff_factors.loc[common_dates]

# Subtract the risk-free rate (RF) to get excess returns
excess_returns = stock_returns.subtract(ff_factors['RF'],
axis=0)

# Function to fit the Fama-French 5-factor model
results = {}
def fama_french_5factor_regression(stock_returns, factors):
```

```
    betas = pd.DataFrame(index=stock_returns.columns,
    columns=['Alpha', 'Mkt-RF', 'SMB', 'HML', 'RMW', 'CMA'])
    for stock in stock_returns.columns:
        Y = stock_returns[stock]  # Stock returns
        X = factors[['Mkt-RF', 'SMB', 'HML', 'RMW',
        'CMA']]  # Fama-French 5 factors
        X = sm.add_constant(X)  # Add constant term
        model = sm.OLS(Y, X).fit()
        results[stock] = model
        betas.loc[stock, 'Alpha'] = model.params['const']
        betas.loc[stock, ['Mkt-RF', 'SMB', 'HML', 'RMW',
        'CMA']] = model.params[1:]  # Exclude constant
    return betas

factors = ff_factors[['Mkt-RF', 'SMB', 'HML', 'RMW',
'CMA']]
betas_table = fama_french_5factor_regression(excess_
returns, ff_factors)

# Display the betas table
print("Betas Table:")
print(betas_table)

# Calculate estimated returns based on the 5-factor model,
including RF
def calculate_annualized_returns(betas_table, factors):
    avg_factors = factors.mean()  # Average daily values
    of the factors
    trading_days = 252  # Approximate number of trading
    days in a year

    # Annualize the average daily factor values
    avg_factors_annualized = avg_factors
    * trading_days

    # Calculate annualized returns for each stock
    annualized_returns = pd.DataFrame(index=betas_
    table.index, columns=['Total Return'])
    for stock in betas_table.index:
        rf_annualized = avg_factors_annualized['RF']
        # Annualized risk-free rate
        factor_contributions = (betas_table.loc[stock]
        * avg_factors_annualized[betas_table.columns[1:]]).
        sum()
        total_return = rf_annualized + factor_contributions

        annualized_returns.loc[stock, 'Total Return'] =
        total_return

    return annualized_returns
```

```
# Calculate annualized returns
annualized_returns = calculate_annualized_returns(betas_
table, ff_factors)
# Display annualized returns
print("\nAnnualized Returns:")
print(annualized_returns)

# Decompose annualized returns into factor
contributions
def decompose_returns(betas_table, factors):
    avg_factors = factors.mean()  # Average daily values
    of the factors
    trading_days = 252  # Approximate number of trading
    days in a year

    # Annualize the average daily factor values
    avg_factors_annualized = avg_factors * trading_days

    # Create a DataFrame to store contributions
    decomposition = pd.DataFrame(index=betas_table.index,
    columns=factors.columns[:-1].tolist() + ['RF',
    'Total'])

    for stock in betas_table.index:
        rf_annualized = avg_factors_annualized['RF']  #
        Annualized risk-free rate
        factor_contributions = betas_table.loc[stock] *
        avg_factors_annualized[betas_table.columns[1:]]
        # Populate the DataFrame
        decomposition.loc[stock, factors.columns[:-1]] =
        factor_contributions
        decomposition.loc[stock, 'RF'] = rf_annualized
        decomposition.loc[stock, 'Total'] = rf_annualized
        + factor_contributions.sum()

    return decomposition

# Calculate the decomposition
returns_decomposition = decompose_returns(betas_table, ff_
factors)

# Make everything numeric, then round
returns_decomposition = returns_decomposition.apply(
    lambda s: pd.to_numeric(s, errors='coerce')
).round(3)


# Display the decomposition
print("\nReturns Decomposition:")
print(returns_decomposition)
```

Output:

```
Betas Table:

          Alpha    Mkt-RF       SMB       HML       RMW       CMA
Ticker
AAPL   0.028172  1.206554 -0.159685 -0.481114  0.533826  0.136813
AMZN   0.036519  1.054358 -0.262607 -0.368618  -0.01635 -1.052201
GOOGL   0.01666  1.066443 -0.212052 -0.217852  0.223145 -0.689456
META   0.042892  1.185856 -0.222065 -0.366692  0.030233 -0.925028
MSFT   0.033989  1.150816 -0.380305 -0.323077  0.323568  -0.38808
NVDA   0.157784  1.655637 -0.058942 -0.913693  0.078834 -0.156412
TSLA   0.115851  1.388878  0.274353 -0.426571 -0.732489 -0.865204


Annualized Returns:

       Total Return
Ticker
AAPL      19.545615
AMZN       17.25089
GOOGL     17.369426
META      18.759755
MSFT      19.067302
NVDA       24.38647
TSLA      17.332862


Returns Decomposition:

        Mkt-RF    SMB    HML    RMW    CMA     RF  Total
Ticker
AAPL    14.802  0.445  0.907  1.805 -0.156  1.743  19.546
AMZN    12.935  0.732  0.695 -0.055  1.201  1.743  17.251
GOOGL   13.083  0.591  0.411  0.754  0.787  1.743  17.369
META    14.548  0.619  0.691  0.102  1.056  1.743  18.760
MSFT    14.118  1.060  0.609  1.094  0.443  1.743  19.067
NVDA    20.312  0.164  1.723  0.267  0.179  1.743  24.386
TSLA    17.039 -0.765  0.804 -2.476  0.988  1.743  17.333
```

7.5 ANALYSING FF FIVE-FACTOR US PORTFOLIOS

The Kenneth R. French Data Library includes various portfolios formed based on factors such as size, value, momentum, profitability, and investment. The data library provides factor portfolios and returns data for various regions, including the U.S., Europe, Japan, and the Asia-Pacific, allowing for both country-specific and global analyses.

The intention behind the portfolios formed based on factors such as size, value, momentum, profitability, and investment in Kenneth R. French's data library is to provide empirical data that helps researchers, academics, and practitioners understand and analyse the drivers of asset returns. By forming portfolios based on these factors, the data library allows users to:

a) Test Asset Pricing Models:

- The primary goal is to test and validate asset pricing models, such as the Fama–French three-factor, five-factor models, and other models that incorporate additional factors like momentum.
- These models aim to explain the variations in stock returns by isolating the influence of specific factors such as size (SMB), value (HML), profitability (RMW), investment (CMA), and momentum.

b) Understand Systematic Risk Factors:

- The portfolios help in identifying and understanding the systematic risk factors that are common across different assets. These factors represent broad economic forces that affect the returns of many securities simultaneously.
- For example, the size factor (SMB) captures the risk associated with small-cap stocks compared to large-cap stocks, while the value factor (HML) captures the risk associated with value stocks compared to growth stocks.

c) Improve Portfolio Management:

- By providing insights into the behaviour of different factors, the portfolios allow investors to design and manage portfolios that align with their risk preferences and return objectives.
- Investors can use this data to construct diversified portfolios that either target specific factors for enhanced returns (e.g., value or momentum) or to hedge against particular risks.

d) Empirical Research and Analysis:

- The data is extensively used for empirical research in finance, helping to validate theories about how markets work, the behaviour of returns over time, and the role of different factors in explaining performance.

- Researchers use these portfolios to analyse trends, anomalies, and the persistence of factor-based returns over different time periods and market conditions.

e) Benchmarking Performance:

- The factor-based portfolios serve as benchmarks for evaluating the performance of active managers, mutual funds, and other investment products.
- Comparing a fund's performance against these factor portfolios helps in attributing performance to specific sources of risk and return, rather than to manager skill alone.

In summary, the intention behind the creation of these factor-based portfolios is to facilitate a deeper understanding of the fundamental drivers of asset returns, support the development and testing of asset pricing models, and provide practical tools for portfolio construction and performance evaluation.

In the following analysis, we will examine the Fama–French five-factor model as it applies to portfolios of the U.S. markets, specifically focusing on portfolios constructed based on the factors of value and size. This model expands on the traditional three-factor model by including factors related to profitability and investment, providing a more comprehensive framework for understanding the drivers of stock returns. Our goal is to assess how these factors interact and contribute to the performance of different portfolios in the U.S. equity market.

PRACTICAL EXERCISE #7.05 ANALYSING FACTOR PORTFOLIOS

Request: Using the 25 portfolios created by Fama–French and the FF five-factor model, and looking at the data from July 1, 1963 to May 31, 2024, calculate the financial performance metrics, and the alphas and betas for each portfolio.

Summary of the script. –

This script performs a comprehensive analysis of stock portfolios using the Fama–French five-factor model and portfolio sorting methodology. The key steps include:

a) Data Acquisition and Preprocessing:
   - Downloading and extracting portfolio and factor data.
   - Cleaning the dataset and converting relevant columns to numeric formats.

b) Portfolio Performance Calculation:
   - Calculating abnormal returns, annualized volatility, and Sharpe ratios.
   - Performing regression analysis to estimate factor exposures.

c) Visualization and Analysis:
   - Generating pivot tables and heatmaps for performance metrics.
   - Displaying results with various statistical insights.

The analysis provides valuable insights into the performance of size and value-sorted portfolios, revealing their exposure to systematic risk factors such as market risk, size, and value premiums. This approach enables investors to assess portfolio performance, optimize asset allocation, and make informed investment decisions based on factor exposures and historical performance trends.

TABLE 7.5 Summary of Key Functions and Their Purposes

Function	Purpose
zipfile.ZipFile(zip_path, 'r')	Extracts the downloaded ZIP file containing portfolio and factor data.
pd.read_csv(filepath, skiprows=18, low_memory=False)	Loads CSV data while skipping header rows.
pd.merge(df1, df2, on='Date', how='outer')	Merges portfolio and factor data on the date column.
df_abnormal_returns.mean( )	Computes daily mean returns to annualize them.
smf.ols(formula=formula, data=df).fit( )	Performs multiple linear regressions using Fama–French factor models.
sns.heatmap(pivot_df, annot=True, cmap=custom_cmap)	Creates heatmaps to visualize metric results.

Script execution and outputs. – Libraries

```
import pandas as pd
import numpy as np
import requests
import zipfile
import os
from datetime import datetime
import statsmodels.formula.api as smf
import seaborn as sns
```

```
import matplotlib.pyplot as plt
from matplotlib.colors import LinearSegmentedColormap
from io import StringIO
```

Portfolios

According to Kenneth French's description, the portfolios, which are constructed at the end of each June, are the intersections of five portfolios formed on size (market equity, ME) and five portfolios formed on the ratio of book equity to market equity (BE/ME). The size breakpoints for year t are the NYSE market equity quintiles at the end of June of t. BE/ME for June of year t is the book equity for the last fiscal year end in t - 1 divided by ME for December of t – 1. The BE/ME breakpoints are NYSE quintiles.

The portfolios for July of year t to June of t + 1 include all NYSE, AMEX, and NASDAQ stocks for which we have market equity data for December of t - 1 and June of t, and (positive) book equity data for t – 1.

```
#FF Data Library file download

url = 'https://mba.tuck.dartmouth.edu/pages/faculty/ken.
french/ftp/25_Portfolios_5x5_daily_CSV.zip'

# Specify the path where you want the file to be saved
zip_path = '25_Portfolios_5x5_daily.zip'

# Make HTTP request to download the file
response = requests.get(url)
with open(zip_path, 'wb') as f:
            f.write(response.content)
            print(f"File downloaded and saved as: {zip_
            path}")

with zipfile.ZipFile(zip_path, 'r') as z:
    # List the names of files in the ZIP to identify the
    CSV
    csv_files = [f for f in z.namelist() if f.endswith('.
    csv')]
    csv_file_name = csv_files[0]
    z.extract(csv_file_name, '.')
    print(f"File '{csv_file_name}'extracted correctly.")

#Review the contents of the file
with open('25_Portfolios_5x5_Daily.csv', 'r') as file:
    for i in range(20):
        print(i, file.readline().strip())
```

```
# Load the CSV file, assuming the first column should be
# named 'Date' and skipping the header

filepath='25_Portfolios_5x5_Daily.csv'
portfolios = pd.read_csv(filepath, skiprows=18, low_
memory=False)
portfolios.rename(columns={portfolios.columns[0]: 'Date'},
inplace=True)

# Remove the first row that is duplicated from the headings
df_portfolios = portfolios.drop(0)

# Convert column 'Date' to datetime
df_portfolios['Date'] = pd.to_datetime(df_
portfolios['Date'], errors='coerce')

# Attempt to convert numeric columns to float, errors will
# be handled as NaN
for col in df_portfolios.columns[1:]:
    df_portfolios[col] = pd.to_numeric(df_portfolios[col],
    errors='coerce')

 # Find the index of the first completely empty row
first_empty_index = df_portfolios[df_portfolios.isnull().al
l(axis=1)].index.min()

# If there is a completely empty row, extract all rows up
to that row.
if pd.notna(first_empty_index):
    df_portfolios = df_portfolios.iloc[:first_empty_
    index-1]
else:
    df_portfolios = df_portfolios   # If there are no
    empty rows, use the whole DataFrame
# Create a replacement dictionary
replacement = {
    'SMALL LoBM': 'ME1 BM1',
    'SMALL HiBM': 'ME1 BM5',
    'BIG LoBM': 'ME5 BM1',
    'BIG HiBM': 'ME5 BM5',
   }

# Rename headings
df_portfolios.rename(columns=replacement, inplace=True)
#Filtering data by date
df_portfolios['Date'] = pd.to_datetime(df_
portfolios['Date'])
start_date = pd.to_datetime('1963-07-01')
end_date = pd.to_datetime('2024-05-31')
try:
```

```
    filtered_portfolios = df_portfolios[(df_
    portfolios['Date'] >= start_date) & (df_
    portfolios['Date'] <= end_date)]
except TypeError as e:
    print("TypeError encountered:", e)
    print("Re-checking the data types...")
    print(portfolios.dtypes)  # This will help identify if
    there's still a data type issue.
```

Factors

The Fama/French five factors (2 × 3) are constructed using the six value-weight portfolios formed on size and book-to-market, the six value-weight portfolios formed on size and operating profitability, and the six value-weight portfolios formed on size and investment. The factors are the following:

- SMB (small minus big) is the average return on the nine small stock portfolios minus the average return on the nine big stock portfolios.
- HML (high minus low) is the average return on the two value portfolios minus the average return on the two growth portfolios.
- RMW (robust minus weak) is the average return on the two robust operating profitability portfolios minus the average return on the two weak operating profitability portfolios.
- CMA (conservative minus aggressive) is the average return on the two conservative investment portfolios minus the average return on the two aggressive investment portfolios.
- Rm – Rf is the excess return on the market.

```
#FF Data Library file download

url = 'https://mba.tuck.dartmouth.edu/pages/faculty/ken.
french/ftp/F-F_Research_Data_5_Factors_2x3_daily_csv.zip'

# Specify the path where you want the file to be saved
zip_path2 = 'F-F_Research_Data_5_Factors_2x3_daily_csv.zip'

# Make HTTP request to download the file
response = requests.get(url)
```

```
with open(zip_path2, 'wb') as f:
            f.write(response.content)
            print(f"File downloaded and saved as: {zip_
            path2}")

with zipfile.ZipFile(zip_path2, 'r') as z:

    # List the names of files in the ZIP to identify the
    CSV
    csv_files2 = [f for f in z.namelist() if f.endswith('.
    csv')]
    csv_file_name2 = csv_files2[0]
    z.extract(csv_file_name2, '.')
    print(f"File '{csv_file_name2}' extracted correctly.")
```

```
#Review the contents of the file
with open('F-F_Research_Data_5_Factors_2x3_daily.csv',
'r') as file:
    for i in range(20):
        print(i, file.readline().strip())
```

```
# Load the CSV file, assuming the first column should be
named 'Date' and skipping the header
csv_name = 'F-F_Research_Data_5_Factors_2x3_daily.csv'

# Load CSV robustly: detect header row and add 'Date' ---
with open(csv_name, "r", encoding="utf-8",
errors="replace") as f:
    lines = f.read().splitlines()

# Find the true header: line that contains 'Mkt-RF' and
starts with a comma after optional spaces
header_idx = next(
    i for i, l in enumerate(lines)
    if "Mkt-RF" in l and l.lstrip().startswith(",")
)

# Prepend 'Date' to the header (turn ",Mkt-RF,..." into
"Date,Mkt-RF,...")
header_line = "Date" + lines[header_idx]

# Build a CSV string from header + all subsequent lines
csv_text = "\n".join([header_line] + lines[header_idx +
1:])
```

```
# Parse; skip initial spaces after commas
raw = pd.read_csv(
    StringIO(csv_text),
    skip_blank_lines=True,
    skipinitialspace=True,
)

# Clean: keep only YYYYMMDD rows, convert types ---
raw.columns = raw.columns.str.strip()
factors = raw[raw["Date"].astype(str).str.match(r"^\s*\
d{8}\s*$", na=False)].copy()

# Convert Date to datetime
factors["Date"] = pd.to_datetime(
    factors["Date"].astype(str).str.strip(),
    format="%Y%m%d",
    errors="coerce"
)
factors = factors.dropna(subset=["Date"])

# Ensure factor columns are numeric
factor_cols = ["Mkt-RF", "SMB", "HML", "RMW", "CMA", "RF"]
missing = [c for c in factor_cols if c not in factors.columns]
if missing:
    raise KeyError(f"Missing expected columns: {missing}")
for c in factor_cols:
    factors[c] = pd.to_numeric(factors[c], errors="coerce")

# --- 5) (Optional) rename, then filter by date range ---
replacement = {"Mkt-RF":"Market","SMB":"Size","HML":"Value
","RMW":"Quality","CMA":"Investment"}
factors = factors.rename(columns=replacement)

start_date = pd.to_datetime("19630701", format="%Y%m%d")
end_date   = pd.to_datetime("20240531", format="%Y%m%d")
filtered_factors = factors[(factors["Date"] >= start_date) &
(factors["Date"] <= end_date)].copy()

print("\nFiltered factors (tail):")
print(filtered_factors.tail())
```

Output:

```
Filtered factors (tail):
            Date  Market  Size  Value  Quality  Investment    RF
15329 2024-05-24    0.71  0.16   0.15     0.29       -0.38  0.02
15330 2024-05-28   -0.04  0.13  -0.88     0.10       -1.12  0.02
15331 2024-05-29   -0.77 -0.40  -0.62     0.46       -0.02  0.02
15332 2024-05-30   -0.53  1.36   1.00     0.32        1.06  0.02
15333 2024-05-31    0.68 -0.02   0.78     0.94        0.78  0.02
```

Combining dataframes

```
#We combine the tables based on the column 'date'.

df1 = pd.DataFrame(filtered_portfolios)
df1['Date'] = pd.to_datetime(df1['Date'])

df2 = pd.DataFrame(filtered_factors)
df2['Date'] = pd.to_datetime(df2['Date'])

df_combined = pd.merge(df1, df2, on='Date', how='outer')

#Sort by date
df_combined = df_combined.sort_values(by='Date')

df_combined.tail()
```

Output:

	Date	ME1 BM1	ME1 BM2	ME1 BM3	ME1 BM4	ME1 BM5	ME2 BM1	...	ME5 BM5	Market	Size	Value	Quality	Investment	RF
15329	2024-05-24	0.28	0.89	0.65	1.24	0.82	1.16	...	1.15	0.71	0.16	0.15	0.29	-0.38	0.02
15330	2024-05-28	0.18	0.17	-0.04	-0.18	-0.19	-0.36	...	-0.67	-0.04	0.13	-0.88	0.10	-1.12	0.02
15331	2024-05-29	-1.39	-0.20	-1.00	-1.47	-1.37	-1.16	...	-1.25	-0.77	-0.40	-0.62	0.46	-0.02	0.02
15332	2024-05-30	0.91	-0.16	0.89	0.90	1.03	0.70	...	-0.08	-0.53	1.36	1.00	0.32	1.06	0.02
15333	2024-05-31	0.60	0.77	0.33	0.26	0.49	0.89	...	1.71	0.68	-0.02	0.78	0.94	0.78	0.02

5 rows × 32 columns

Volatility

```
#Calculation of annual volatility

#Ensure that the date column is in the index.

df_combined.set_index('Date', inplace=True)

#Ensure that all columns except 'date' are numeric
for col in df_combined.columns:
    if col != 'Date':
        df_combined[col] = pd.to_numeric(df_combined[col],
        errors='coerce')

#Excluded columns
excluded_columns= ['Market', 'Size', 'Value','Quality',
'Investment', 'RF']
```

```
#Select the columns you want to process
columns_to_process = [col for col in df_combined.columns
if col not in excluded_columns]

#Calculate daily volatility
daily_volatility = df_combined[columns_to_process].std()

#Convert daily volatility to annual volatility
annual_volatility = daily_volatility * np.sqrt(252)

#Create a DataFrame for the annual volatility row
summary_volatility = pd.DataFrame(annual_volatility,
columns=['volatility_annual']).T


#Ensure that all columns are present and in the
# same order as the original DataFrame.
summary_volatility = summary_volatility.reindex(columns=df_
combined.columns)

#Concatenate results to original DataFrame
df_combined_volatility = pd.concat([df_combined, summary_
volatility])
```

Abnormal returns

```
#Create a copy for the result
df_abnormal_returns= df_combined.copy()

#Select the reference column
col_ref = 'RF'

#Indicate the columns to be excluded
exclude_columns = ['Market', 'Size', 'Value','Quality',
'Investment']


#Subtract the reference column from all other numeric
columns
for column in df_combined.select_dtypes(include='number').
columns:
    if column != col_ref and column not in exclude_
    columns:
        df_abnormal_returns[column] = df_combined[column] -
df_combined[col_ref]
```

Sharpe ratio

```
#Calculation of annual abnormal returns and Sharpe
ratio

#Columns to be excluded in the calculation
excluded_columns= ['Market', 'Size', 'Value','Quality',
'Investment', 'RF']

#Select the columns you want to process
columns_to_process = [col for col in df_abnormal_
returns.columns if col not in excluded_columns]

# Calculate the abnormal returns daily average
# for the selected columns
daily_mean = df_abnormal_returns[columns_to_
process].mean()

#Convert to annual average
annual_mean = daily_mean * 252
Sharpe_ratio=annual_mean/annual_volatility

#Create series with the results and keep the original
portfolio names.
summary_mean = pd.Series(annual_mean, name='AbnRet mean
annual')
summary_volatility = pd.Series(annual_volatility,
name='Volatility annual')
summary_Sharpe=pd.Series(Sharpe_ratio, name='Sharpe')

#Add the excluded columns with NaN
for col in exclude_columns:
    summary_mean[col] = np.nan
    summary_volatility[col] = np.nan
    summary_Sharpe[col]=np.nan

#Convert the Series to DataFrames and reorder the
columns
# to match the original DataFrame.
summary_mean = summary_mean.reindex(df_abnormal_
returns.columns).to_frame().T
summary_volatility = summary_volatility.reindex(df_
combined_volatility.columns).to_frame().T
summary_Sharpe=summary_Sharpe.reindex(df_abnormal_
returns.columns).to_frame().T

#Delete rows of previous results if they exist
df_abnormal_returns= df_abnormal_
returns.drop(index=['AbnRet mean annual', 'Volatility
annual', 'Sharpe'], errors='ignore')
```

```
#Concatenate results to original DataFrame
df_abnormal_returns = pd.concat([df_abnormal_returns,
summary_mean, summary_volatility, summary_Sharpe])

#Convert the date index to a simplified string format only
# if they are not summary indexes
df_abnormal_returns.index = df_abnormal_returns.index.
map(lambda x: x.strftime('%Y-%m-%d') if isinstance(x,
pd.Timestamp) else x)
df_abnormal_returns.tail()
```

Output:

	ME1 BM1	ME1 BM2	ME1 BM3	ME1 BM4	ME1 BM5	ME2 BM1	ME2 BM2	...
2024-05-30	0.890000	-0.180000	0.870000	0.880000	1.010000	0.680000	0.560000	...
2024-05-31	0.580000	0.750000	0.310000	0.240000	0.470000	0.870000	0.020000	...
AbnRet mean annual	2.122874	8.623808	8.988539	11.316736	12.631096	5.997826	9.355108	...
Volatility annual	21.285060	19.304405	17.426310	16.978977	16.771903	21.732639	18.847136	...
Sharpe	0.099735	0.446727	0.515803	0.666515	0.753110	0.275982	0.496368	...

5 rows × 31 columns

Fama/French 5 Factors (2x3) [Daily]

```
# Assume df_combined is your already loaded DataFrame
df = df_combined.copy()

# Clean up column names to ensure they have no spaces or
special characters.
df.columns = df.columns.str.replace('[^A-Za-z0-9_]+', '_',
regex=True)

# Assume that the first 25 columns are the dependent
columns and the last 5 are the independent columns.
dependent_columns = df.columns[:25]
independent_columns = df.columns[25:30]


# Generate regression formulas
formulas = [f'{dep} ~ {" + ".join(independent_columns)}'
for dep in dependent_columns]

# Perform regressions and extract coefficients and p-values.
results = {}
for formula in formulas:
    model = smf.ols(formula=formula, data=df).fit()
```

```
    params = model.params
    pvalues = model.pvalues
    results[formula] = {'coefficients': params, 'pvalues':
    pvalues}

# Show coefficients and p-values
for formula, result in results.items():
    print(f'Resultados para la fórmula "{formula}":')
    print('Coeficientes:')
    print(result['coefficients'])
    print('P-values:')
    print(result['pvalues'])
    print('\n')
```

Output (only for the first regression):

```
Results for regression "ME1_BM1 ~ Market + Size + Value +
Quality + Investment":
Coefficients:
Intercept    -0.002774
Market        1.031183
Size          1.117418
Value        -0.290387
Quality      -0.374662
Investment    0.007250
dtype: float64
P-values:
Intercept      4.463687e-01
Market         0.000000e+00
Size           0.000000e+00
Value         6.104077e-299
Quality       1.666708e-307
Investment     5.557633e-01
dtype: float64
```

```
# Initialisation of dictionaries to store coefficients and
p-values separately
coefficients = {}
pvalues = {}

# Run regressions and extract coefficients and p-values
for formula in formulas:
    model = smf.ols(formula=formula, data=df).fit()
    dep = formula.split('~')[0].strip()  # Obtener el
    nombre de la variable dependiente
    coefficients[dep] = model.params
    pvalues[dep] = model.pvalues
```

```
# Converting dictionaries to DataFrames
coefficients_df = pd.DataFrame(coefficients)
pvalues_df = pd.DataFrame(pvalues)

# Simplifying column names and replacing underscores with
spaces
coefficients_df.columns = [col.replace('_', ' ') for col in
coefficients_df.columns]
pvalues_df.columns = [col.replace('_', ' ') for col in
pvalues_df.columns]


# Create the final DataFrame ensuring that the above data
does not accumulate
df_abnormal_returns= df_abnormal_
returns.drop(index=['AbnRet mean annual', 'Volatility
annual', 'Sharpe'], errors='ignore')
df_updated = pd.concat([df_abnormal_returns, summary_mean,
summary_volatility, summary_Sharpe, coefficients_df])

# Ensure the index is called 'Date'.
if df_updated.index.name != 'Date':
    df_updated.index.name = 'Date'
df_updated.tail(11)
```

Output:

Date	ME1 BM1	ME1 BM2	ME1 BM3	ME1 BM4	ME1 BM5	ME2 BM1	ME2 BM2	...
2024-05-30	0.890000	-0.180000	0.870000	0.880000	1.010000	0.680000	0.560000	...
2024-05-31	0.580000	0.750000	0.310000	0.240000	0.470000	0.870000	0.020000	...
AbnRet mean annual	2.122874	8.623808	8.988539	11.316736	12.631096	5.997826	9.355108	...
Volatility annual	21.285060	19.304405	17.426310	16.978977	16.771903	21.732639	18.847136	...
Sharpe	0.099735	0.446727	0.515803	0.666515	0.753110	0.275982	0.496368	...
...	...	...	...	...	...	...	...	...
Market	1.031183	0.965961	0.914055	0.895099	0.874087	1.103549	1.032954	...
Size	1.117418	1.058733	0.999582	0.974733	0.943422	1.008844	0.947120	...
Value	-0.290387	-0.150877	0.085228	0.306067	0.367199	-0.398994	-0.069456	...
Quality	-0.374662	-0.291324	-0.045907	0.003642	0.009015	-0.307149	-0.061309	...
Investment	0.007250	0.083110	0.078750	0.041054	0.166500	-0.114657	0.049293	...

11 rows × 31 columns

FF 5-Factor Matrix

We construct double-entry matrices where one entry is one factor and the other entry is the other factor, in order to study the performance of the portfolios in terms of the impact of different combinations of two factors.

```
# Filter the first 25 relevant columns
df_filtered = df_updated.iloc[:, :25]

# Define the metrics to create individual DataFrames and
# their respective pivots
metrics = [
    'AbnRet mean annual', 'Volatility annual', 'Sharpe',
    'Intercept',
    'Market', 'Size', 'Value', 'Quality', 'Investment'
]

# Dictionary to store the pivot DataFrames
pivot_dfs = {}

# Process each metric, extract data, create pivot and
# store in dictionary
for metric in metrics:
    temp_df = df_filtered.loc[metric].reset_index()
    temp_df[['ME', 'BM']] = temp_df['index'].str.split('
    ', expand=True)
    temp_df.drop(columns=['index'], inplace=True)
    pivot_dfs[metric] = temp_df.pivot(index='BM',
    columns='ME', values=metric)

# Print each rounded DataFrame pivot
for metric, df in pivot_dfs.items():
    print(f'{metric}'); print(round(df, 2 if metric !=
    'Sharpe' else 3))
```

Output (only for AbnRet mean annual, Volatility annual):

```
AbnRet mean annual

ME      ME1    ME2    ME3    ME4    ME5
BM
BM1    2.12   6.00   6.31   8.09   7.82
BM2    8.62   9.36   9.67   8.01   7.35
BM3    8.99  10.58   9.33   8.95   7.67
BM4   11.32  10.94  10.82  10.46   7.12
BM5   12.63  11.98  12.13  10.67   9.20
```

```
Volatility annual

ME      ME1    ME2    ME3    ME4    ME5
BM
BM1   21.29  21.73  20.77  19.17  17.67
BM2   19.30  18.85  17.49  16.51  16.48
BM3   17.43  17.75  16.58  16.54  16.55
BM4   16.98  17.58  17.01  16.86  18.17
BM5   16.77  19.67  19.70  19.94  21.71
```

Heatmap FF Five-Factor Matrix

To make the analysis more intuitive, we constructed the same double-entry matrices transformed into heat maps.

```
# Filter the first 25 relevant columns
df_filtered = df_updated.iloc[:, :25]

# Defining metrics and their colours for heat maps
metrics = [
    'AbnRet mean annual', 'Volatility annual', 'Sharpe',
    'Intercept',
    'Market', 'Size', 'Value', 'Quality', 'Investment'
]
colors = ["#ff0000", "#ff6600", "#ffff00", "#99ff99",
"#00cc00"]
n_bins = 100  # Use 100 discrete colors
cmap_name = 'custom_heatmap'
custom_cmap = LinearSegmentedColormap.from_list(cmap_name,
colors, N=n_bins)

# Process each metric and generate heat maps
for metric in metrics:
    # Filtering the data relevant to the metric
    temp_df = df_filtered.loc[metric].reset_index()

    # Separating variables to obtain row and column
    categories
    temp_df[['ME', 'BM']] = temp_df['index'].str.split('
    ', expand=True)

    # Delete the original index column
    temp_df.drop(columns=['index'], inplace=True)

    # Create a pivot matrix with ME as columns and BM as
    rows
    pivot_df = temp_df.pivot(index='BM', columns='ME',
    values=metric)
```

```
    # Create the heat matrix
    plt.figure(figsize=(6, 4))
    sns.heatmap(pivot_df, annot=True, cmap=custom_cmap,
    cbar_kws={'label': f'{metric} Range'})
    plt.title(f'{metric} Heatmap')
    plt.show()
# Dictionary to store the pivot DataFrames
pivot_dfs = {}

# Process each metric, extract data, create pivot and
# store in dictionary
for metric in metrics:
    temp_df = df_filtered.loc[metric].reset_index()
    temp_df[['ME', 'BM']] = temp_df['index'].str.split('
    ', expand=True)
    temp_df.drop(columns=['index'], inplace=True)
    pivot_dfs[metric] = temp_df.pivot(index='BM',
    columns='ME', values=metric)

# Print each rounded DataFrame pivot
for metric, df in pivot_dfs.items():
    print(f'{metric}'); print(round(df, 2 if metric !=
    'Sharpe' else 3))
```

Output:

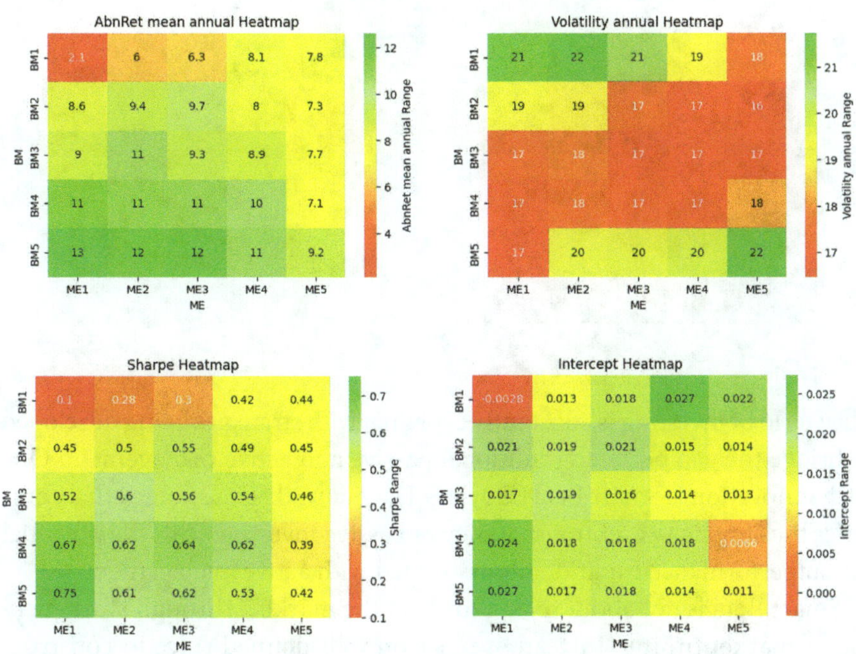

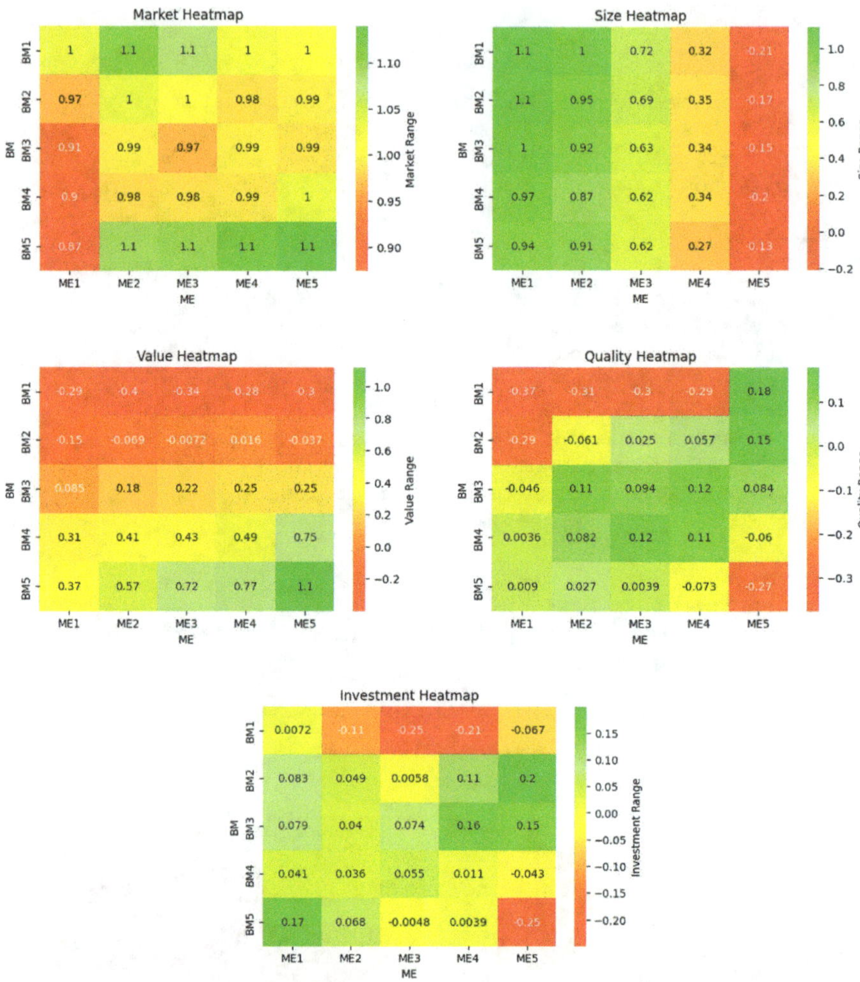

7.6 SMART BETA STRATEGY

7.6.1 Introduction to Smart Beta

The world of investing is constantly evolving, with strategies being developed to bridge the gap between traditional passive and active management. One such innovation is Smart Beta (Doyle & Hayman, 2024), a strategy that combines the simplicity and transparency of passive investing with the potential for outperformance traditionally associated with active management.

Smart Beta is not about trying to "beat the market" through stock picking or market timing. Instead, it relies on well-defined rules to construct portfolios that target specific characteristics - or factors - that have been shown to explain differences in asset returns over time. By doing so, Smart Beta provides a structured, systematic approach to enhancing returns, reducing risk, or both.

7.6.2 What Is Smart Beta?

At its core, Smart Beta rethinks how securities are selected and weighted in a portfolio. Traditional index funds, like those tracking the S&P 500, use market capitalization as the sole criterion for weighting assets. This means the largest companies, by market value, dominate the portfolio. While straightforward, this approach can lead to inefficiencies, such as excessive exposure to overvalued stocks.

Smart Beta challenges this convention by introducing alternative ways to select and weight assets. These strategies may focus on specific factors, such as value, size, momentum, low volatility, quality and investment. By moving beyond market capitalization, Smart Beta portfolios aim to harness these factors to achieve better risk-adjusted performance.

7.6.3 How Smart Beta Works

A Smart Beta strategy typically involves two key steps:

- Security Selection: Securities are selected based on a predefined factor or set of factors. For example, a "value" strategy might filter for stocks with low price-to-book ratios, while a "momentum" strategy focuses on stocks with the highest 12-month returns.
- Alternative Weighting: Unlike traditional indexes, which weight securities by market capitalization, Smart Beta uses alternative methods such as:
    - Equal weighting: All selected securities receive equal weights, reducing concentration in larger companies.
    - Factor weighting: Securities are weighted based on their exposure to the targeted factor(s).

7.6.4 Why Choose Smart Beta?

Investors are drawn to Smart Beta for several reasons:

- Enhanced Returns: By targeting factors with proven historical performance, Smart Beta aims to outperform traditional market-capitalization indexes over the long term.

- Improved Risk Management: Strategies like low volatility or quality focus on reducing portfolio risk during market downturns.
- Cost Efficiency: Smart Beta is generally less expensive than traditional active management, offering a cost-effective way to access factor-based strategies.
- Transparency: The rules for selecting and weighting securities are clearly defined, providing investors with clarity on how their portfolios are constructed.
- Customization: Smart Beta allows investors to align their portfolios with specific goals, such as achieving steady income or minimizing drawdowns.

7.6.5 Challenges and Considerations

While Smart Beta has many advantages, it is not without limitations:

- Cyclicality: Factors like value or momentum can underperform for extended periods, testing the patience of investors.
- Overcrowding: As more investors adopt the same factors, their effectiveness may diminish due to increased demand.
- Complexity: Implementing a Smart Beta strategy requires a deep understanding of factors, data, and portfolio construction.
- Tracking Error: Smart Beta portfolios often deviate significantly from traditional benchmarks, which may be unsettling for some investors.

7.6.6 Conclusion

Smart Beta represents a middle ground between passive and active investing, offering the transparency and cost-effectiveness of index strategies while systematically targeting factors that drive returns. As investors seek more sophisticated and tailored approaches to portfolio construction, Smart Beta has become an essential tool for navigating the complexities of modern markets. Its blend of simplicity, science, and strategy ensures that it remains at the forefront of innovation in investment management.

PRACTICAL EXERCISE #7.06 SMART BETA PORTFOLIO (EQUALLY WEIGHTED) VERSUS INDEX

Request: We will construct a portfolio using the stocks from the IBEX 35, assigning an equal weight to each stock. We will compare this portfolio with the IBEX 35 over the period 2019–2024.

Summary of the script. –

This script analyses an equally weighted portfolio composed of IBEX 35 stocks and compares its performance against the IBEX 35 index. Key steps:

a) Data Collection:
   - Fetch historical adjusted closing prices for IBEX 35 stocks and the IBEX 35 index from Yahoo Finance.
   - Handle missing data using forward and backward filling.

b) Portfolio Construction:
   - Construct an equally weighted portfolio where each stock receives an equal allocation.

c) Backtesting:
   - Compute daily returns for the portfolio and IBEX 35 index.
   - Calculate cumulative returns over time for performance comparison.

d) Performance Metrics Calculation:
   - Evaluate key metrics such as annualized return, volatility, and the Sharpe ratio to assess risk-adjusted performance.

e) Visualization and Interpretation:
   - Compare the cumulative returns of the equally weighted portfolio with the IBEX 35 index.
   - Print the computed performance metrics for analysis.

The equally weighted IBEX 35 portfolio provides a useful benchmark against the index. By evaluating key metrics such as return, volatility, and Sharpe ratio, investors can assess whether the portfolio offers better risk-adjusted performance compared to the market. The visualization aids in identifying trends and deviations between the portfolio and index, helping in strategic decision-making for asset allocation and portfolio management.

TABLE 7.6 Summary of Key Functions and Their Purposes

Function	Purpose
yf.download( )	Downloads historical stock and index price data from Yahoo Finance.
pct_change( )	Calculates daily percentage returns.
cumprod( )	Computes cumulative returns over time.
std( )	Calculates the standard deviation (volatility) of returns.
portfolio_annualized_return	Computes annualized return for portfolio and index.
portfolio_sharpe_ratio	Evaluates risk-adjusted return based on risk-free rate.

Script execution and outputs. –

```
import yfinance as yf
import pandas as pd
import numpy as np
import matplotlib.pyplot as plt

# Step 1: Define IBEX 35 Tickers
ibex35_tickers = [
    "SAN.MC", "TEF.MC", "ITX.MC", "BBVA.MC", "IBE.MC",
"ACS.MC", "ANA.MC",
    "AENA.MC", "FER.MC", "CLNX.MC", "REP.MC", "ENG.MC",
"RED.MC", "AMS.MC",
    "GRF.MC", "MAP.MC", "NTGY.MC", "MEL.MC", "CABK.MC",
"SAB.MC",
    "COL.MC", "ELE.MC", "LOG.MC", "IAG.MC", "MRL.MC",
"MTS.MC", "ACX.MC",
    "IDR.MC", "SCYR.MC", "ROVI.MC", "UNI.MC", "ANE.MC",
"FDR.MC", "SLR.MC", "BKT.MC"
]

# Fetch historical price data for valid tickers
price_data = yf.download(ibex35_tickers,
start="2019-01-01", end="2025-01-01",auto_adjust=False,
actions=False)['Adj Close']

# Step 2: Handle Missing Data
price_data = price_data.ffill().bfill()  # Fill missing data

# Step 3: Create Equally-Weighted Portfolio
equal_weights = 1 / len(price_data.columns)
portfolio_weights = pd.DataFrame(equal_weights,
index=price_data.index, columns=price_data.columns)

# Step 4: Backtesting
returns = price_data.pct_change().dropna()
portfolio_returns = (portfolio_weights.shift() *
returns).sum(axis=1)
cumulative_returns = (1 + portfolio_returns).cumprod()

# Fetch and process IBEX 35 data
ibex35_index = "^IBEX"
ibex_index_data = yf.download(ibex35_index,
start="2019-01-01", end="2025-01-01", auto_adjust=False,
actions=False)['Adj Close']

ibex_index_data = ibex_index_data.ffill().bfill()  # Fill
missing data
ibex_index_returns = ibex_index_data.pct_change().
dropna()
```

```
# Calculate annualized volatility
portfolio_volatility = portfolio_returns.std() *
np.sqrt(252)
index_volatility = ibex_index_returns.std() * np.sqrt(252)

# Convert to scalar if necessary
portfolio_volatility = portfolio_volatility.iloc[0]
if isinstance(portfolio_volatility, pd.Series) else
portfolio_volatility
index_volatility = index_volatility.iloc[0] if
isinstance(index_volatility, pd.Series) else index_
volatility

# Plot cumulative returns
plt.figure(figsize=(12, 6))
plt.plot(cumulative_returns, label="Equally-Weighted
Portfolio (IBEX 35)", color="green")
plt.plot((1 + ibex_index_returns).cumprod(), label="IBEX
35 Index", color="blue")
plt.title("Comparison of Equally-Weighted Portfolio vs.
IBEX 35 Index")
plt.xlabel("Date")
plt.ylabel("Cumulative Returns")
plt.legend()
plt.grid()
plt.show()

# Step 5: Performance Metrics
portfolio_annualized_return = (cumulative_returns.iloc[-1]
** (1 / (cumulative_returns.index[-1].year - cumulative_
returns.index[0].year))) - 1
index_annualized_return = ((1 + ibex_index_returns).cumpro
d().iloc[-1] ** (1 / (ibex_index_returns.index[-1].year -
ibex_index_returns.index[0].year))) - 1

# Convert to scalar using iloc[0] if necessary
portfolio_annualized_return = portfolio_annualized_
return.iloc[0] if isinstance(portfolio_annualized_return,
pd.Series) else portfolio_annualized_return
index_annualized_return = index_annualized_return.iloc[0]
if isinstance(index_annualized_return, pd.Series) else
index_annualized_return

# Sharpe Ratios
risk_free_rate = 0.01
portfolio_sharpe_ratio = (portfolio_annualized_return -
risk_free_rate) / portfolio_volatility
index_sharpe_ratio = (index_annualized_return - risk_free_
rate) / index_volatility
```

```
# Display Results
print("\nPerformance Comparison:")
print(f"Equally-Weighted Portfolio Annualized Return:
{portfolio_annualized_return:.2%}")
print(f"IBEX 35 Index Annualized Return: {index_
annualized_return:.2%}")
print(f"Equally-Weighted Portfolio Volatility: {portfolio_
volatility:.2%}")
print(f"IBEX 35 Index Volatility: {index_volatility:.2%}")
print(f"Equally-Weighted Portfolio Sharpe Ratio:
{portfolio_sharpe_ratio:.2f}")
print(f"IBEX 35 Index Sharpe Ratio: {index_sharpe_
ratio:.2f}")
```

Output:

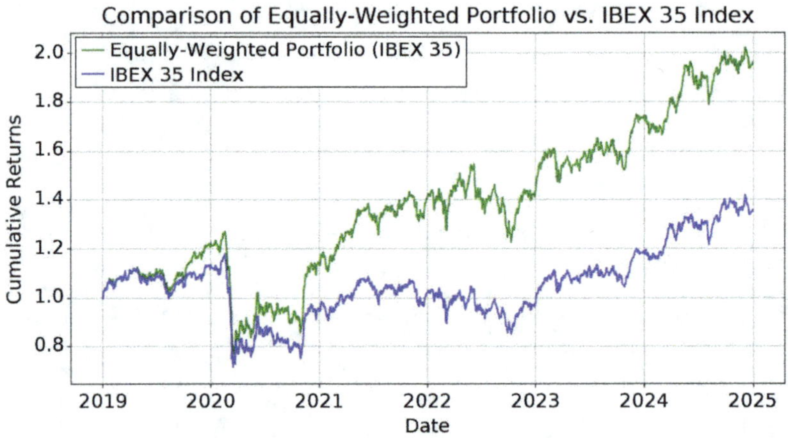


```
Performance Comparison:
Equally-Weighted Portfolio Annualized Return: 14.39%
IBEX 35 Index Annualized Return: 6.28%
Equally-Weighted Portfolio Volatility: 19.41%
IBEX 35 Index Volatility: 19.58%
Equally-Weighted Portfolio Sharpe Ratio: 0.69
IBEX 35 Index Sharpe Ratio: 0.27
```

PRACTICAL EXERCISE #7.07 SMART BETA PORTFOLIO (MOMENTUM) VERSUS INDEX

Request: We will construct a portfolio using the stocks from IBEX 35, assigning weights based on the momentum factor. We will compare this portfolio with the IBEX 35 over the period 2019–2024.

Summary of the script. –

This script constructs and evaluates a momentum-based Smart Beta portfolio using the IBEX 35 stocks. Momentum investing involves selecting stocks that have demonstrated strong past performance, with the expectation of continued performance in the future. The goal is to compare this strategy's performance against the IBEX 35 index using key financial metrics such as annualized return, volatility, and the Sharpe ratio. Key steps:

a) Data Collection:
   - Download historical adjusted closing prices for IBEX 35 stocks and the IBEX 35 index from Yahoo Finance.
   - Handle missing data by forward and backward filling.

b) Momentum Factor Calculation:
   - Compute 1-year momentum for each stock based on a 252-day rolling period.
   - Filter out negative momentum values and normalize the remaining weights.

c) Portfolio Construction:
   - Assign portfolio weights based on momentum scores.
   - Ensure weights sum to 100% by normalizing the calculated values.

d) Backtesting:
   - Calculate daily portfolio returns.
   - Compute cumulative returns over time for performance comparison.

e) Performance Evaluation:
   - Assess portfolio risk and return by calculating annualized return and volatility.
   - Compare with IBEX 35 index using the Sharpe ratio.

f) Visualization and Interpretation:
   - Plot the cumulative return performance of the momentum portfolio against the IBEX 35 index.
   - Print key performance metrics to understand the strategy's effectiveness.

TABLE 7.7 Summary of Key Functions and Their Purposes

Function	Purpose
yf.download( )	Downloads historical stock and index price data from Yahoo Finance.
pct_change( )	Calculates daily percentage returns for stocks and index.
shift( )	Adjusts weights based on prior period values.
clip(lower=0)	Removes negative momentum values.
div( )	Normalizes the portfolio weights to ensure full allocation.
cumprod( )	Computes cumulative returns over time.
std( )	Calculates portfolio volatility.
sqrt(252)	Annualizes the volatility assuming 252 trading days.
Sharpe Ratio formula	Evaluates risk-adjusted return based on risk-free rate.

Script execution and outputs. –

```
import yfinance as yf
import pandas as pd
import numpy as np
import matplotlib.pyplot as plt

# Step 1: Define IBEX 35 Tickers
ibex35_tickers = [
    "SAN.MC", "TEF.MC", "ITX.MC", "BBVA.MC", "IBE.MC",
    "ACS.MC", "ANA.MC",
    "AENA.MC", "FER.MC", "CLNX.MC", "REP.MC", "ENG.MC",
    "RED.MC", "AMS.MC",
    "GRF.MC", "MAP.MC", "NTGY.MC", "MEL.MC", "CABK.MC",
    "SAB.MC",
    "COL.MC", "ELE.MC", "LOG.MC", "IAG.MC", "MRL.MC",
    "MTS.MC", "ACX.MC", "IDR.MC", "SCYR.MC", "ROVI.MC",
    "UNI.MC", "ANE.MC",
    "FDR.MC", "SLR.MC", "BKT.MC"
]

# Fetch historical price data for valid tickers
price_data = yf.download(ibex35_tickers,
start="2019-01-01", end="2025-01-01", auto_adjust=False,
actions=False)['Adj Close']

# Step 2: Handle Missing Data
price_data = price_data.ffill().bfill()  # Fill missing data

# Step 3: Calculate Momentum Factor
momentum = (price_data / price_data.shift(252)) - 1
momentum = momentum.iloc[-1]  # Use the most recent
momentum values
```

```
momentum = momentum.clip(lower=0).dropna()  # Remove
negative or invalid values
momentum_weights = momentum / momentum.sum()  # Normalize
weights

# Step 4: Portfolio Construction
portfolio_weights = pd.DataFrame(index=price_data.index,
columns=price_data.columns)
for ticker in price_data.columns:
    portfolio_weights[ticker] = momentum_
weights.get(ticker, 0)
portfolio_weights = portfolio_weights.div(portfolio_
weights.sum(axis=1), axis=0)

# Step 5: Backtesting
returns = price_data.pct_change().dropna()
portfolio_returns = (portfolio_weights.shift() *
returns).sum(axis=1)
cumulative_returns = (1 + portfolio_returns).cumprod()

# Fetch and process IBEX 35 data
ibex35_index = "^IBEX"
ibex_index_data = yf.download(ibex35_index,
start="2019-01-01", end="2025-01-01", auto_adjust=False,
actions=False)['Adj Close']
ibex_index_data = ibex_index_data.ffill().bfill()  # Fill
missing data
ibex_index_returns = ibex_index_data.pct_change().dropna()

# Calculate annualized volatility (ensure scalar)
portfolio_volatility = portfolio_returns.std() *
np.sqrt(252)
index_volatility = ibex_index_returns.std() * np.sqrt(252)

# Convert to scalar using iloc[0] if necessary
portfolio_volatility = portfolio_volatility.iloc[0]
if isinstance(portfolio_volatility, pd.Series) else
portfolio_volatility
index_volatility = index_volatility.iloc[0] if
isinstance(index_volatility, pd.Series) else index_
volatility

# Plot cumulative returns
plt.figure(figsize=(12, 6))
plt.plot(cumulative_returns, label="Smart Beta Portfolio
(Momentum)", color="green")
plt.plot((1 + ibex_index_returns).cumprod(), label="IBEX
35 Index", color="blue")
plt.title("Comparison of Momentum-Based Portfolio vs. IBEX
35 Index")
plt.xlabel("Date")
```

```
plt.ylabel("Cumulative Returns")
plt.legend()
plt.grid()
plt.show()

# Step 6: Performance Metrics
portfolio_annualized_return = (cumulative_returns.iloc[-1]
** (1 / (cumulative_returns.index[-1].year - cumulative_
returns.index[0].year))) - 1
index_annualized_return = ((1 + ibex_index_returns).cumpro
d().iloc[-1] ** (1 / (ibex_index_returns.index[-1].year -
ibex_index_returns.index[0].year))) - 1

# Convert to scalar using iloc[0] if necessary
portfolio_annualized_return = portfolio_annualized_
return.iloc[0] if isinstance(portfolio_annualized_return,
pd.Series) else portfolio_annualized_return
index_annualized_return = index_annualized_return.iloc[0]
if isinstance(index_annualized_return, pd.Series) else
index_annualized_return

# Sharpe Ratios
risk_free_rate = 0.01
portfolio_sharpe_ratio = (portfolio_annualized_return -
risk_free_rate) / portfolio_volatility
index_sharpe_ratio = (index_annualized_return - risk_free_
rate) / index_volatility

# Display Results
print("\nPerformance Comparison:")
print(f"Momentum Portfolio Annualized Return: {portfolio_
annualized_return:.2%}")
print(f"IBEX 35 Index Annualized Return: {index_
annualized_return:.2%}")
print(f"Momentum Portfolio Volatility: {portfolio_
volatility:.2%}")
print(f"IBEX 35 Index Volatility: {index_volatility:.2%}")
print(f"Momentum Portfolio Sharpe Ratio: {portfolio_
sharpe_ratio:.2f}")
print(f"IBEX 35 Index Sharpe Ratio: {index_sharpe_
ratio:.2f}")
```

Output:

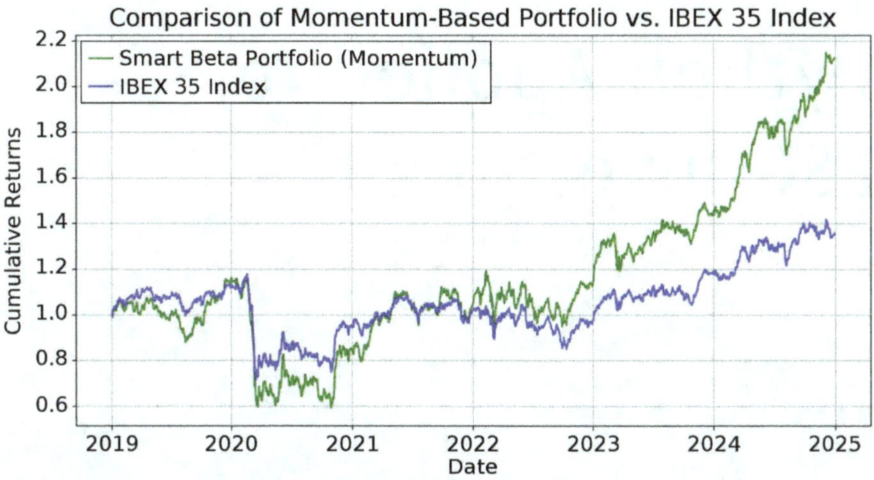


```
Performance Comparison:
Momentum Portfolio Annualized Return: 16.47%
IBEX 35 Index Annualized Return: 6.28%
Momentum Portfolio Volatility: 25.52%
IBEX 35 Index Volatility: 19.58%
Momentum Portfolio Sharpe Ratio: 0.61
IBEX 35 Index Sharpe Ratio: 0.27
```

NOTES

1 http://mba.tuck.dartmouth.edu/pages/faculty/ken.french/Data_Library/f-f_factors.html

2 http://mba.tuck.dartmouth.edu/pages/faculty/ken.french/Data_Library/f-f_5_factors_2x3.html

CHAPTER 8

Python Applied to ESG Investment

8.1 CHAPTER OVERVIEW

This chapter introduces environmental, social, and governance (ESG) as a modern, financially material framework that has evolved far beyond early socially responsible investing (SRI) exclusion lists into a core pillar of professional asset management and quantitative finance. It explains how ESG information – spanning environmental exposures, social and human-capital dynamics, and governance quality – now functions as a forward-looking lens for assessing long-term risks, resilience, and cash-flow durability, increasingly shaped by regulation, client mandates, and improved disclosure infrastructure. The chapter then focuses on the practical challenges of ESG implementation, including data heterogeneity, provider disagreement, methodological opacity, and the need to transform raw indicators into standardized, industry-relative signals suitable for systematic modelling. Building on this foundation, it maps the main pathways through which ESG enters the investment process – from universe construction and screening, to ESG-constrained optimization, to the construction of ESG-driven factors such as momentum and carbon beta – showing how sustainability metrics can be treated with the same statistical discipline applied to traditional-style factors. Finally, the chapter positions Python as the key enabling tool for replicable ESG strategy design, offering detailed code-based workflows that translate ESG narratives into scalable, testable portfolio rules and quantitative signals.

DOI: 10.1201/9781003781394-8

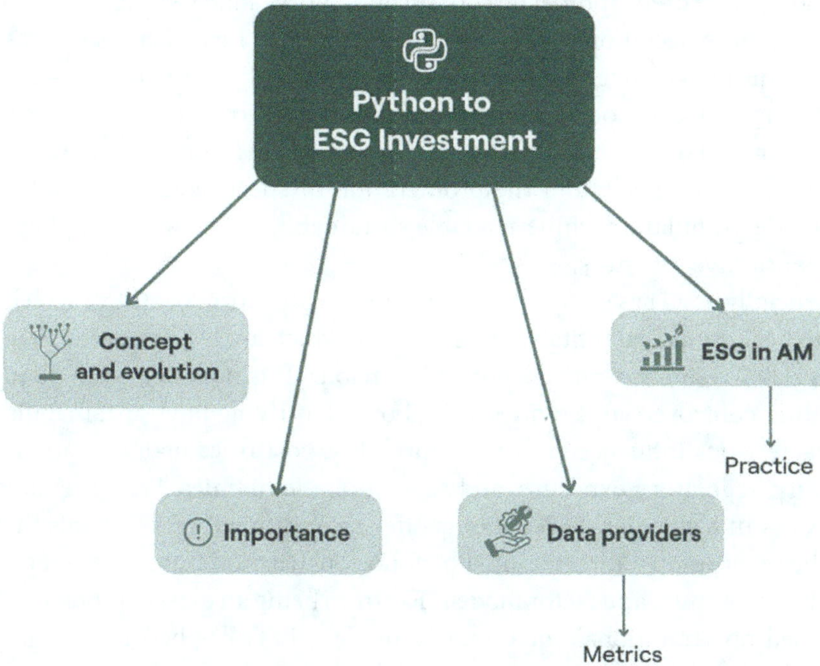

FIGURE 8.1 Python to ESG Investment

8.2 INTRODUCTION

In recent years, the role of environmental, social, and governance considerations in investment decision-making has expanded dramatically. What began several decades ago as a niche initiative – often dismissed as a marketing exercise, a public-relations tool, or a concession to values-based investors – has matured into a central pillar of professional asset management. Whereas early "socially responsible investing" focused narrowly on exclusion lists, ESG has evolved into a comprehensive analytical framework used to evaluate material risks and opportunities that traditional financial statements often fail to capture.

Today, ESG integration is embedded in the mandates of pension funds, sovereign wealth funds, insurance companies, endowments, and asset managers across all major markets. Regulatory scrutiny has intensified: global authorities now demand standardized disclosure of climate risks, human-capital metrics, and governance practices, forcing investors to develop structured approaches to sustainability analysis. At the same time, client expectations have shifted substantially. Beneficiaries increasingly require evidence that their investments are aligned with long-term environmental and social stability and that portfolios are insulated from emerging sustainability-related risks. Parallel to this, corporate ESG disclosure has improved, and the proliferation of specialized data vendors has made granular, machine-readable sustainability data widely available to quantitative investors.

Crucially, ESG has shifted from being primarily a form of ethical screening to becoming a quantitative lens through which analysts examine long-term risks, resilience, and corporate behaviour. It is no longer only about avoiding controversial activities; it is about identifying how sustainability characteristics influence cash-flow durability, cost of capital, operational stability, regulatory exposure, and reputational dynamics. For systematic investors in particular, ESG datasets offer an additional set of signals that can be incorporated directly into portfolio construction frameworks, optimization routines, and factor models. Far from being an external constraint imposed on "traditional" quantitative models, ESG has become a legitimate source of information with potential alpha implications and, at minimum, material risk-management value. The ability to translate qualitative ESG narratives into structured, testable, and scalable indicators is rapidly emerging as a core technical competency in modern asset management.

This transformation has been accelerated by methodological advances in data science and computational finance. Modern portfolio platforms can now ingest millions of ESG datapoints, process alternative datasets such as satellite-based emissions detection or natural-language sentiment on governance controversies, and incorporate them into multi-factor risk models. As a result, ESG is increasingly analysed with the same statistical rigor applied to value, momentum, quality, or low-volatility strategies. This convergence between sustainability research and quantitative modelling is reshaping how investment teams think about portfolio construction and risk attribution.

The aim of this chapter is to provide a rigorous yet practical introduction to ESG for quantitative finance practitioners, with special emphasis on how Python can be used to implement ESG strategies in a systematic and replicable manner. The chapter begins by clarifying the meaning and relevance of ESG, drawing distinctions between traditional ethical investing, modern ESG integration, and emerging approaches related to climate-risk modelling and impact measurement. It then provides an overview of major data providers and key metrics, highlighting the challenges of data heterogeneity, rating disagreement, and methodological opacity. Building on this foundation, the chapter examines the different ways in which ESG is embedded into investment processes -from universe construction and signal design to optimization constraints and risk-factor specification.

The second half of the chapter turns fully practical, presenting three canonical approaches to quantitative ESG integration: (1) screening methodologies, which shape the investable universe; (2) ESG-tilted optimization routines, which incorporate sustainability targets directly into mathematical portfolio frameworks; and (3) ESG factor construction, including momentum-style signals, climate-risk premia, and carbon-beta estimation. Each approach is illustrated with detailed Python examples that emphasize conceptual clarity and reproducibility.

8.3 UNDERSTANDING ESG: CONCEPT AND EVOLUTION

The term environmental, social, and governance refers to a multidimensional framework designed to evaluate companies beyond conventional financial reporting by systematically incorporating non-financial drivers of risk and performance. Rather than functioning as a fixed set of ethical criteria, ESG represents an analytical architecture that captures how environmental practices, social behaviours, and governance structures shape a firm's exposure to long-term risks and ability to generate sustainable cash flows. As economies confront climate change, demographic shifts, technological disruption, and regulatory transformation, these dimensions have become central to understanding corporate value creation (Friede et al., 2015).

Historically, ESG emerged from earlier forms of socially responsible investing, which primarily focused on ethical exclusions – removing firms involved in activities such as tobacco, gambling, weapons manufacturing, or environmental degradation. These early frameworks were rooted in moral or religious values rather than financial materiality, and as a result, they were often criticized for limiting diversification and reducing expected returns. Over time, however, empirical research and corporate reporting practices revealed that many sustainability-related issues correlate strongly with operational risk, regulatory exposure, capital costs, and reputational stability (Bolton & Kacperczyk, 2021; Khan et al., 2016; Eccles et al., 2014). This marked the shift from value-driven exclusions to risk-driven analysis, setting the foundation for modern ESG integration (Sjöström, 2011; Kotsantonis et al., 2016).

The environmental (E) pillar encompasses a firm's interaction with the natural environment and its exposure to ecological and climate-related risks. This includes greenhouse gas emissions, energy efficiency, pollution levels, water management, biodiversity impacts, and the environmental footprint of supply-chain operations. Investors have come to recognize that companies failing to manage environmental risks may face intensified regulatory scrutiny, carbon taxation, litigation, or the physical consequences of climate change – ranging from disrupted production to damaged infrastructure (Clark et al., 2015). Moreover, heavy carbon emitters increasingly face the prospect of stranded assets, particularly in energy and extractive industries where policy shifts toward decarbonization render traditional business models less viable (Weber et al., 2020).

The social (S) pillar deals with how firms manage relationships with employees, customers, suppliers, and communities. This includes labour conditions, worker health and safety, union relations, diversity and inclusion practices, human rights compliance, data privacy protocols, and product safety controls. Though social metrics are inherently complex, as they involve qualitative assessments and long temporal lags between cause and effect, yet their importance is clear: firms with poor labour practices experience higher employee turnover, supply-chain disruptions, and costly litigation. Conversely, firms with strong human-capital development strategies tend to display higher innovation rates, stronger customer loyalty, and greater adaptability during crises. As the global economy becomes increasingly knowledge based, human capital has become a primary driver of competitive advantage, making social considerations more financially material than ever (Edmans, 2011; Friede et al., 2015).

The governance (G) pillar examines the quality of a company's leadership, oversight mechanisms, and institutional safeguards. It includes board independence and diversity, executive compensation alignment, shareholder rights, audit quality, internal controls, and exposure to corruption or unethical practices. Among the three pillars, governance is often considered the most directly linked to financial outcomes. Failures in governance have repeatedly resulted in catastrophic corporate collapses – Enron, Parmalat, Lehman Brothers, Olympus, Wirecard – each demonstrating how weak oversight, misaligned incentives, or fraudulent behaviour can destroy shareholder value and destabilize financial markets (La Porta et al., 1998; Coffee, 2005). Effective governance enhances transparency, improves capital allocation, and reduces the likelihood of operational or strategic mismanagement.

As ESG evolved, its conceptual foundation broadened from a moral framework to a material risk assessment system. This shift is reinforced by a growing body of academic research linking ESG characteristics to firm performance, cost of capital, downside protection, and long-term valuation (Friede et al., 2015; Berg et al., 2022). For investors, ESG is therefore not – or at least not solely – an ethical statement; it is increasingly a financial lens through which to assess the robustness of a company's business model in a changing world. This evolution explains why ESG has been embraced across investment philosophies: fundamental analysts see ESG as a source of qualitative insight, while quantitative investors treat ESG data as structured signals that can be normalized, ranked, and incorporated into factor models or portfolio constraints.

Above all, the modern ESG framework is dynamic rather than static. As disclosure standards, regulatory expectations, and societal preferences evolve, ESG metrics continue to expand and mature. Today's ESG analysis incorporates climate-transition scenarios, supply-chain traceability, cybersecurity resilience, and artificial intelligence governance – topics that were absent even a decade ago. Consequently, ESG's evolution reflects broader economic and technological shifts, and its conceptual boundaries will continue to adapt as sustainability considerations become increasingly intertwined with corporate strategy and financial performance (Kotsantonis et al., 2016; European Commission, 2019).

8.4 WHY ESG MATTERS FOR FINANCE

The growing relevance of environmental, social, and governance considerations in financial markets is not the result of a single trend but rather the convergence of multiple structural forces – economic, regulatory, social, and technological – that have reshaped the way investors perceive risk and value creation. ESG matters for finance because it addresses dimensions of corporate behaviour that, although historically underexamined, have demonstrated clear financial materiality. In this section, we explore the four major drivers underpinning ESG's ascendance within the investment industry (Khan et al., 2016).

8.4.1 Financial Materiality

A rapidly expanding body of empirical research shows that certain ESG characteristics have measurable implications for long-term performance, volatility, and downside risk. Environmental exposures, for instance, can create significant contingent liabilities: carbon-intensive companies face heightened vulnerability to regulatory shocks, carbon taxes, and shifts in consumer behaviour. These exposures can affect operating margins, asset valuations, and ultimately cost of capital (Lins et al., 2017; Bolton & Kacperczyk, 2021).

Governance is particularly well documented in academic literature as a financially material dimension. Firms with weak internal controls, concentrated power, or misaligned managerial incentives are more prone to fraud, earnings manipulation, and severe operational setbacks. The collapses of Enron, Lehman Brothers, Volkswagen (diesel emissions scandal), and Wirecard illustrate how governance failures can destroy billions in market value almost overnight (Coffee, 2005; Bebchuk et al., 2009).

Social issues – long dismissed as "soft" or non-material – have also proved economically significant (Khan et al., 2016). Poor labour standards, unsafe working conditions, or deficient data-privacy practices generate operational disruptions, litigation, and reputational damage. In contrast, firms that invest effectively in human capital tend to benefit from enhanced innovation capacity, employee retention, customer loyalty, and greater resilience during crises such as COVID-19.

Taken together, ESG indicators help investors identify hidden risks that are not captured by conventional accounting metrics or short-term performance indicators. By broadening the informational set available to analysts, ESG contributes to a more comprehensive assessment of corporate risk profiles.

8.4.2 Regulatory Pressure

Regulation has become one of the most powerful forces accelerating ESG integration. In the European Union, the Sustainable Finance Disclosure Regulation (SFDR) imposes stringent requirements on asset managers to measure, report, and justify their sustainability practices. The EU Taxonomy further establishes a classification system that defines which economic activities can be considered environmentally sustainable, directly influencing fund labelling, product design, and investment constraints (European Union, 2019; European Commission, 2019; SEC, 2022; NGFS, 2021).

This regulatory shift is not confined to Europe. In the United States, the Securities and Exchange Commission has advanced climate-related disclosure requirements. Across Asia, regulators in jurisdictions such as Singapore, Hong Kong, and Japan are implementing their own sustainability reporting frameworks. Latin America is following a similar path, with Brazil and Chile adopting mandatory ESG disclosure standards.

As a result, ESG integration is rapidly transitioning from a discretionary initiative used by a subset of thematically oriented funds to a general compliance obligation for all major asset managers. Firms that fail to meet these evolving standards face reputational damage, regulatory sanctions, or exclusion from institutional mandates.

8.4.3 Client Expectations and Fiduciary Duty

Institutional investors – including pension funds, endowments, insurance companies, and sovereign wealth funds – are increasingly demanding robust ESG integration from their asset managers. Clients expect not only transparency but also evidence that investment decisions incorporate sustainability-related risks that could impair long-term returns.

The concept of fiduciary duty has expanded accordingly (Principles for Responsible Investment, 2019; United Nations & PRI, 2019). Historically interpreted as the obligation to maximize financial returns, fiduciary duty is now widely understood to include the obligation to consider material ESG risks. Ignoring climate exposure, weak governance, or social liabilities is increasingly seen as neglecting relevant financial information. Many asset owners explicitly incorporate ESG metrics into manager selection, performance evaluation, and mandate structure.

This shift has created a feedback loop: as asset owners demand higher ESG standards, asset managers invest in analytics, datasets, and modelling capabilities to meet those expectations. Over time, ESG sophistication becomes a competitive differentiator.

8.4.4 A Broader Notion of Risk

Traditional financial risk models focus on volatility, correlation structures, and factor sensitivities. While these models are powerful, they overlook a wide range of non-financial yet financially material risks that ESG metrics are designed to capture. For example:

- Reputational risk: A corporate scandal or data breach can lead to market-cap losses far greater than any model-predicted volatility shock (Gatzert, 2015).
- Climate transition risk: High emitters face increasingly unfavourable capital-market conditions, regulatory penalties, and investor divestment (Bolton & Kacperczyk, 2021).
- Cultural and human-capital risk: Toxic corporate cultures can lead to high turnover, regulatory actions, or loss of market confidence (Edmans, 2011).
- Governance risk: Fraud, accounting manipulation, or board dysfunction can devastate shareholder value (Bebchuk et al., 2009; Coffee, 2005).

ESG metrics therefore serve as risk-signal augmentations, enriching conventional quantitative models with forward-looking, structural, and sometimes qualitative insights that would otherwise remain invisible.

By integrating ESG into portfolio construction, investors gain a more complete understanding of the true risk landscape - one that reflects not only short-term price dynamics but also long-term sustainability pressures and structural transformations affecting global markets.

8.5 ESG DATA PROVIDERS: ACCESSING AND UNDERSTANDING THE DATA

Despite its rapidly growing importance in financial analysis and portfolio construction, ESG data remains highly heterogeneous, inconsistent, and methodologically fragmented. Unlike traditional financial metrics - governed by standardized accounting rules, audit requirements, and regulatory frameworks - ESG metrics lack universally accepted definitions, measurement techniques, and disclosure protocols. Firms vary widely in what they report, how they report it, and the granularity and frequency of their disclosures. As a result, third-party ESG data providers have emerged to fill informational gaps, interpret corporate sustainability reports, and produce standardized scores. Yet because these providers use divergent methodologies, the resulting ESG ratings frequently disagree with each other.

This lack of convergence among ESG ratings is well documented. Academic research, most notably Berg, Koelbel and Rigobon (2020), shows that correlations between major ESG rating providers are surprisingly low - often between 0.38 and 0.71 - contrasting sharply with the near-perfect correlation observed between major credit rating agencies. These discrepancies arise from differences in scope (what indicators are included), measurement (how raw data is interpreted), and weighting (how indicators are aggregated). For practitioners, this creates both a challenge and an opportunity: ESG data must be interpreted with caution, but raw datasets - when cleaned, normalized, and contextualized - can provide powerful inputs to systematic models.

8.5.1 Major Providers and Their Characteristics

Because of the complexity and diversity of ESG information, multiple specialized providers have emerged. Although they share similar objectives, their methodologies differ significantly, making it essential for investors to understand their underlying assumptions and analytical frameworks.

8.5.1.1 MSCI ESG

MSCI operates one of the most widely used ESG rating systems in the asset-management industry. Its approach combines structured indicators, industry-adjusted scorecards, forward-looking assessments, and a rich dataset on controversies. MSCI places strong emphasis on sector-relative performance, meaning that companies are evaluated relative to peers facing similar sustainability challenges. Additionally, MSCI produces dedicated climate datasets – such as the Low Carbon Transition Scores – which are frequently used by index providers and passive funds.

8.5.1.2 Sustainalytics

Sustainalytics adopts a different philosophy. Instead of classifying firms as "good" or "bad," it generates a risk-based score, estimating the degree to which a firm's ESG exposures are manageable or unmanageable. This approach highlights vulnerability rather than virtue: firms are scored not on sustainability achievements but on their residual ESG risk after accounting for mitigation strategies. This makes Sustainalytics particularly valuable for risk-focused investment strategies.

8.5.1.3 LSEG ESG (Formerly Refinitiv, Formerly Thomson Reuters)

LSEG maintains one of the largest repositories of raw ESG datapoints, collected from corporate reports, regulatory filings, sustainability disclosures, and third-party documents. LSEG's strength is its breadth: hundreds of individual indicators across governance, environmental practices, and human-capital management. Because it emphasizes raw inputs over subjective interpretations, LSEG data is well suited for quantitative investors who prefer to build custom scoring frameworks rather than relying on provider-generated ratings.

8.5.1.4 TruValue Labs (FactSet)

TruValue Labs, now part of FactSet following its 2020 acquisition, pioneered the use of artificial intelligence and natural-language processing to generate real-time ESG insights from unstructured data sources such as news, NGO publications, regulatory reports, and industry research. Its methodology is explicitly aligned with the SASB materiality framework, focusing on the ESG issues most financially relevant to each industry. TruValue Labs produces several dynamic metrics, including Insight, Momentum, and Pulse Scores, that capture both long-term ESG behaviour and short-term event-driven shifts. Because it prioritizes timely external information rather than company-reported disclosures, TruValue Labs is particularly valuable for investors seeking to identify emerging ESG risks and opportunities, incorporate momentum-based signals into quantitative strategies, or integrate financially material ESG factors into valuation and risk-management processes.

8.5.1.5 Bloomberg ESG

Bloomberg ESG integrates sustainability data directly into the Bloomberg Terminal ecosystem, enabling analysts to seamlessly cross-reference ESG metrics with financial data, market news, and regulatory filings. Bloomberg excels in *timeliness*, as it continuously updates datasets based on new disclosures and developments. It also provides proprietary analytics such as carbon-emissions estimates for non-disclosing companies.

8.5.1.6 Trucost (S&P Global)

Trucost is the industry leader in carbon accounting and environmental footprinting. It provides detailed Scope 1, 2, and 3 emissions data, carbon intensity metrics adjusted for revenue or production output, and supply-chain emissions modelling. Trucost datasets are foundational for climate-risk analysis, carbon-beta modelling, and regulatory reporting under frameworks such as the EU's SFDR and TCFD.

8.5.1.7 CDP (Carbon Disclosure Project)

CDP collects self-reported environmental information from companies, cities, and regions, with particular focus on climate risk, water use, and forest impacts. CDP questionnaires provide qualitative and quantitative data on emissions management, governance of climate issues, scenario analysis, and environmental risk governance. CDP's transparency initiative has become a *de facto* global standard for environmental disclosure, though coverage varies by region and sector.

8.5.2 Interpreting ESG Data: Challenges and Best Practices

Because ESG datasets are heterogeneous, asset managers rarely rely on a single provider. Instead, they typically aggregate multiple datasets or build internal ESG scoring frameworks that transform raw indicators into structured, comparable metrics. This approach offers several advantages:

- Mitigating provider bias through cross-provider reconciliation
- Improving signal reliability by blending raw data from different sources

- Enhancing comparability through unified normalization techniques
- Allowing customization to reflect firm-specific or mandate-specific priorities

However, analysts must navigate several challenges:

- Disclosures are incomplete and inconsistent.
- Methodologies evolve, which introduces time-series discontinuities unless scores are reconstructed retroactively.
- Providers differ in geographic and sectoral coverage, requiring careful merging and validation.
- Composite scores obscure the underlying data, making them potentially unsuitable for quantitative factor construction.

For these reasons, advanced ESG integration typically relies on raw inputs rather than composite ratings, enabling quants to build factor signals that are transparent, reproducible, and aligned with portfolio objectives.

8.6 ESG METRICS AND THEIR TRANSFORMATION

ESG analysis relies on a wide array of metrics that vary substantially in scope, granularity, transparency, and methodological construction. Unlike financial accounting data – structured by uniform standards such as IFRS or US GAAP – ESG indicators lack globally harmonized definitions (Berg et al., 2022). As a result, practitioners must navigate a complex landscape of raw indicators, composite scores, and derived metrics, ensuring that each is transformed appropriately before being incorporated into investment models. Understanding the nature, strengths, and limitations of each metric type is crucial for building robust quantitative ESG strategies.

8.6.1 Raw Indicators

Raw ESG indicators are the foundational building blocks from which most sustainability assessments are derived. These indicators represent directly observable and, in principle, objective measurements of a firm's environmental footprint, social practices, or governance structure.

Raw indicators are the most transparent and analytically flexible inputs for quantitative modelling. They allow investors to construct customized factor definitions, perform industry-relative benchmarking, and evaluate time-series evolution. However, they also tend to be fragmented, with varying levels of completeness, inconsistent reporting methodologies, and significant gaps in coverage -particularly for smaller firms and emerging markets.

Because of this fragmentation, working with raw ESG data typically requires extensive data cleaning, imputation, verification against disclosures, and sometimes cross-referencing across multiple providers.

8.6.2 Composite ESG Scores

To simplify the complexity of raw indicators, most ESG data providers generate composite ESG scores -single numerical ratings (Berg et al., 2022) intended to summarize a company's sustainability performance. These scores blend dozens or even hundreds of underlying datapoints through proprietary weighting schemes and aggregation rules.

Composite scores offer clear benefits:

- They are easy to interpret and compare across firms.
- They provide a broad, multidimensional perspective.
- They reduce the analytical burden for investors lacking internal modelling capabilities.

However, composite scores also carry significant limitations. Each provider's score reflects subjective methodological choices regarding:

a) Scope – which indicators are included or excluded.

b) Measurement – how data gaps are handled and how controversies are incorporated.

c) Weighting – how environmental, social, and governance components are balanced.

d) Normalization – whether scores are sector relative, region relative, or absolute.

These design choices introduce a substantial amount of model risk. Two companies may receive dramatically different ESG ratings from different providers not because their sustainability performance differs, but because methodologies diverge. For this reason, composite scores are rarely used directly in systematic investment strategies, which typically require transparent, reproducible, and interpretable inputs.

Instead, quants frequently decompose composite scores into their raw subcomponents or reconstruct their own composite metrics using raw data.

8.6.3 Standardization and Normalization

To integrate ESG metrics into quantitative models, data must be made comparable across firms, industries, and time periods (Amel-Zadeh & Serafeim, 2018). Without normalization, raw ESG metrics can lead to biased signals: utilities naturally emit more CO_2 than technology firms; extractive industries face different risks than financial institutions; smaller firms disclose less data than multinationals.

To correct for these biases, practitioners employ a range of statistical transformations, each aligned with typical quantitative-finance workflows.

8.6.3.1 Z-Scoring within Industry Groups

Z-scores allow analysts to standardize metrics relative to sector peers:

$$z_i = \frac{x_i - \mu_{\text{industry}}}{\sigma_{\text{industry}}}$$

This is essential when comparing firms in inherently heterogeneous industries, such as energy vs. software.

8.6.3.2 Rank Transformations (Percentile Ranks)

Rank-based metrics mitigate the influence of outliers and reporting noise:

```
Python

esg['E_pct_rank'] =
esg.groupby('industry')['E_raw'].rank(pct=True)
```

Percentile ranks are especially useful for factor construction and cross-sectional regressions.

8.6.3.3 Winsorization

Extreme values – common in emissions or controversies data – can distort optimization and regression outputs. Winsorizing reduces the influence of outliers by capping values at predefined percentiles (e.g., 1st and 99th). This stabilizes factor behaviour and enhances robustness.

8.6.3.4 Rescaling (0–1 or 0–100)

Rescaling puts all ESG indicators on a common scale, which is essential when aggregating multiple metrics. Examples include min–max normalization or linear scaling to a 0–100 range.

8.6.4 From Raw Metrics to Analytical Signals

After transformation, ESG metrics become suitable inputs for quantitative processes:

- Factor construction (e.g., ESG momentum, carbon intensity factors)
- Portfolio optimization constraints (e.g., minimum portfolio-level ESG score)
- Risk modelling (e.g., governance risk factors or carbon beta exposures)
- Scenario analysis and stress testing

Raw indicators give flexibility, composite scores offer simplicity, and transformations ensure analytical rigor. The interplay of these elements determines the quality and reliability of ESG integration in practice.

8.7 ESG IN ASSET MANAGEMENT PRACTICE

The integration of ESG considerations into professional asset management has evolved from a niche practice into a diversified and sophisticated set of approaches that permeate nearly every stage of the investment process. ESG integration varies substantially across asset classes, investment philosophies, regulatory environments, and client mandates, but the underlying objective is consistent: to incorporate sustainability-related information in a manner that enhances risk-adjusted returns or aligns portfolios with specified ethical or environmental goals. As data availability and analytical techniques have advanced, ESG has shifted from a peripheral constraint to an integral part of mainstream investment management (Kotsantonis et al., 2016).

Historically, the earliest applications of ESG in finance consisted of values-based screening, often implemented by faith-based institutions, foundations, or public pension funds. These approaches typically excluded sectors deemed incompatible with the investor's principles – for example tobacco, gambling, weapons, or fossil fuels (Sjöström, 2011). While these exclusion lists remain in use today, modern ESG integration goes well beyond simple screening. Contemporary frameworks view ESG information as a set of material financial indicators that can improve portfolio construction, identify hidden risks, and detect long-term structural trends.

A second evolution occurred through the adoption of best-in-class selection. Under this approach, asset managers overweight or exclusively select firms with superior ESG performance relative to sector peers. The focus is not on penalizing entire industries but on identifying companies that manage environmental, social, and governance challenges more effectively. This aligns with the view that firms demonstrating strong sustainability practices are likely to exhibit greater operational efficiency, lower regulatory exposure, and more resilient business models.

More recently, ESG has become a key component of quantitative multi-factor frameworks (Pedersen et al., 2021). Rather than treating ESG as an external constraint, systematic managers increasingly incorporate ESG-derived signals directly into alpha models and risk models. ESG characteristics are evaluated alongside traditional style factors such as value, momentum, size, low volatility, and quality. The use of ESG as a factor is supported by growing empirical evidence that environmental and governance characteristics, in particular, can influence long-term return premia or explain cross-sectional patterns in risk.

At the portfolio level, asset managers use ESG in a variety of structured ways, each serving a different analytical purpose:

a) Screening:

   Screening remains the most common ESG application. Positive screens include selecting companies with superior ESG performance, while negative screens remove firms involved in controversial activities or with severe governance deficiencies. Screening defines the investable universe, shaping all subsequent decisions.

b) Portfolio tilting:

   Tilting involves overweighting stocks with high ESG scores and underweighting those with poor sustainability performance, usually within a risk-controlled framework (Pedersen et al., 2021). Tilts can be implemented through optimization or rule-based scoring, allowing managers to improve the portfolio's ESG profile without significantly altering its risk–return characteristics.

c) Risk control:

ESG metrics are increasingly used for enhanced risk management (Bolton & Kacperczyk, 2021). Portfolios may enforce constraints on carbon intensity, limit exposure to firms with ongoing controversies, or cap governance risk. These constraints reflect the recognition that ESG deficiencies translate into non-traditional but financially material risks, complementing conventional risk models.

d) Factor integration:

ESG-based factors are incorporated alongside traditional risk premia factors (Covachev et al., 2025). This approach requires transforming raw ESG data into quantitative signals that can be backtested, normalized, and integrated into cross-sectional models. Factor integration is the hallmark of advanced systematic ESG.

e) Impact alignment:

Beyond risk and return, some investors aim to align portfolios with specific environmental or social outcomes, such as the Paris Agreement, the UN Sustainable Development Goals, or national decarbonization pathways (NGFS, 2021). Impact-oriented strategies include low-carbon indices, climate-transition portfolios, and funds designed to contribute to Net Zero objectives through capital allocation and engagement.

These diverse applications illustrate that ESG integration is not monolithic. For some investors, ESG serves primarily as a compliance or risk-management tool. For others, it is a source of alpha signals. For many, it is a mechanism for aligning investments with societal or environmental objectives. What unites these approaches is the need for transparent, high-quality data and the ability to translate ESG concepts into rigorous analytical frameworks.

8.8 PRACTICAL ESG INTEGRATION

This section presents three of the most widely used quantitative approaches to integrating ESG into systematic portfolios.

a) Screening and Exclusions

Screening is the oldest ESG technique and remains one of the most operationally important. From a quantitative perspective, it simply involves filtering the investment universe based on ESG eligibility rules, such as excluding companies from controversial industries (e.g., those involved in thermal coal, tobacco, or weapons), applying rating thresholds (e.g., excluding firms with ESG scores below the 20th percentile), and handling controversies (where incidents like fraud, accidents, or corruption cases often trigger immediate exclusion).

b) Tilting and ESG-Constrained Optimization

Unlike screening, tilting adjusts portfolio weights to favour companies with stronger ESG characteristics while preserving diversification and risk controls, typically by incorporating ESG constraints or objectives into a quadratic (mean-variance) optimization problem. In the standard formulation, the objective minimizes risk while maximizing expected returns for a vector of portfolio weights, subject to a constraint on the portfolio's aggregate ESG score. In practice, ESG constraints can be far more complex, including sector-level ESG minima, carbon-intensity limits, or dynamic ESG thresholds that evolve over time.

c) ESG as Factors: Momentum, Climate Premia, and Carbon Beta

Quantitative managers increasingly view ESG as a source of alpha or a risk factor rather than a constraint, supported by research showing ESG signals (especially environmental) are priced into returns. ESG momentum tracks score improvements over time, with studies indicating outperforming firms enable long-short strategies (long top quintile, short bottom). Carbon beta, built from Trucost or CDP data, measures stock sensitivity to carbon shocks by constructing a carbon factor (e.g., changes in aggregate intensity) and regressing stock returns against it.

PRACTICAL EXERCISE #8.01 ESG-EQUITY PORTFOLIO OPTIMIZATION

Request: Let us construct portfolios of stocks from companies of the US market using ESG criteria.

Summary of the script. –

The script builds three ESG-oriented equity portfolios from the S&P 500. It performs four main tasks:

a) Data Collection
   - Scrapes S&P 500 tickers.
   - Downloads historical daily prices via *yfinance*.
   - Computes log returns.
   - Loads ESG Materiality scores from a FactSet (Truvalue SASB) Excel file.[1]

b) Utility Tools
   - Equal-weight portfolios.
   - Tilting weights based on ESG, Sharpe, or combined scores.
   - Calculating portfolio return/volatility/Sharpe metrics.

c) Portfolio Construction
   Portfolio 1: Top-50 ESG firms + tilt by ESG.
   Portfolio 2: Combined ESG+Sharpe score → Top-50 + tilt by combined score.
   Portfolio 3: ESG filter (top 200) → Top-50 by Sharpe → tilt by Sharpe.

d) Main Execution
   - Runs the full workflow, builds the three portfolios, and prints weights and metrics.

TABLE 8.1 Summary of Key Functions and Their Purposes

Function	Purpose
tickers_sp500( )	Scrape S&P 500 ticker list.
download_daily_prices( )	Download adjusted close/close prices for all tickers.
calculate_logarithmic_returns( )	Compute log returns.
esg_scores( )	Load ESG materiality scores from Excel (truvalue modified).
tilt_weights( )	Apply tilt to weights based on a score (ESG/Sharpe).
portfolio_characteristics( )	Compute expected return, volatility, and Sharpe.
equal_weight_portfolio( )	Generate equal-weight vector.
building_esg_top_tilt_portfolio( )	Portfolio 1: Top ESG + tilt by ESG.
building_esg_sharpe_top_tilt_portfolio( )	Portfolio 2: Combined ESG+Sharpe score + tilt.
building_esg_filter_sharpe_top_tilt_portfolio( )	Portfolio 3: ESG filter → Sharpe Top-50 → Sharpe tilt.

Script execution and outputs.

```
import pandas as pd
import numpy as np
import yfinance as yf
from datetime import date
from pandas.tseries.offsets import DateOffset
from io import StringIO

# ============================================================
# 1) S&P 500 tickers (StockAnalysis with Wikipedia fallback)
# ============================================================

def tickers_sp500(use_fallback=True):
    """
    Try StockAnalysis first (with browser headers). If
    blocked/format changes, fallback to Wikipedia.
    Yahoo-compatible tickers (BRK.B -> BRK-B).
    """
    url = "https://stockanalysis.com/list/sp-500-stocks/"
    try:
        import requests
        headers = {
            "User-Agent": (
                "Mozilla/5.0 (Windows NT 10.0; Win64; x64) "
                "AppleWebKit/537.36 (KHTML, like Gecko) "
                "Chrome/121.0.0.0 Safari/537.36"
            ),
            "Accept-Language": "en-US,en;q=0.9",
            "Referer": "https://stockanalysis.com/",
        }
        r = requests.get(url, headers=headers, timeout=20)
        r.raise_for_status()

        tabla = pd.read_html(StringIO(r.text))[0]
        # avoids FutureWarning
        tickers = tabla["Symbol"].astype(str).str.strip()
        tickers = tickers.str.replace(".", "-", regex=False)
        # BRK.B -> BRK-B
        return tickers.tolist()

    except Exception:
        if not use_fallback:
            raise

    url2 = "https://en.wikipedia.org/wiki/List_
    of_S%26P_500_companies"
    tabla2 = pd.read_html(url2, attrs={"id":
    "constituents"})[0]
```

```
    tickers2 = tabla2["Symbol"].astype(str).str.strip()
    tickers2 = tickers2.str.replace(".", "-", regex=False)
    return tickers2.tolist()

# ========================================================
# 2) Download daily prices (ONE simple call)
# ========================================================

def download_daily_prices(tickers, start_date, end_date):
    data = yf.download(
        tickers,
        start=start_date,
        end=end_date,
        interval="1d",
        progress=True,
        auto_adjust=False,
        actions=False
    )

    if isinstance(data.columns, pd.MultiIndex):
        lvl0 = data.columns.get_level_values(0)
        if "Adj Close" in lvl0:
            prices = data["Adj Close"].copy()
        elif "Close" in lvl0:
            prices = data["Close"].copy()
        else:
            raise ValueError(f"'Adj Close'/'Close' not
            found in level 0. Columns: {lvl0.unique()}")
    else:
        cols = data.columns
        if "Adj Close" in cols:
            prices = data[["Adj Close"]].copy()
            if len(tickers) == 1:
                prices.columns = [tickers[0]]
        elif "Close" in cols:
            prices = data[["Close"]].copy()
            if len(tickers) == 1:
                prices.columns = [tickers[0]]
        else:
            raise ValueError(f"'Adj Close'/'Close' not
            found. Columns: {list(cols)}")

    prices.index = pd.to_datetime(prices.index)
    prices.sort_index(inplace=True)
    prices = prices.dropna(axis=1, how="all")
    return prices
# ========================================================
# 3) Log returns
# ========================================================
```

```
def calculate_logarithmic_returns(prices):
    returns = np.log(prices / prices.shift(1))
    return returns.dropna(how="all")

# ========================================================
# 4) ESG Scores
# ========================================================

ESG_FILE = "TruValue Modified.xlsx"  # <-- change if needed

def esg_scores(path=ESG_FILE, sheet_name="Truvalue
Modified"):
    """
    Reads the Excel.
    Expected columns (case-insensitive):
      - Symbol (or Ticker)
      - Modified Score (or a close variant)
      - optional: Name

    Returns:
      esg_scores (Series), df (DataFrame)
    """
    df = pd.read_excel(path, sheet_name=sheet_name,
    header=0)
    df = df.dropna(how="all").copy()

    # Normalize column names (strip)
    df.columns = [str(c).strip() for c in df.columns]

    # Find symbol column
    col_lower = {c: c.lower() for c in df.columns}
    symbol_col = next((c for c in df.columns if col_
    lower[c] in ["symbol", "ticker"]), None)
    if symbol_col is None:
        symbol_col = next((c for c in df.columns if "symbol"
        in col_lower[c] or "ticker" in col_lower[c]), None)
    if symbol_col is None:
        raise KeyError(f"No Symbol/Ticker column found.
        Columns: {list(df.columns)}")

    # Find score column
    score_col = next((c for c in df.columns if "modified"
    in col_lower[c] and "score" in col_lower[c]), None)
    if score_col is None:
        score_col = next((c for c in df.columns if "score"
        in col_lower[c]), None)
    if score_col is None:
        raise KeyError(f"No score column found. Columns:
        {list(df.columns)}")
```

```
    # Clean and normalize tickers for Yahoo
    df[symbol_col] = df[symbol_col].astype(str).str.strip()
    df[symbol_col] = df[symbol_col].str.replace(".", "-",
    regex=False)  # BRK.B -> BRK-B

    df["ESG_Materiality"] = pd.to_numeric(df[score_col],
    errors="coerce")
    df = df.dropna(subset=[symbol_col, "ESG_
    Materiality"]).copy()

    df.set_index(symbol_col, inplace=True)
    esg_scores = df["ESG_Materiality"].copy()

    return esg_scores, df

# ========================================================
# 5) Utilities: tilt, metrics, equal weight
# ========================================================

def tilt_weights(w_base, score, k=1.0):
    """
    w'_i ∝ w_i * (1 + k * (score_i - mean(score)))
    then normalize to sum=1, clip at 0.
    """
    score_centered = score - score.mean()
    w_raw = w_base * (1 + k * score_centered)
    w_raw = w_raw.clip(lower=0)
    return w_raw / w_raw.sum()

def portfolio_characteristics(w, daily_returns):
    ret_port = (daily_returns * w).sum(axis=1)

    mu_d = ret_port.mean()
    vol_d = ret_port.std()

    mu_a = mu_d * 252
    vol_a = vol_d * np.sqrt(252)
    sharpe = mu_a / vol_a if vol_a > 0 else np.nan

    return {
        "Expected daily return": mu_d,
        "Expected annual return": mu_a,
        "Daily volatility": vol_d,
        "Annual volatility": vol_a,
        "Sharpe annual": sharpe
    }
def equal_weight_portfolio(assets):
    n = len(assets)
    return pd.Series(1 / n, index=assets)
```

```
# ==========================================================
# 6) Portfolio 1 - ESG TOP-50 + tilt (ESG only)
# ==========================================================

def building_esg_top_tilt_portfolio(daily_returns, esg_
scores, top_n=50, k=1.0):
    assets = daily_returns.columns
    esg = esg_scores.reindex(assets).dropna()
    valid_assets = esg.index
    valid_returns = daily_returns[valid_assets]

    esg_z = (esg - esg.mean()) / (esg.std() + 1e-8)

    top_n = min(top_n, len(valid_assets))
    top_assets = esg_z.sort_values(ascending=False).
    head(top_n).index

    top_returns = valid_returns[top_assets]
    esg_top = esg.loc[top_assets]
    esg_z_top = esg_z.loc[top_assets]

    w_base_top = equal_weight_portfolio(top_assets)
    w_top = tilt_weights(w_base_top, esg_z_top, k=k)

    metrics = portfolio_characteristics(w_top, top_returns)
    esg_avg = (w_top * esg_top).sum()

    w_full = pd.Series(0.0, index=assets)
    w_full.loc[top_assets] = w_top

    return w_full, metrics, esg_avg

# ==========================================================
# 7) Portfolio 2 - Combined Score ESG+Sharpe TOP-50
+ tilt
# ==========================================================

def building_esg_sharpe_top_tilt_portfolio(daily_returns,
esg_scores, top_n=50, k=1.0, alpha=0.5):
    """
    combined score = alpha * Sharpe_z + (1-alpha)
    * ESG_z
    """
    assets = daily_returns.columns
    esg = esg_scores.reindex(assets).dropna()
    valid_assets = esg.index
    valid_returns = daily_returns[valid_assets]

    esg_z = (esg - esg.mean()) / (esg.std() + 1e-8)
```

```
    mean_ret = valid_returns.mean()
    vol = valid_returns.std()
    sharpe = mean_ret / (vol + 1e-8)
    sharpe_z = (sharpe - sharpe.mean()) / (sharpe.std() + 1e-8)

    score_comb = alpha * sharpe_z + (1 - alpha) * esg_z

    top_n = min(top_n, len(valid_assets))
    top_assets = score_comb.sort_values(ascending=False).
    head(top_n).index

    returns_top = valid_returns[top_assets]
    esg_top = esg.loc[top_assets]
    score_top = score_comb.loc[top_assets]

    w_base_top = equal_weight_portfolio(top_assets)
    w_top = tilt_weights(w_base_top, score_top, k=k)

    metrics = portfolio_characteristics(w_top, returns_top)
    esg_avg = (w_top * esg_top).sum()

    w_full = pd.Series(0.0, index=assets)
    w_full.loc[top_assets] = w_top

    return w_full, metrics, esg_avg

# ========================================================
# 8) Portfolio 3 - ESG filter (top ESG) + Sharpe TOP-50 +
  Sharpe tilt
# ========================================================

def building_esg_filter_sharpe_top_tilt_portfolio(daily_
returns, esg_scores, top_esg=200, top_n=50, k=1.0):
    assets = daily_returns.columns
    esg = esg_scores.reindex(assets).dropna()
    valid_assets = esg.index
    valid_returns = daily_returns[valid_assets]

    esg_z = (esg - esg.mean()) / (esg.std() + 1e-8)

    top_esg = min(top_esg, len(valid_assets))
    universe_esg = esg_z.sort_values(ascending=False).head
    (top_esg).index

    returns_esg = valid_returns[universe_esg]
    esg_esg = esg.loc[universe_esg]

    mean_ret = returns_esg.mean()
    vol = returns_esg.std()
    sharpe = mean_ret / (vol + 1e-8)
```

```
    sharpe_z = (sharpe - sharpe.mean()) / (sharpe.std() +
    1e-8)

    top_n = min(top_n, len(universe_esg))
    top_assets = sharpe_z.sort_values(ascending=False).
    head(top_n).index

    returns_top = returns_esg[top_assets]
    esg_top = esg_esg.loc[top_assets]
    sharpe_z_top = sharpe_z.loc[top_assets]

    w_base_top = equal_weight_portfolio(top_assets)
    w_top = tilt_weights(w_base_top, sharpe_z_top, k=k)

    metrics = portfolio_characteristics(w_top,
    returns_top)
    esg_avg = (w_top * esg_top).sum()

    w_full = pd.Series(0.0, index=assets)
    w_full.loc[top_assets] = w_top

    return w_full, metrics, esg_avg

# ====================================================
# 9) MAIN
# ====================================================

if __name__ == "__main__":
    # 9.1 Tickers
    sp500_tickers = tickers_sp500()
    print(f"S&P 500 tickers downloaded: {len(sp500_
    tickers)}")

    # 9.2 Prices
    end_date = date.today()
    start_date = end_date - DateOffset(years=5)

    prices = download_daily_prices(sp500_tickers, start_
    date, end_date)
    print("Shape prices:", prices.shape)

    # 9.3 Returns
    daily_returns_log = calculate_logarithmic_
    returns(prices)
    print("Shape returns:", daily_returns_log.shape)

    # 9.4 ESG
    esg_scores, esg_df = esg_scores()
    print(f"ESG rows loaded: {len(esg_scores)}")
```

```
# Parameters
top_n = 50
top_esg = 200
k_tilt = 1.0
alpha = 0.5

# Portfolio 1
w1, m1, esg1 = building_esg_top_tilt_portfolio(
    daily_returns=daily_returns_log,
    esg_scores=esg_scores,
    top_n=top_n,
    k=k_tilt
)
print(f"\n=== PORTFOLIO 1: ESG TOP-{top_n} + TILT
(ESG) - TOP 10 WEIGHTS ===")
print(w1.sort_values(ascending=False).head(10))
print("\nMETRICS PORTFOLIO 1:")
for k, v in m1.items():
    print(f"{k}: {v:.6f}")
print(f"Weighted average ESG (P1): {esg1:.4f}")

# Portfolio 2
w2, m2, esg2 = building_esg_sharpe_top_tilt_portfolio(
    daily_returns=daily_returns_log,
    esg_scores=esg_scores,
    top_n=top_n,
    k=k_tilt,
    alpha=alpha
)
print(f"\n=== PORTFOLIO 2: ESG+Sharpe TOP-{top_n} +
TILT - TOP 10 WEIGHTS ===")
print(w2.sort_values(ascending=False).head(10))
print("\nMETRICS PORTFOLIO 2:")
for k, v in m2.items():
    print(f"{k}: {v:.6f}")
print(f"Weighted average ESG (P2): {esg2:.4f}")

# Portfolio 3
w3, m3, esg3 = building_esg_filter_sharpe_top_tilt_
portfolio(
    daily_returns=daily_returns_log,
    esg_scores=esg_scores,
    top_esg=top_esg,
    top_n=top_n,
    k=k_tilt
)
print(f"\n=== PORTFOLIO 3: Filter ESG TOP-{top_esg} +
Sharpe TOP-{top_n} + TILT - TOP 10 WEIGHTS ===")
print(w3.sort_values(ascending=False).head(10))
```

```
    print("\nMETRICS PORTFOLIO 3:")
    for k, v in m3.items():
        print(f"{k}: {v:.6f}")
    print(f"Weighted average ESG (P3): {esg3:.4f}")
```

Output:

```
S&P 500 tickers downloaded: 501
[*********************100%***********************]  501 of 501
completed
Shape prices: (1255, 501)
Shape returns: (1254, 501)
ESG rows loaded: 497

=== PORTFOLIO 1: ESG TOP-50 + TILT (ESG) - TOP 10 WEIGHTS ===
Ticker
VLTO    0.043255
WELL    0.039431
UDR     0.035606
FRT     0.031781
O       0.029868
REG     0.029868
KIM     0.026043
ARE     0.026043
EXR     0.024131
PFG     0.024131
dtype: float64

METRICS PORTFOLIO 1:
Expected daily return: 0.000432
Expected annual return: 0.108973
Daily volatility: 0.011705
Annual volatility: 0.185803
Sharpe annual: 0.586497
Weighted average ESG (P1): 78.9927

=== PORTFOLIO 2: ESG+Sharpe TOP-50 + TILT - TOP 10 WEIGHTS ===
Ticker
GEV     0.040321
WELL    0.039830
EME     0.036364
PWR     0.029685
PH      0.029100
TRGP    0.028867
IRM     0.026383
HUBB    0.025065
GWW     0.024966
```

```
VLTO     0.024122
dtype: float64

METRICS PORTFOLIO 2:
Expected daily return: 0.000959
Expected annual return: 0.241656
Daily volatility: 0.011835
Annual volatility: 0.187882
Sharpe annual: 1.286213
Weighted average ESG (P2): 75.2958

=== PORTFOLIO 3: Filter ESG TOP-200 + Sharpe TOP-50 + TILT -
TOP 10 WEIGHTS ===
Ticker
GEV      0.070068
EME      0.044746
TRGP     0.043125
PWR      0.035138
WELL     0.032458
APH      0.032211
GWW      0.029480
PH       0.028177
CAT      0.027853
CEG      0.027804
dtype: float64

METRICS PORTFOLIO 3:
Expected daily return: 0.001107
Expected annual return: 0.278963
Daily volatility: 0.012369
Annual volatility: 0.196356
Sharpe annual: 1.420698
Weighted average ESG (P3): 71.8657
```

NOTE

1 As this is proprietary data, we cannot deposit the file in a public repository. We have therefore modified it by adding a random percentage between 1% and 10% to the TruValue scores. It is clear that the final data is fictitious and serves only a methodological purpose, enabling it to be deposited in a public repository.

Bibliography

Amel-Zadeh, A., & Serafeim, G. (2018). Why and how investors use ESG information. *Financial Analysts Journal*, 74(3), 87–103.

Bebchuk, L., Cohen, A., & Ferrell, A. (2009). What matters in corporate governance? *Review of Financial Studies*, 22(2), 783–827.

Berg, F., Kölbel, J. F., & Rigobon, R. (2022). Aggregate confusion: The divergence of ESG ratings. *Review of Finance*, 26(6), 1315–1344.

Black, F., Jensen, M. & Scholes, M. (1972). The capital asset pricing model: Some empirical tests. In: M. Jensen (ed.), *Studies in the Theory of Capital Markets*. Praeger.

Blitz, D. C. (2015). Factor investing revisited. *The Journal of Index Investing*, 6(2), 7–17.

Blitz, D. C., & van Vliet, P. (2007). The volatility effect: Lower risk without lower return. *The Journal of Portfolio Management*, 34(1), 102–103.

Bolton, P., & Kacperczyk, M. (2021). Do investors care about carbon risk? *Journal of Financial Economics*, 142(2), 517–549.

Breeden, D. T. (1979). An intertemporal asset pricing model with stochastic consumption and investment opportunities. *The Journal of Finance*, 7, 265–296.

Brinson, G. P., & Fachler, N. (1985). Measuring non-US equity portfolio performance. *The Journal of Portfolio Management*, 11(3), 73–76.

Brooks, C. (2019). *Python Guide for Introductory Econometrics for Finance*. Cambridge University Press.

Carhart, M. M. (1997). On persistence in mutual fund performance. *The Journal of Finance*, 52(1), 57–82.

Clark, G. L., Feiner, A., & Viehs, M. (2015). *From the Stockholder to the Stakeholder: How Sustainability Can Drive Financial Outperformance*. SSRN.

Coffee, J. C. (2005). A theory of corporate scandals: Why the USA and Europe differ. *Oxford Review of Economic Policy*, 21(2), 198–211.

Covachev, S., Martel, J., & Brito-Ramos, S. (2025). Are ESG factors truly unique? *The North American Journal of Economics and Finance*, (77), 102386.

Doyle, J., & Hayman, G. (2024). *Smart Beta, Direct Indexing, and Index Based Investment Strategies. A Framework*. CFA Institute Research and Policy Center.

Eccles, R. G., Ioannou, I., & Serafeim, G. (2014). The impact of corporate sustainability on organizational processes and performance. *Management Science*, 60(11), 2835–2857.

Edmans, A. (2011). Does the stock market fully value intangibles? Employee satisfaction and equity prices. *Journal of Financial Economics*, 101(3), 621–640.

European Commission. (2019). *EU Taxonomy for Sustainable Activities.* European Commission. Available at (April 23, 2026): https://finance.ec.europa.eu/sustainable-finance/tools-and-standards/eu-taxonomy-sustainable-activities_en

European Union. (2019). Regulation (Eu) 2019/2088 of the European Parliament and of the Council. *Official Journal of the European Union*, 317, 1–16.

Fabozzi, F. J. (2007). *Fixed Income Analysis.* John Willey.

Fabozzi, F. J. (2010). *Bond Markets, Analysis, and Strategies.* Prentice Hall.

Fama, E. (1970). Efficient capital markets: A review of theory and empirical work. *The Journal of Finance*, 25(2), 383–417.

Fama, E. (1991). Efficient capital markets: II. *Journal of Finance*, 46(5), 1575–1617.

Fama, E. (1998). Market efficiency, long term returns, and behavioral finance. *The Journal of Financial Economics*, 49(1), 283–306.

Fama, E., & French, K. R. (1992). The cross-section of expected stock returns. *The Journal of Finance*, 47(3), 427–465.

Fama, E., & French, K. R. (1993). Common risk factors in the returns on stocks and bonds. *The Journal of Financial Economics*, 33(3), 3–56.

Fama, E., & French, K. R. (2004). The capital asset pricing model: Theory and evidence. *The Journal of Economic Perspectives*, 18(3), 25–46.

Fama, E., & French, K. R. (2015). A five-factor asset pricing model. *The Journal of Financial Economics*, 116(1), 1–22.

Febrero, R. (1991). Markowitz, Sharpe y Miller o el reconocimiento de Finanzas como disciplina económica. *Revista de Economía*, 689, 63–82.

Fernández, P., & Carabias, J. M. (2015). *El Peligro de utilizar Betas Calculadas (The Danger of Using Calculated Betas).* SSRN.

Finnerty, J. E. (1976). Insiders and market efficiency. *The Journal of Finance*, 31(4), 1141–1148.

Fisher, I. (1930). *The Theory of Interest.* The Macmillan Company.

Friede, G., Busch, T., & Bassen, A. (2015), ESG and financial performance: Aggregated evidence from more than 2000 empirical studies. *Journal of Sustainable Finance & Investment*, 5(4), 210–233.

Gatzert, N. (2015). The impact of corporate reputation and reputation damaging events on financial performance: Empirical evidence from the literature. *European Management Journal*, 33(6), 485–499.

Grossman, S., & Stiglitz, J. (1980). On the impossibility of informationally efficient markets. *American Economic Review*, 70(3), 393–408.

Heydt, M. (2015). *Mastering Pandas for Finance.* Packt Publishing.

Hilpish, Y. (2019). *Python for Finance: Mastering Data-Driven Finance.* O'Reilly.

Jaffe, J. (1974). Special information and insider trading. *Journal of Business*, 47, 410–428.

Jegadeesh, N., & Titman, S. (1993). Returns to buying winners and selling losers: Implications for stock market efficiency. *The Journal of Finance*, 48(1), 65–91.

Khan, M., Serafeim, G., & Yoon, A. (2016). Corporate sustainability: First evidence on materiality. *The Accounting Review*, 91(6), 1697–1724.

Kotsantonis, S., Pinney, C., & Serafeim, G. (2016). ESG integration in investment management: Myths and realities. *Journal of Applied Corporate Finance*, 28(2), 10–16.

La Porta, R., Lopez-de-Silanes, F., Shleifer, A., & Vishny, R. (1998). Law and finance. *Journal of Political Economy*, 106(6), 1113–1155.

Lins, K. V., Servaes, H., & Tamayo, A. (2017). Social capital, trust, and firm performance: The value of corporate social responsibility during the financial crisis. *Journal of Finance*, 72(4), 1785–1824.

Lintner, J. (1965). The evaluation of risky assets and the selection of risky investments in stock portfolios and capital budgets. *Review of Economics and Statistics*, 73, 13–37.

Lucas, R. E. (1978). Asset prices in an exchange economy. *Econometrica*, 46, 1429–1446.

Malkiel, B. G. (1999). *A Random Walk Down Wall Street: The Best Investment Advice for the New Century Completely Revised and Updated.* W.W. Norton y Company.

Malkiel, B. G. (2003). The efficient market hypothesis and its critics. *The Journal of Economic Perspectives*, 17(1), 59–82.

Malkiel, B. G. (2005). Reflections on the efficient market hypothesis: 30 years later. *Financial Review*, 40(1), 1–9.

Markowitz, H. M. (1952). Portfolio selection. *The Journal of Finance*, 7(1), 77–91.

Markowitz, H. M. (1959). *Portfolio Selection: Efficient Diversification of Investments.* John Wiley & Sons.

Merton, R. (1973). An intertemporal capital asset pricing model. *Econometrica*, 41, 867–887.

Mossin, J. (1966). Equilibrium in a capital asset market. *Econometrica*, 34, 768–783.

NGFS. (2021). *Climate scenarios for central banks and supervisors.* NGFS. Available at (April 21, 2026): https://www.ngfs.net/en/publications-and-statistics/publications/ngfs-short-term-climate-scenarios-central-banks-and-supervisors

Pedersen, L. H., Fitzgibbons, S., & Pomorski, L. (2021). Responsible investing: The ESG-efficient frontier. *Journal of Financial Economics*, 142(2), 572–597.

Principles for Responsible Investment. (2019). *ESG Integration in Investment Management.* PRI. Available at (April 21, 2026): https://www.unpri.org

Ramalho, L. (2015). *Fluent Python: Clear, Concise, and Effective Programming.* O'Reilly.

Roll, R. (1977, Marchm). A critique of the asset pricing theory's tests Part I: On past and potential testability of the theory. *Journal of Financial Economics*, 4(2), 129–176.

Ross, S. (1976). The arbitrage pricing theory of capital asset pricing. *Journal of Economics Theory*, 13, 341–360.

Rubinstein, M. (1976). The valuation of uncertain income streams and the price of options. *Bell Journal of Economics*, 7, 407–425.

Ruiz, G., Jiménez, J. I., y Torres, J. J. (2000). *La gestión del riesgo financiero.* Pirámide.

SEC. (2022). *Proposed rule: The Enhancement and Standardization of Climate-Related Disclosures*. Proposed rule. Release Nos. 33-11042; 34-94478; File No. S7-10-22. Available at (April 21, 2026): https://www.sec.gov/newsroom/speeches-statements/lizarraga-statement-mandatory-climate-risk-disclosures-030624

Seyhun, H. N. (1986). Insiders' profits, costs of trading, and market efficiency. *The Journal of Financial Economics*, 16(2), 189–212.

Sharpe, W. F. (1964). Capital asset prices: A theory of market equilibrium under conditions of risk. *The Journal of Finance*, 19(3), 425–442.

Sjöström, E. (2011). *The Performance of Socially Responsible Investment – A Review of Scholarly Studies Published 2008–2010*. SSRN.

Tobin, J. (1958). Liquidity preference as behavior towards risk. *Review of Economic Studies*, 25(1), 65–86.

Treynor, J. L. (1961). *Market Value, Time and Risk*. Unpublished manuscript.

United Nations & PRI. (2019). *Fiduciary Duty in the 21st Century*. Final Report. Available at (April 23, 2026): https://www.unepfi.org/industries/investment/fiduciary-duty-in-the-21st-century-final-report/

Weber, O., Dordi, T., & Oyegunle, A. (2020). Stranded assets and the transition to low-carbon economy. In: M. Migliorelli, & P. Dessertine (eds.), *Sustainability and Financial Risks: Palgrave Studies in Impact Finance*. Palgrave Macmillan.

Weiming, J. L. (2015). *Mastering Python for Finance*. Packt Publishing.

Yang, Y. (2014). *Python for Finance*. Packt Publishing.

Index

Note: *Italic* page numbers indicate figures, **bold** page numbers indicate tables, and references following 'n' refer to notes.

E

F

G

H

I

T

V

W

Y

Z

For Product Safety Concerns and Information please contact our EU representative GPSR@taylorandfrancis.com
Taylor & Francis Verlag GmbH, Kaufingerstraße 24, 80331 München, Germany

www.ingramcontent.com/pod-product-compliance
Lightning Source LLC
LaVergne TN
LVHW011846200926
848484LV00002B/405

* 9 7 8 1 0 4 1 3 0 8 3 2 4 *